491 Days

491 Days

Prisoner Number 1323/69

By

WINNIE MADIKIZELA-MANDELA

PICADOR AFRICA

First published in 2013 by Picador Africa
an imprint of Pan Macmillan South Africa
Private Bag X19, Northlands
Johannesburg, 2116

www.panmacmillan.co.za

ISBN 978-1-77010-330-6

ePub ISBN 978-1-77010-331-3

Editing by Sally Hines
Proofreading by Valda Strauss
Design and typesetting by Triple M Design, Johannesburg
Cover design by K4
Front cover photograph (taken on the day of Mrs Madikizela-
    Mandela's release on 14 September 1970) from Bailey's African
    History Archive/Africa Media Online
Printed and bound by Ultra Litho (Pty) Limited, Johannesburg

To little Zenani Mandela,
my great granddaughter
who lost her life on 11 June 2010

I struggled like her mother and the family at large to deal with the pain of her loss. I felt faith flagging as I introspectively questioned God, asking secretly how much pain can any one human being endure.

I was consoled by a quotation on the cover of a book my eldest daughter Princess Zenani, Her Excellency, Her Royal Highness, Ambassador to Argentina gave me. Max Depree wrote of how we are led 'through the darkness of loss and pain and into the light of grace'.

Grasping at the straws of my faith, I know that God will provide justice and closure to this unbearable grief.

'I had to wait for 2 weeks before I could send you my warmest congratulations for serving 491, and still emerge the lively girl you are, and in high spirits. To you and your determined friends I say welcome back! Were I at home when you returned I should have stolen a white goat from a rich man, slaughtered it and given you *ivanya ne ntloya* to down it. Only in this way can a beggar like myself fete and honour his heroes.'
— Nelson Mandela in a letter to his wife written on
1 October 1970 shortly after her release

'In a way during the past two years I felt so close to you. It was the first time we were together in similar surroundings for that length of time. Eating what you were eating and sleeping on what you sleep on gave me that psychological satisfaction of being with you.'
— Winnie Mandela in a letter to her husband written on
26 October 1970 shortly after her release

Contents

As the South African security system sought to destroy all opposition after Nelson Mandela was sentenced to life imprisonment in 1964, his wife Nomzamo Winnie Mandela experienced almost constant harassment. Her longest and most tortuous period of police detention lasted sixteen months, from 12 May 1969 to 14 September 1970. This little-known period is documented in a recently recovered prison journal she kept secretly and details the trauma this young mother of two small children endured. Her words and those in letters by her and Nelson Mandela reproduced here highlight both the effect of apartheid's brutality and the strength of a defiant spirit.

Foreword

Ahmed Kathrada

I met Mrs Winnie Mandela in about 1957 or 1958 – a little before she and Madiba were married. Not long after her marriage, and five months' pregnant, she had her first taste of detention. At the threshold of what should have been a happy, healthy and peaceful married life, little did the mother-to-be, or Madiba, foresee that this was going to be the beginning of her increasingly turbulent and full-time way of life.

In 1959, their first daughter, Zenani, was born. And during 1960, their second daughter, Zindziswa, was born.

For over two years after their marriage, Madiba was still involved in the marathon Treason Trial in Pretoria. He was among the last 30 accused in the case that started in 1956. He had to travel daily to Pretoria, which meant he was obliged to leave home when the girls were not quite awake, and often return home when they were about to go to bed.

Following the Sharpeville massacre of 1960, a state of emergency was declared, during which Madiba and his fellow Treason Trialists were detained for five months, and the African National Congress and the Pan-Africanist Congress were banned. Oliver Tambo was sent into exile, and the law firm of Mandela & Tambo closed down. This negatively affected Madiba's income, which in turn impacted on the household.

Soon after the acquittal of him and 29 other Treason Trialists on 29 March 1961, Madiba went underground, and lived the life of an outlaw. He could not live at home with his family while he was in the country, and nine months later he left on a clandestine trip abroad. He only returned in July 1962 and was arrested soon thereafter.

All the above happenings meant that from the time they were married in 1958 and had their first child in 1959, Winnie's life was virtually that of a single parent. From 1959 to 1961, Zenani and Zindzi lived with an occasional father. From Madiba's arrest on 5 August 1962, until his release on 11 February 1990, for 27 years Zenani and Zindzi and their brothers and sister from Madiba's first marriage grew up with an absent father.

It is a privilege to be invited to write a foreword to this book. Like Winnie, I too know something about bannings and detentions. Although there are basic similarities in detentions, there are also unique features about each.

Winnie has been arrested, detained or faced trials about a dozen times. She has been banned, placed under house arrest, and worst of all, banished to the little rural town of Brandfort in the Free State. Over a period of thirteen years, she was free of banning orders for only ten months. In one instance, despite suffering from a heart condition, she was interrogated by the security police continuously without a break for days and nights!

This was when she was detained in May 1969 under the Terrorism Act and charged with 21 others. Two of the detainees, Shanti Naidoo, whose father was in the Treason Trial with Madiba, and Nondwe Mankahla, refused to give evidence against Winnie, and were sentenced to two months' imprisonment. Another detainee, Caleb Mayekiso, was tortured to death. Caleb and I were fellow accused in the Treason Trial. I knew, respected and admired him, and mourned his death when I got news of it on Robben Island.

Because of her commitment, loyalty, courage, determination and resilience, Winnie emerged from this long spell in detention unshaken and proud, with her head held high.

Something can be written about every one of Winnie's detentions.

However, this book is about one of her highly risky, dramatic, unique and per-haps unprecedented initiatives.

During her detention, Winnie managed to keep a secret journal of her experi-ences. She handed it over to her lawyers, and practically forgot about it. Forty-one years later, in 2011, Greta Soggot turned up at Winnie's office in parliament and pre-sented the original journal to her.

While Winnie was going through unimaginable harassment at the hands of the police, she remained constant in her thoughts about her beloved husband on far-away Robben Island. Likewise, Madiba's days and nights were no less filled with concern and anxiety about Winnie. I personally witnessed his pain at her detention and saw his countless representations to the authorities. And he was equally worried about his children.

Here are extracts written by both Madiba to Winnie and vice versa. In one of his letters from Robben Island he wrote:

Since the dawn of history, mankind has honoured and respected brave and honest

people, men and women like you darling – an ordinary girl who hails from a coun-
try village ... My sense of devotion to you precludes me from saying more in public
than I have already done in this note ... One day we will have the privacy which will
enable us to share the tender thoughts which we have kept buried in our hearts.

In another letter, he wrote:

Our short lives together, my love, have always been full of expectation ... In these
hectic and violent years I have grown to love you more than I ever did before.

In a letter to Winnie after he was convicted and sentenced to five years in 1962:

One of my precious possessions here is the first letter you wrote to me ... I have read
it over and over again and the sentiments it expresses are as golden and fresh now
as the day I received it.

I never cease to be amazed that 23 years after my release the interest in our prison experience continues unabated. One of the questions most frequently asked is: 'How did you manage to keep up your spirit and morale?' My response is simple, but true.

The 26 years on Robben Island and in Pollsmoor Prison were difficult.

The thirteen years of hard labour with picks and shovels for eight hours a day were not easy. The unchanging everyday monotony of the same food; the cold showers for about ten years; sleeping on two mats on the ground for fourteen years; the first period with two letters and two visits a year; the absence of children. In my case, for the first time I saw a child at close quarters, and actually touched and held her was after twenty years! There were no newspapers for sixteen years.

I must emphasise, prison is no bed of roses. Yes, with all the deprivations and trauma, those were undoubtedly difficult years. What then kept up our morale?

There were a number of factors. It may not be easy to believe. In our case, uppermost in our undiminished thoughts and reminders were: Yes, we were suffering. But after taking every hardship and every deprivation into account, it could not be disputed that we were protected! No policeman could barge onto Robben Island or into Pollsmoor Prison and start shooting. This was not the case with our comrades outside prison. They were at the very coalface of the struggle. They had no protection. Comrades such as Winnie Mandela; the 600 unarmed, defenceless schoolchildren who were slaughtered in the Soweto uprising of 1976; the leaders and members of the United Democratic Front and the Congress of South African Students. Individually and collectively, in the face of adversity and danger, they kept the flag flying.

Their sacrifices, courage and concern must never be forgotten.

Introduction

Forty-one years after she was released from sixteen months in detention, Mrs Winnie Madikizela-Mandela MP received a surprise visitor at her office in South Africa's parliament. It was Greta Soggot, the widow of David Soggot, one of her advocates. She had come from England armed with a stack of papers that turned out to be a journal and notes Mrs Madikizela-Mandela had written while she was in detention between 12 May 1969 and 14 September 1970.

She and scores of others had been detained under the repressive Terrorism Act, which had been passed just two years earlier. It placed them beyond the reach of the courts and under the total control of the security police.

The delivery of the documents to Mrs Madikizela-Mandela brought vivid and horrific memories rushing back to the then 75-year-old woman of the traumatic time when, as a young wife and mother of two small children, she was left alone when her husband Nelson Mandela was jailed for life for sabotage. She had decided to join with others to continue the struggle for freedom in South Africa, and she paid the price.

She and her comrades were interrogated by the notorious security police's Sabotage Squad, which included Theunis Jacobus 'Rooi Rus' Swanepoel, whose reputation for brutality grew during this period and beyond.

After almost six months in detention, Mrs Mandela and her 21 co-accused appeared in court charged under the Suppression of Communism Act. The state claimed that among other charges they attempted to revive the banned African National Congress (ANC) and to commit sabotage by inspecting trains and railway installations as potential targets. They were not charged with a single act of violence.

Of the expected 80 state witnesses only twenty were ultimately called to testify. Many of them had been held for months in solitary confinement and were tortured, including Shanti Naidoo and Nondwe Mankahla who refused to testify against Mrs Mandela.

In what became known as the 'Trial of the 22' or more officially the 'State vs Ndou and others', the defence raised the issue of torture under interrogation. Four months later, the charges were dropped and they were free to go. But their exit from the court was thwarted by security police who simply re-detained them. About a year after her detention had begun, Mrs Mandela started writing a journal, recording the still-fresh memories of her incarceration and subsequent trial. In July 1970, all but three of the accused were recharged with similar offences, but this time under the Terrorism Act. They were joined by an Umkhonto we Sizwe operative, Benjamin Ramotse, who had nothing to do with them.[1] In June 1970, he became accused number one in the new trial of the 'State vs Benjamin Ramotse and 19 others.'

On 14 September 1970, the nineteen accused were acquitted. Mr Ramotse stood trial alone and eventually was convicted and sentenced to fifteen years in prison. Mrs Mandela and some of the other accused attended his sentencing to give him moral support.

Her journal written on loose pages is published here, not strictly in chronological order, along with letters between her and Nelson Mandela, then in Robben Island Prison, and other correspondence about her plight.

---

1. He was one of the members of Umkhonto we Sizwe who launched the armed wing of the ANC on 16 December 1961. His comrade Petrus Molefe was killed when their device exploded in Soweto. Mr Ramotse was injured and captured. After being charged, he jumped bail and left South Africa to undergo military training. He was kidnapped by Rhodesian security forces in Botswana and brought back to South Africa.

Part One

Journal

Chapter 1

Arrest

On a freezing-cold winter's morning some hours before dawn, on Monday 12 May 1969, security police arrived at the Soweto home of Winnie Mandela and detained her in the presence of her two young daughters.

At the time, she was banned and restricted to Orlando township and unable to leave or even to visit her husband, Nelson Mandela, who was in the fifth year of his life sentence.[2]

Mrs Mandela and at least 40 others were rounded up and detained under Section 6 of the Terrorism Act, which was passed in 1967 and designed for the security police to hold people and to interrogate them for as long as they chose. One of those detained, Caleb Mayekiso, died just days after his arrest.

She was driven to Pretoria Central Prison and held incommunicado, not knowing what would happen to her children Zenani and Zindzi, aged ten and nine, who had been left in the small hours on their own. She was not allowed to bring her medication for an existing heart condition.

Her first interrogation started on 26 May and lasted for five days and five nights. On the second day she began having dizzy spells and palpitations. A day later, the blackouts began.

One of her sisters, Iris Madikizela, brought a case against the minister to stop her and her fellow accused from being assaulted.

Mrs Mandela and 21 others appeared five months later in the Old Synagogue in Pretoria, the same makeshift court where her husband was sentenced to five years in prison on 7 November 1962.

The trial, known as 'The Trial of the 22' or the 'State vs Samson Ndou and 21

---

2. Nelson Mandela and seven of his comrades were sentenced to life imprisonment on 12 June 1964. He had already been in custody for 22 months, having been arrested on 5 August 1962 and sentenced to five years on 7 November 1962.

others', started on 1 December 1969. All pleaded not guilty to charges under the Suppression of Communism Act. These charges included:

> Establishing groups or committees within the banned African National Congress; taking or administering the oath of the ANC; recruiting members for the ANC; arranging, attending or addressing meetings of the ANC; inspecting trains to find sabotage targets; devising means for obtaining explosives; discussing, distributing or possessing publications by the ANC in exile; preparing, discussing, distributing or possessing ANC literature; propagating the Communist doctrine; discussing the establishment of contact with guerrilla fighters; arranging a funeral under the auspices of the ANC; encouraging people to listen to radio broadcasts of the ANC in Tanzania; discussing sending people outside the country; informally discussing and issuing instructions related to the affairs of the organisation.

After a range of witnesses testified and after Shanti Naidoo and Nondwe Mankahla were sentenced to two months for refusing to testify against her, the court adjourned to February 1970, when all 22 accused were acquitted but immediately re-detained by police.

Six months later they reappeared in court to face similar charges – this time under the Terrorism Act. Three of the accused turned state witness and MK operative Benjamin Ramotse was added to the list of accused. Mrs Mandela wrote in her journal of Mr Ramotse: 'I have never been involved with him in any of my political activities nor am I aware of his activities.'

On 14 September 1970, Mrs Mandela and all the accused except Mr Ramotse were acquitted.

Judge Gerrit Viljoen accepted that the alleged acts were so similar to the first that the prosecution was 'oppressive, vexatious and an abuse of the process of the court'.

As soon as she was able to, Mrs Mandela kept a secret journal, which she shared with her advocate David Soggot and did not see it again until 2011 when his widow Greta Soggot brought it to her office in parliament.

> *On the 10th of May I had been referred by my doctor to the specialist Dr Berman*
> *[who gave me a prescription] which I took to the chemist in West Street. I did not get*
> *all the tablets at the chemist, I was told to get the rest on a Monday as the 10th was*
> *a Saturday. I just had enough tablets for the weekend.*
> *When Maj Viktor[3] of the Johannesburg Security Branch told me that I would have*

---

3. Johannes Viktor.

to accompany him as he was detaining me under the Terr[orism] Act I wrote down the name of the chemist and the prescription No., and requested Peter Magubane who knew the chemist to fetch the rest of the tablets with a message that the tablets should be given to my attorney.

THE ARREST

12 MAY 1969

On the night of the Security Branch raid and my arrest I was reading the biography of Trotsky which I fetched the previous night from Mrs Betty Miya's house together with some documents.

On Friday the 9th of May 1969 I sent my 10yr old daughter to Mrs Miya to find out if I could visit her. She understood this to mean, 'is the coast clear,' she said I should not come, but that I could visit her the following day. It is not possible that I was followed to her house. I had used Mrs Miya's place for the past ten years. I sometimes sent Olive[4] with a paper bag parcel to give to Mrs Miya and I always put clothes on top if there were documents underneath. Mrs Miya was a child welfare foster mother; this was arranged by me to assist her with some income as she was unemployed and sickly. I gave her clothes for the children in her care from time to time.

On the night of the raid I put some of the documents in the stove with the book I was reading. The one copy of the Loabile[5] speech was brought by Sikosana[6] during that same week. He had taken it to No 1[7] earlier and I told him to return it so that I could destroy it.

When the police kicked the door open I had just taken it out of the kitchen units, I put it in the pocket of my gown. They started raiding the bedroom for almost two hours. I have a set of suitcases in which my husband's clothes, my new clothes and my children's clothes are kept besides the wardrobes. Major[8] went through the contents of each suitcase, he removed all my photographs, my husband's military attire which was sent back to me by the police after the

---

4. Her niece, Olive Nomfundo Mandela.
5. Lameck Loabile, an activist. The accused had arranged his funeral and an ANC flag, which they were charged for.
6. Joseph Sikosana turned out to be a police informer.
7. Accused No. 1, Samson Ndou.
8. Major Viktor of the security police.

Rivonia Trial. I protested and told this major that the police gave the attire back, he said that may well be and that was before his time – he was taking it.

As I packed the contents back into my husband's suitcase I managed to put the Loabile speech into the pocket of one of his folded jackets which I put back into the suitcase. I put the case back on top of the wardrobe with the assistance of the police.

This is the speech said to have been found with Maud.[9] It could have been found by a person who went through each garment looking for something. I cannot understand all this business about the removal of my clothes by Maud herself from my bedroom with the aid of a librarian from the *Rand Daily Mail*. Nor do I understand why the police who in any case had the speech naturally from Sikosana who kept it for a while before he brought it to me from No 1, should want to use Maud whom they have protected for so long.

I appreciate No 22's[10] desire to assist me by keeping my husband's clothes and mine in a safe place but my sister-in-law who is so adamant that no one have them, should in fact have kept them herself. She says she was very annoyed because none of the members of my family came near my house after my arrest for a whole month, but they went to Mr Carlson.[11] The fact that nobody paid rent, electricity and there was no one to look after Olive and the house was not important. She made all the arrangements for my children to return to school.

---

9. Maud Katzenellenbogen, a friend who Winnie Mandela later mistrusted as an informer.
10. Peter Magubane.
11. Attorney Joel Carlson.

Chapter 2

Detention

The first thing you do when you get into a cell is to do a calendar, the very first day because you lose track of days when you are in solitary confinement because the light was on for 24 hours and it was the brightest light – they never switched it off. You didn't know when it was sunset or daybreak; they never switched off the lights and in my case I was held in the death cell with three doors.
— WINNIE MADIKIZELA-MANDELA 2012

A DAY IN THE LIFE OF A DETAINEE

In the dim grim dark walls with the electric light burning day and night, the difference between day and night or daybreak and dawn is hard to tell when you can't sleep and all you do is to doze off now and again whenever the mind decides to stop over functioning for a while.

The cell measures 15' x 5'[12] or is it? I've walked miles and miles in this cell, round and round, backwards and forwards in a desperate attempt to kill the empty long lonely minutes, hours, weeks, months which drag by at a snail's pace gnawing at the inner cores of my soul, corroding it, scarring it, battering it about, tearing it to pieces in the second bout round number two[13] of the Terrorism Act boxing match between the 22 and the Security Branch.

The trouble with this match is that it has a biased referee; it may go on for years. The referee wants my side to lose, and he goes out of his way to break my

---

12. This is in feet. South Africa metricated between 1971–73. This would measure 4.5 x 1.5 metres.
13. The journal was started after Mrs Mandela and her co-accused were acquitted and immediately re-detained.

side. No rules and regulations have to be observed by his side whilst my boxers are forced at gunpoint to observe rules and regulations. The match has already had a bad start for someone; history will decide who of these two teams had this bad start. All I know is that both sides are determined to win the main match at whatever cost.

The first bell rings at 6am means it is time to get up, make my 'bed' and clean my cell. To make up my bed takes about five minutes for I have just two sisal mats, four blankets, the bitterly cold cement floor as my bed. I roll up the two mats, leaving about one foot of the mat underneath sticking out so that I can put my cold feet on this when I sit on the folded mats on top of which I put the neatly folded blanket to make my chair higher and a little more comfortable.

Both the blankets and the mats tell many tales each time I fold them up. Perhaps the mat underneath has the worst story to tell for about a quarter of this mat is full of blood, may be the blood all over this mat on top is the same but how did it come to appear to have been sprinkled all over the top mat? I wonder if it's the same blood which seems to have been scrubbed hurriedly off the wall, beneath the window and right at the corner which I have chosen for my bed. Whoever scrubbed it used a lot of [V]im, the hands must have been shaking badly or trembling for some reason, it's very untidily scrubbed.

I am next to the assault chamber. As long as I live I shall never forget the nightmares I have suffered as a result of the daily prisoners' piercing screams as the brutal corporal punishment is inflicted on them. As the cane lashes at them, sometimes a hose pipe, you feel it tearing at your own flesh mercilessly. It's hard to imagine women inflicting so much punishment. I have shed tears time without number quite unconsciously and often forget even to wipe them off. These hysterical screams pierce through my heart and injure my dignity so much. The hero of these assaults is barely 23 years old, very often the scream-ing voice appealing for mercy is that of a mother twice her age but of course she is white, a matron [at] that, this qualifies her for everything. The prisoner is at her mercy, life and all. She even bangs their heads against my cell wall in her fury. As the blood spurts from the gaping wounds she hits harder.

This matron has formidable assistants too in this business from what I hear through my cell window just above the assault chamber. They are Scantsu and Joyce.[14] Scantsu is also known as Maureen, she has recently been paroled to the Minister of Justice because of her 'exceptionally good conduct' which earned her ten months remission because once in 1968 she chased and caught an escaped female prisoner whom she assaulted mercilessly as part of her 'good

---

14. Fellow detainee and co-accused Joyce Sikakane.

conduct'. These 'assistants' receive prisoners on their arrival daily from court after the formalities of entering them into the huge reception book in the front office where matron Wessels spends most of her time. There is so much change of staff you never know who is doing what at a time, where and when.

I have been in this prison for over a year but I only have a vague idea of sections which I have been transferred to one time or another. I am whisked away so fast that I have been unable to draw a sketch in my mind of this prison. I know the row of six cells and the high wall in front of the cells. My door faces west, the wall on the extreme right of my cell is built very high, it is made in the shape of an entrance to the church cathedral, it looks so odd and out of place in these surroundings. This wall must be very old or rather the prison must be old. It's full of cracks and looks like it will tumble down at the slightest earth tremor. Just where my cell ends there is a corrugated iron wall extending from the corner of my cell right up to the stone wall, almost enclosing the church-like porch – this is the assault chamber – on the other side of the corrugated iron wall. The distance between my cell door and high stone wall is 1½ yards.[15] On the extreme left where cell number 1 is occupied by Acc. No. 7[16] there is a big grille gate which is permanently locked shutting us off completely from the rest of the prison. The exercise yard in front of our six cells is therefore 5½ x 1½ yards.[17]

Monday morning sounds like the busiest day in this prison but to me it's just like any other day or even Sunday for that matter. In solitary confinement my daily routine is full of nothing. My cell inventory is highly limited too, it's as follows:

(a) Two mats (sisal)
(b) 4 blankets
(c) 1 filthy plastic bottle in which is my drinking water
(d) 1 'pon' (sanitary bucket)
(e) 1 metal mug
(f) Soap (blue and carbolic) the latter for my face
(g) All my clothes

On my detention I was stripped of my suitcase, books, handbag, hangers, nails on the wall which were my wardrobe, tinned food. All my clothes were savagely thrown on the floor, scattered all over the black cell floor as if in anger.

15. 1.37 metres.
16. Joyce Sikakane.
17. 5 x 1.37 metres.

They were tramped on too, they are full of foot marks with the black floor polish. I have three blankets to fold in the morning, the fourth is my suitcase and pillow at night. The seams of all four blankets are broken. Someone must have wanted to keep her mind occupied just like I did at the Johannesburg Fort in September 1968 when I served four days on a suspended sentence. I served the four days in solitary confinement. I was given six blankets, soft and clean. At the end of the four days I had undone the seams of all six blankets and had derived a great deal of pleasure from this. I was really highly privileged then, new blankets are a rare luxury in prison, how lovely it was to pull that lovely white cotton.

I have a small rag, my floor cloth which I use for polishing my cell floor, this rag is too filthy to be touched with the hands before breakfast and in prison we do things the other way round. It's common practice to eat breakfast before you wash. I have therefore never knelt down to polish, besides I feel I should not kneel down when I am a convicted prisoner. My feet are already used to the simple process – just one foot on the cloth and reach the floor with the toes. It's an enjoyable warming up exercise especially in winter, you end up almost jiving as you change the feet quickly. The only trouble is that the cell floor is very rough, rugged in fact. My feet used to get caught in some of the holes but I can now polish with my eyes closed after such long practice.

My colour scheme has an ominous effect on me, it is so depressing. My corrugated iron ceiling, home for the fattest and noisiest rats in Pretoria was originally white. The upper wall light grey and the bottom dark grey, the door is painted light grey, the peep hole is surrounded with black paint. In the evening I welcome the company of rats up there in the ceiling, at least it's something to listen to as they dart all over the ceiling. I often wonder if they are playing or fighting, or perhaps they are as cold as I am and therefore trying to warm themselves up.

In this cell so many of my people have spent tortuous moments. The walls are an encyclopaedia on the different types of persons held in the cell at one time or another. I scrutinise the cell walls daily to discover some rude and angry insults hurled at some prison official on the grey paint and underneath the dark dull layers of years of paint. It's so easy to tell what state of mind each prisoner was in, this mute expression – writing on the wall is the only emotional catharsis for a prisoner in solitary confinement. Why, you may even guess the prisoner's personality from this writing.

Most of the visible handwriting is extremely vulgar, it is mostly directed to 'Ma Britz se ...' 'Mrs Britz's something ...' scrawled all over the door in deep letters. Then below the peep hole is 'Unkulu-nkulu ukhona ndizophuma mntakwethu, ungandilahle dudu'. This is Zulu meaning 'God is there my dear, I will be released, don't reject me my love'. On the right side of the wall is a drawing of house and flowers, the house has twelve steps on which stand an emaciated (picture) drawing of a woman clutching two sinewy armed children with extended tummies, a thin dog, the apparent father of the children who is the fattest of all this group is walking right ahead of his wife. The faces of all are grim. There is an arrow pointing at the woman with the worlds below 'Le nto ephalwa ngeminwe, le jna ethanda isnanga-nanga.' I have since discovered that 'isinanga-nanga' is the prisoners' lingo for homosexual practice. 'This dog. You love homosexualism, you allow fingers to be used on you.'

On the lift wall is a 1964 calendar drawn from beginning of April. Above it is 'my third wedding anniversary'. This is covered with layers of paint. In the same handwriting, 'I will not be terrorised', beneath this is, 'Mandela your wife is a sell out', then, 'my mother is'. I burst out laughing alone when I discovered this in October 1969, a day after I was charged in the Pretoria Supreme Court with twenty-one others. I recognised the handwriting as that of Zozo Mahlasela. I learned from Swanepoel, the head of my country's Gestapo during my interrogation of five days and six nights that this Zozo Mahlasela was sent to my in-laws in the Transkei to take certain letters when my husband was facing the Rivonia Trial. The Mahlaselas fled the country in 1965 or 1964 after long spells of detention under 90 days.

In a frail handwriting almost at the corner, hardly visible is 'Ndopho was here from the 22nd of May on account of Joyce Sikhakhane's sake'. In the same handwriting, 'Joyce was also here'. This is Nondwe Makahla's piece. She looked as frail as her handwriting when I saw her for the first time the day she stood in the dock and declared, 'I refused to give evidence against my people.' Ndopho is her nickname.

Scribbled almost hurriedly it seems or perhaps in deep meditation two feet[18] from the floor on the door is, 'Trust in the Lord thy God, in Him I shall be saved. Pray no matter how difficult times may be, never lose faith. He will answer your prayers.' This was Shanti Naidoo whom I still see vividly in my mind, her dark hollow eyes, her thin arms hanging loosely out of that pale yellowish sleeveless dress, her slanted head when she craned her neck in the dock with her misty eyes strained to hear Justice Bekker[19] on that memorable day when she declared in a firm voice which left no doubt, 'I will not be able to live with my conscience for the rest of my life if I give evidence.'

18. 0.6 metres.
19. The trial judge, Simon Bekker.

How I loved her always and even more now. My admiration and respect for her is doubled. Only a person who has been through solitary confinement would realise the amount of sacrifice that lies behind those few words. To my horror hot tears rolled down my checks in the Supreme Court when Shanti said those words – I concealed my face from the press reporters by shielding behind accused No. 5's[20] shoulder, then No. 4.[21] The prospect of screaming headlines in the so called non-white papers, 'Mandela's wife weeps in court' was not a very palatable thought.

Scrawled untidily in cursive is 'October 17th I shall never forget' followed by a number of scratches. This is my sister's mark. Beneath this is a half hearted attempt to draw a calendar, she recorded just the first few days of each month. It's amazing she is just like that at home too. Nonyaniso Madikizela is as stubborn as a mule, has no continuity of purpose. If she cleans the house she will do all the rooms at the same time and leave them halfway if she feels like it. She can be exceptionally neat and just as exceptionally untidy. As a child only father managed to discipline her when she started with her tantrums. He had to give up placing her in boarding school because she packed her clothes and went home if she was fed up with the teachers. That's how she ended up in day schools whilst all the other children were in boarding schools. I can never get over the shock of seeing her as a submissive docile witness for the state in our trial with half her weight gone with the brutality of solitary confinement. At that moment I felt so bitter that time will never heal the bleeding wounds inflicted on me by this experience. From now henceforth I prefer my feelings left at that, perhaps this will justify my own attitude of tomorrow.

That reminds me that this is the third cell I've occupied since my arrival on the 12th of May 1969. On this date I was taken to a cell upstairs. At the entrance to the prison there is a big door on the left. From inside this door there are 39 shiny black steps which lead to the cells upstairs. There is one cell however separated by a locked grille/gate from the rest of the two long rows of cells with a long passage between. The door of this isolated cell faces north west, one small window faces east and another large one much higher facing west. The first three days I spent in this cell were the most wonderful days I've ever had in prison because of the small window which I reached with ease, opened it and gazed at the outside world from the moment I finished my breakfast.

My daily routine in all three cells was the same, full of nothing. After cleaning the cell I washed my mouth, face and hands into the sanitary buckets with

---

20. Elliot Shabangu.
21. Jackson Mahluale.

the drinking water poured into the mug. There are no lavatories in all three cells so I had to use the same bucket for everything. I trained my stomach to work once a day, in the morning just after washing my mouth, face and hands because this 'pon' is changed once a day, in the morning only.

When the second bell rings at 7am the wardress opens the cell door. I take out my 'pon', bottle of drinking water, the mug and the Dixie.[22] These I put just outside my door where I find already waiting for me a bucket of washing water, a plate of porridge, a clean 'pon' rarely with a disinfectant. Once when my 'pon' was the enamel type with a flat lid, my dixie was put on top of the pon. The wardress then pours into my mug black sugarless coffee or just so little sugar it makes very little difference. The door is closed. The porridge is seldom cooked, often I am compelled to do without breakfast. This porridge is dished up about 40–50 yards[23] from my cell, by the time I take it it's already cold and covered with dust. No hygienic rules are observed in prison, the food is not covered. I also bring in drinking water.

I eat before I wash as I would like to eat warm food, then I wash and get dressed, I wash my teeth with toothpaste if I have it, into the washing bucket. I also wash my mug and spoon into the washing bucket. After about an hour the door is opened again for me to take my washing water out with the breakfast dixie. Sometimes I also go out at this time for exercise for about 15 to 20 minutes. I exercise by going round and round the exercise yard. When the wardress is not looking I knock on the doors of my colleagues to greet them. For months this was our only means of communication until we decided the Aucamp[24] lot could go to hell, we just shouted to each other at night and pretended we did not hear the Afrikaans-speaking wardress screaming at us to keep quiet. This is down at the punishment cells. The lunch is served at 11.30am. Our menu is as follows:

---

22. A steel plate.
23. 36.5–45.7 metres.
24. Commissioner of Prisons Brigadier Aucamp.

	Breakfast	Lunch	Supper
Monday	Uncooked porridge Black coffee	Porridge, sugar beans, beetroot	Dry cooked mealies and phuzamandla
Tuesday	Uncooked porridge Black coffee	Porridge, over-cooked spinach and fried fish	Dry cooked mealies and phuzamandla
Wednesday	Uncooked porridge Black coffee	Porridge, sugar beans, sometimes overcooked spinach	Dry cooked mealies and phuzamandla
Thursday	Uncooked porridge Black coffee	Porridge, overcooked spinach, half ounce meat	Dry cooked mealies and phuzamandla
Friday	Uncooked porridge Black coffee	Porridge, sugar beans overcooked spinach	Dry cooked mealies and phuzamandla
Saturday	Cooked porridge and coffee	Porridge, beetroot, half ounce meat. Sometimes sweet potatoes	Dry cooked mealies and phuzamandla
Sunday	Cooked porridge and coffee	Porridge, beetroot, half ounce meat. Sometimes sweet potatoes	Dry cooked mealies and phuzamandla

Chapter 3

Acquittal and Re-detention

On 16 February 1970 Winnie Mandela and her co-accused appeared in court after an adjournment of more than a month. The Attorney General himself, Kenneth Donald McIntyre Moodie, made a rare appearance in court and declared that he was with-drawing the charges against all 22 of the accused. The judge pronounced that they could leave but the Security Police re-detained them and took them back to Pretoria Central Prison. They also confiscated the notes that they had been preparing for their defence team.

THE NEW DETENTION SINCE FEBRUARY 16, 1970

ARRIVAL FROM COURT ON 16TH

On our arrival from court on the 16th of February 1970 we found members of the Security Branch waiting for us in the matron's office. In court I had left my plastic bag containing all my documents on the bench with the hope that my attorney would see the bag and take it. I anticipated what would happen later on and although the documents were mostly court records of the case I have all my draft notes on certain portions of the Saga[25] and the biographical data

---

25. Mrs Mandela had titled the journal and collection of notes as the 'Saga' after the name given to their detention and trial by Advocate David Soggott.

on the two accused 17[26] and 18[27]. Unfortunately Victor Mazituleli[28] thought I had forgotten the bag and he picked it up and brought it to me. I was stopped by the police at the entrance of the court trying to take it back to my attorney. The members of the SB[29] called us into the office one by one and took everything we had on us including pens, cigarettes etc.

BACK IN THE CELLS

No. 7 was the first to be called by the matron to go to the cell. She kissed us goodbye and was promptly told by Britz that she would be deprived of three meals the following days for this act. I was the last to be taken to the cells after standing outside for about an hour. At the entrance to my cell I found everything outside including the suitcase and the handbag which had my clothes.

I was stripped naked outside and entered the cell naked after the matron had searched my naked body. Inside the cell my clothes were on the floor, four stinking blankets, one sanitary bucket and drinking water plus two sisal mats. I asked the matron what I was expected to do with the clothes on the floor without a suitcase. She said she was acting on instructions. Even the nails on which I hung some of my clothes had been removed.

I wrapped the clothes with one blanket and used them as my pillow. Normally every prisoner has six blankets so that one can use two as pillows. From that very day I noticed the food ration was almost half of what we usually get when we were served with supper. We were back to the usual mental agony of solitary confinement.

We saw Brig Aucamp for the first time on the 24th of February. He saw us one by one in our cells. He was in a very jovial mood. He told me that we were re-detained because we violated prison conditions with all those letters we had been writing. I said I thought we were detained in terms of the Terrorism Act and I asked if letters were acts of terrorism. He said it was no use cracking my head over that because in any case we would be kept at least for the next eight years, that I could be sure of. He further said (with amusement) that if he was in my position he would seriously consider escaping from prison. (I

26. Douglas Mvembe.
27. Venus Thokozile Mngoma.
28. A fellow accused.
29. Security Branch of the South African Police.

took this to be a sarcastic reference to the portion of the Saga which deals with my husband's suggested escape from the Fort.)[30] I thought the Saga must have been confiscated from my defence the day we were detained as no mention is made of this in the chronological order draft which they must have made a photostat copy of.

THE VISITING MAGISTRATE

That same week the visiting magistrate called on a Thursday. We almost all made similar complaints.

(a) That our suitcases be returned as we had nothing in which to put our clothes.

(b) That we be allowed reading matter.

(c) I requested that charges be brought against me, that Brig Aucamp said we violated prison conditions and that surely General Nel has efficient staff who wouldn't take so long to investigate such charges.

(d) That we be allowed to exercise together as the time allocated to our exercises was at the most ten minutes, and that twice or thrice a week.

(e) Later on we complained about the little food, the stinking blankets and the dirty overcooked vegetables.

There was only a slight improvement on exercises and cleaner blankets were exchanged for the filthy one, otherwise we got tired of complaining to the visiting magistrate as there was just no point.

The SB's followed up each magistrate's visit to tell us we shall be charged when they feel like doing so and that we shall never get reading matter.

On the 17th of March Dirker came to tell me (thumbing his chest as he spoke), 'We shall decide when to charge you, you must stop at once telling the magistrate every time you want to be charged.' I screamed back and said who is he to tell me that. I asked if he had been promoted to the post of attorney general and that I thought he was a warrant officer, a rank he held before I was born. Britz who was with them screamed at me, 'I am sick and tired of your

---

30. Mrs Mandela had written notes about a plot to have her husband escape from prison in 1962. It was not carried out due to fears that it was part of a plan to kill him.

nonsense, you must stop talking like that' – the cell door was banged. I had long sat down and disregarded the whole lot. Later on matron Zeelie came to tell me I would be deprived of three meals that following day.

On the 18th I was therefore punished, the girls also boycotted the food in protest except Acc. 17.[31] The following day there was a complete change of attitude, the staff was more friendly. That following Sunday and Monday we were visited by the most senior members of the prison department to ask us if we had any specific complaints against the prison conditions. Unfortunately they were never introduced so we never knew who they were but from the number of stars and medals I suspected one was General Nel.

That was the first and last time I personally saw Dirker.

THE EASTER WEEKEND

During the second week of March we had a shower specially installed next to our cells with the hot water system as well.[32] It is just an enclosure with corrugated iron in an open space and has no roof. We had showers only then. This can only be used in summer although the wardresses daily ask if we want to shower which is impossible in this weather. On a Saturday of the Easter weekend Brig Aucamp visited me in the cell. He said, 'I was with your husband this week, he is full of nonsense as usual. He is putting on weight for the first time ever since he has been in prison all these years – very happy that his wife is in prison I suppose – strange love! The last time he ever looked as he does [was] in the early 60s.' He mumbled something else, by then the cell door was long closed before I could say anything.

DURING MARCH 1970

During the 1st week of March we were given Bibles and hymn books. The first few days I read the Bible but soon discovered that I read one sentence more

31. Venus Thokozile Mngoma.
32. Access to showers resulted from legal action by the attorneys of the accused.

than four or five times and still absorbed nothing at all.

Up to this stage the wardresses and the matrons hardly spoke to us at all and they wore long faces and were very nasty. The maximum exercise period was about ten minutes thrice a week at the most. Often we were locked up from Thursday to Monday continuously.

After the quarrel and my punishment of the 18th March referred to in my first notes I developed a new type of attack at night mostly.

THE ATTACKS

It would start off as a blackout although I would be lying flat and slightly propped up. I then felt completely numb, the whole body – I lose complete control over my muscles and struggle to breathe and [have an] irregular heart beat. The body then jerks into functioning in a very painful spasm. I then breathe very fast and sweat a lot. I grew afraid to sleep and sat up the whole night. I literally became afraid of nightfall and started getting anxious towards the afternoon. On two occasions when the attacks were very bad at night I banged on the wall of my cell neighbour Acc. No. 17 who is a very heavy sleeper. Acc. No. 18[33] who is four cells away from me heard me but I could not shout to her as we were not allowed to communicate.

RETENTION OF URINE AND EXCESSIVE BLEEDING

During the third week of March I had difficulty with passing water. This often happened after the attacks described above. I would struggle for hours especially during the night. I would try seven or eight times before I passed a little drop of water. I asked to see the doctor. In prison you merely give the history of your illness and the doctor prescribes. The doctor who saw me on this occasion is not the one who usually treats me, he stood outside the cell and asked

33. Martha Dlamini.

me to give him the history of my illness. He prescribed something. I was also bleeding profusely for eight days, my normal period is three days. This was also a complication I had suffered on my previous detention. The hospital orderly gave me something for bleeding.

During the first week of April the retention of urine grew worse even though I was taking the new treatment. I was then taking eight different drugs three times a day. The sleeping tablets were increased by the doctor who had seen me before and I was able to sleep half the night at least. I found out however that if I did not get the sleeping tablets I did not have a wink of sleep and that is the position to this day. The bleeding continued endlessly until the doctor prescribed something else.

I was convinced in my mind that I was becoming a drug addict. I was frightened when I thought of what I would go through if I got a long prison term and I knew that I would never get my treatment then.

The bitter taste in my mouth which I suffered as a result of loss of appetite grew worse. I did not feel like eating at all.

Chapter 4

State of Mind

The thought of beginning another period of detention was almost too much to bear.

MY STATE OF MIND DURING THE FIRST TWO WEEKS OF MY RE-DETENTION

Perhaps because I already had experience of what I would go through in solitary confinement, the first two weeks were the most gruesome period I've ever gone through. I went through the following phases:

(a) I was lucky if I got my three times a day treatment once a day. I had to literally beg for my tablets from the matrons and the wardresses. I just could not sleep at all even when I did get all the tablets sometimes. I was alarmed when I found myself walking in my sleep. On four occasions I remember finding myself standing near the door. I tried to think how I got there but could not reconstruct any movements. This happened when I did fall asleep for a short while.

(b) I had horrible nightmares and woke up screaming in the night. I discovered I spoke aloud when I thought of my children and literally held conversations with them. I cried almost hysterically when I recalled their screams on the night of my arrest. I just cannot get this out of my mind up to date. I spent the whole day walking up and down my cell hoping to exhaust myself so that I could sleep at night.

(c) I realised that although I was not sleeping I did not either feel tired or drowsy during the day. I could not bear the glare of the light day and night. I was growing more and more tense each day.

(d) I suffered from loss of appetite and because I ate so little, my colleagues' food was reduced to almost a quarter of our daily rations. This was enough for me but serious punishment for my colleagues. I then decided to throw my food in the sanitary bucket. [Unnamed accused] suffered most as she is a heavy eater. I told No. 9 and 7 who were also poor eaters to dispose of their food as I did if they had not finished it. We whispered to each other at night.

(e) The blackouts which I have now had for the whole year of my detention grew worse and lasted longer. If I stood up suddenly I fell down. When I recovered I felt the blood rushing to the upper part of my body especially the head. I would then put my head between my knees.

(f) I filled the long and empty endless hours by reconstructing the story of my life in my mind. I was nine years old when I lost my mother, I can hardly remember her but I longed for her and cried bitterly when I thought of her. I remembered my hard childhood years without her, how poor my family was although my father was the school principal. I recalled how I had to wash his khaki shirt and iron it overnight, his baggy trousers often full of holes and I ironed them so badly because I was too young. The secret childhood tears I shed when the school children teased me about my shabbily dressed father. Mother's illness had drained his pockets and we were nine children. Mother was ill for years and every penny was spent on doctor's fees all over the district. When she died I had to nurse my three-month-old baby brother. All this came to my mind as though it had happened yesterday. I cried when I remembered how I cried as I was forced to leave school, put my baby brother on my back and go to look after cattle. Father could not afford even to hire a herd boy which was common practice those days.

(g) I could feel the blood pressure was dropping again. My pulse was raised and I had the attacks of breathlessness even during the day, this I never had before. I often had these at night if I lay flat.

(h) I worried a great deal about how I felt and worried more about the 'boys' in our group. I thought endlessly about how I could save my colleagues from this mental agony. I felt it was my duty to do something to save them no matter how drastic it would be as long as Nelson and my people would understand.

Chapter 5

The Decision

APRIL 1970

MY DECISION

During the second week of April I just could not take solitary confinement any more. I realised it might go on for another year before we were charged. There was no sign that we were going to be interrogated again. It suddenly dawned on me that if I took my life there would be no trial and my colleagues would be saved from the tortuous mental agony of solitary confinement. The long and empty hours tore through the inner core of my soul. There were moments when I got so fed up I banged my head against the cell wall. Physical pain was more tolerable.

I decided I would commit suicide but would do so gradually so that I should die of natural causes to spare Nelson and the children the pains of knowing I had taken my life. I thought there would be no better method of focusing the world attention on the terror of the Terrorism Act than this. I wanted also to avoid my death being interpreted as an act of cowardice hence the decision to make it look a natural death. I made up my mind I would first find out what was happening outside, try and establish contact with my attorney and my family so that I could leave a farewell note for my husband and my children which I would smuggle during the last few days of my life. I decided to take the following steps in preparation for my suicide:

(a) I remembered that it was possible for F.B.[34] to communicate with one from the prison hospital, so if I landed myself in prison hospital, I might find a way of communicating with my attorney. I stopped taking my treatment. If the wardress stood in the cell to see that I took my tablets I put them under my tongue and spat them into the sanitary bucket as soon as the door was locked.

(b) I stopped eating. I drank my black cup of coffee in the morning. It is not sugared at all and it acted as a stimulant to my weak heart so the pulse was raised daily. I did not even attempt to sleep, I sat up through the night thinking of the step I had decided to take. I convinced myself that my own contribution to the struggle of my people was too infinitesimal and that at the moment there were too many odds against us in my country for any positive action and that my death would be a major contribution which would stir up world opinion and touch the conscience of those fellow South Africans who still have some conscience, especially the church and student groups. But I later decided I would say in my farewell note that I had taken my life in protest to the Terrorism Act. I wondered how many of my people had died in prison without anyone knowing, especially those who were arrested during the border clashes between SA's security forces and our men.

(c) I stopped asking for permission to see the doctor. I lost weight rapidly. When I had my attacks they lasted longer each time. Towards the last week of April I noticed that during the attack certain parts of the body would jerk and twitch (almost epileptic like). Strangely enough I felt very happy within myself. I enjoyed the bitter sweetness of unjust suffering and was quite excited when I thought how dramatic my death would be. I was so happy at times I fell asleep and hoped I would not get up the following day even if I had not gone as far as the hospital, I did not care anymore.

---

34. Unknown.

ACC. 4 24.6.70

MY DECISION CONTINUED

I continued with my plans until the 1st of May when I was taken to Compol Building[35] for interrogation. The rest of the information as to what took place thereafter is contained in my first notes already submitted. The following however was omitted for fear that the notes may be perused as before by the wardresses before they are handed to my attorney.

Brig Aucamp visited me on my return from the Compol Building. He had not seen me for quite a long time. This is the day I screamed at him about our suitcases and the conditions of our detention. He expressed his alarm about my loss of weight. It is him who arranged for me to be examined on the 6th of May. That was the day the doctor recommended urgent hospitalisation.

On the evening of the 1st of May Rita[36] spoke to me at night. She said she had never heard me scream before the way I did when I spoke to Brig Aucamp. I think they were all generally concerned that I might make things worse for them. I explained that I personally thought that was the only way to deal with Brig as he completely misunderstands respect, he mistakes it for submission. They all expressed their gratitude when they got the suitcases, and realised that the screaming had achieved results after all.

During the exercise time on the 6th of May I managed to whisper through the peep hole of my cell door to No. 7 and told her I was going to hospital. I told her to tell the others not to worry because I had aggravated my condition deliberately to force the Aucamp group into taking some sort of decision concerning us even if it was re-interrogation for that matter. I told her I hoped to bring back some news from the hospital.

AFTER THE MEDICAL EXAMINATION OF THE 6TH OF MAY

I think the doctor became suspicious that I had not been taking treatment or that something else had developed other than the heart condition. He

---

35. Security police headquarters.
36. Rita Ndzanga, fellow detainee and co-accused.

withdrew all the treatment and told matron Zeelie that he would not risk giving me any treatment until I was seen by the specialist. He said my condition was too bad. The very first night I spent in hospital I managed to speak to the prisoner who was ordered by Brig to sleep with me in hospital. Brig Aucamp gave me strict orders that I was not to speak to the said prisoner at all. There had to be someone with me because the doctor said I was very ill.

The hospital was cleared of very sick patients and I was locked up alone in hospital. When food was brought the wardress sat in hospital to see that I ate. Because I had not eaten for so long the stomach was immediately upset. I brought up all the food. The hospital orderly was called and he gave me tablets to stop the vomiting but I got worse.

By the 7th I had all the latest information about what was going on outside. I was checked daily by the hospital orderly. I continued vomiting and getting weaker. The appointment for the specialist was for the 20th of May. In the meantime the prison doctor prescribed something else I had not taken before (some red tablets).

I learned of new developments outside, the students' protests,[37] the press uproar etc. I then realised those concerned would soon be forced to issue a statement which might reveal our fate. I saw the statement issued by the Minister of Justice to the effect that we would be charged or released soon and the various statements issued by the Bar Council, Mr Wentzel, our attorney, Mr Mncube, Maponya,[38] Dr Nkomo, Bishop Stranling[39] etc. I could not wait to be back with my colleagues. All my plans were now changed. I was thrilled at the prospect of facing a trial at last. After seeing all the specialists as fully described in the notes already submitted I begged the matron to have me discharged back to the cell.

On the 13th or 14th of May I managed to smuggle a note to my family and attorney. That was when I still had the original plans in mind. I was very ill at the time. I was discharged on the 10th of June upon my request. That night I told my colleagues all the latest developments. But I was still too weak to have returned to the cell hence my re-admission on 15th June.[40]

---

37. Students from the University of the Witwatersrand had protested against the continued detention of Mrs Mandela and her group.

38. Richard Maponya.

39. Anglican bishop of Johannesburg.

40. Mrs Mandela was not at the next court appearance on 18 June 1970 because of her hospitalisation.

Chapter 6

Health

MY PRESENT STATE OF HEALTH

My monthly periods have just been continuous this month since the new complication of bronchitis and anaemia and something else I do not know. I saw the long medical term in my file when the Pretoria District Surgeon examined me on the 18th. I am feeling very weak possibly due to too much loss of weight and the poor appetite has not improved at all although Dr Morgan had said the anti-depressant would also improve my appetite but she did say we should not expect miracles, it would be a long process and it will be slow.

THE PRESENT TREATMENT

The heart treatment is as it was before my re-detention. The original treatment which was originally prescribed by the specialist last year and subsequently withdrawn and substituted with something else (yellow capsules and three other drugs) by the prison doctor is what I am getting at the moment since my admission to hospital. It is four drops which I take three times a day. The ones I know are Inderal, Roche [sic], Mondex and the fourth one is the psychiatrist's prescription.

For the bleeding I get two injections every other day. I usually stop bleeding the day I get the injections and start bleeding again the second day before I get the next injections. I have not had those awful attacks since I have been taking the psychiatrist's treatment. So perhaps I needed psychiatrist's treatment after all! My defence once said after reading a portion of the Saga, 'You have really suffered brain damage.' 'Are you in touch with reality?'

I also remember that I just could not remember what day of the week it was when Dr Morgan wanted to know. I get so shocked when the mind just gets completely blank and I can't remember the simplest things no matter how hard I try to remember sometimes.

EVENTS FROM THE 6TH OF MAY

On the 6th of May I was seen by the doctor. I was at that stage taking eight different drugs three times a day. The black-outs had developed into bouts of semi-unconsciousness which would last for about 15 minutes. I was also suffering from the retention of urine, an unbearable condition which kept me awake the whole night no matter how heavily drugged I was.

After examining me the doctor was very shocked. He said my condition was very bad. He ordered that I should be hospitalised urgently. He said all treatment should be stopped until I am seen by the cardiac specialised Dr Weiss. I was taken back to the cell. Within half an hour Brig Aucamp arrived – I was taken to the matron's office. He told me he had decided that I should be admitted to the prison hospital and that the specialist would come and see me in prison. (The prison doctor had said I should be admitted to the General Hospital.) I know the problem was security in a public hospital.

In the afternoon of the 6th I was admitted to the prison hospital which was cleaned and I was solitary confined in it. The poor patients were returned to their cells. I got worse in hospital, I could not retain any solids, I brought up all the food except porridge. The senior hospital orderly gave me treatment until the 13th of May when I refused to take anymore treatment because I continued bringing up the food. I demanded to see the doctor who came the following day.

He prescribed the original treatment I took on my arrival in prison, a double dose of Inderal, Roche and two other drugs. He told me my appointment to see the specialist was for the 20th of May.

20TH OF MAY

The Security Branch took me to Dr Weiss' consulting rooms. I was examined for two hours by another specialist. Dr Weiss was also present. He told me they had held a conference and decided I should be seen by this other specialist as two opinions are better than one. After the exhaustive examination, taking of blood specimens, ECG test, X-rays and the usual heart tests the doctor told me his diagnosis was Hyperventilation. That the heart is working against unimaginable odds. It triggers off certain electrons which result in my breathing abnormally fast to such an extent that the required amount of carbon dioxide to maintain the blood is consumed.

That there were very many causes for the condition e.g. lack of calcium, iron, sugar, proteins but the commonest is acute tension, anxiety and mental strain. He said only a series of blood tests would reveal the cause, there was no point in treating the symptoms. He said he would arrange for a gynaecologist to see me as anaemia had also set in and that was possibly due to the fact that I get my monthly periods twice a month since my detention. He also said arrangements would be made with the prison doctor for me to have a 'sleeping bag' into which I would breathe in the same carbon dioxide I exhaled at night.

26TH OF MAY

On the 26th I was taken by the SBs to the 7th floor of the Pretoria Medical Centre. I have forgotten the name of the doctor, but it is a laboratory. Several blood specimens were taken and urine specimens.

27TH OF MAY

The prison doctor saw me again in hospital. He told me he had received the cardiac specialist's report, it was obvious that my condition was deteriorating due to acute tension and mental strain. He told me they have arranged for a psychiatrist to see me, that I should not worry as they did not think I am mad, they merely wanted his opinion. That my treatment would be changed only when he had received all the reports. It was also noted that I had lost 18 lbs[41] of weight on the 20th.

28TH OF MAY

On the 28th of May I was taken from the hospital to the matron's office where I found two doctors (psychiatrists) from Weskoppies. One was a woman doctor, Dr Morgan, and she is the one who carried out the interview. (I have always had trouble distinguishing between the psychiatrist and the mental patient.) On this date I was however more convinced than ever that psychiatrists are really mentally sick people. The absurd questions I was asked were as follows; to mention a few –

    (a) 'My assistant and I have come to find out how we can help you solve your problems – would you like to tell us the nature of the additional problems that seem to have disturbed you so much lately.'

    Reply – 'yes certainly – my problems are solitary confinement and the political ones do not belong to a psychiatrist's diary. In fact the person who needs your interview is the one who subjects human beings to solitary confinement for over a year.'

    (b) 'Please bear with us Mrs Mandela we are merely here to help you, we understand how you feel. How old are your children, where are they and who looks after them now that you are here?'

    Reply – I gave the ages – told them I do not know the rest of the information as I am cut off from the outside world. I do not communicate with my family and therefore do not know where the children are.

    (c) 'Do you sometimes feel [hallucinatory] and have you ever had any doubts about your mind or thought of consulting a psychiatrist in your private life?'

---

41. 8 kilograms.

I laughed and did not bother myself by replying to this. I just said I was feeling very amused. I told her however that I have a schizophrenic brother and I happen to know that he suffered from this as a result of our unhappy childhood – that was however a family matter I did not wish to discuss any further – I was interrogated enough on why I went to visit him in Sterkfontein without permission. I knew this Dr Morgan was driving to this point – possibly to find out if there were more mentally ill members of the family.

(d) The most pathetic of all questions was, 'Do you feel you are chosen by God for the role you are playing amongst your people – the leadership role? Do you hear God's voice sometimes telling you to lead your people?'

Reply: 'Dr Morgan, I would like to co-operate with you, I would not like to display my temper before you as you have nothing to do with my being here unless of course you are one of those who voted for the people who locked me up. If you have no more questions to ask I suggest we put an end to the interview. I deeply resent the indirect insult on my national pride and my husband's. Would you ask Vorster's[42] wife the same question if the situation was reversed?'

'You are quite right Mrs Mandela in feeling the way you do, I'm very sorry I have no intention of upsetting you. It's just that you look so depressed and strained my desire is simply to try and assist you.'

'Of course I am depressed and tense naturally – how else can I be when I am subjected to the brutal conditions we have been subjected to for a whole year?'

Dr Morgan: 'Do not worry about your gross loss of weight, it is natural under the circumstances. I will however prescribe an anti-depressant for you to help you ease the tension and we shall see you again next week.'

That was the last I saw of this nauseating couple. My informant told me an urgent meeting with Brig Aucamp, the General, members of the Security Branch

---

42. The then South African prime minister, John Vorster.

and all the matrons was held with the psychiatrist immediately I left the office. All the windows and doors were closed and all the prisoners who normally work in the office were ordered off the premises. When she took the tea she was met at the door by the matron (normally she serves the tea) and she overheard the words 'some sort of trial will have to take place urgently if we are to justify' ... the door was closed. She could not recognise the voice, she assumed it was one of the doctors.

2ND OF JUNE 1970

The gynaecologist called at the prison hospital and I underwent a very painful examination which last approximately an hour. Specimens were taken for further tests to establish the cause of fortnightly periods and anaemia. After the examination the doctor told me he was satisfied the cause was mental strain and stress. He also said he will submit his report after the completion of the tests to the Commissioner of Police.

On the 10th of June I was discharged from the hospital and sent back to the cell. Towards the early hours of the following morning all the symptoms started all over again. I asked to see the doctor on the 12th. Brig visited me in the cell late in the afternoon with the matron. He told me the doctor would see me on Monday the 15th. On Saturday the 13th my condition grew much worse, the senior hospital orderly came to take my temperature and found that I was running a very high temperature. I was ordered back to bed which was brought to my cell. The temperature got worse, our cells have no window panes and the draft is terrible during the night.

On Monday 15th I was re-admitted to the prison hospital. On Tuesday the 16th members of the Security Branch visited me to take fingerprints. Brig Aucamp later visited me and told me he was going to Robben Island. He granted me permission to write a note to my husband on condition I wrote nothing political, no date and no address. I wrote a very short note informing Nelson that I was not well. I also wrote that he should arrange with Brig to see our attorney to appoint the children's guardian so that the guardian should include the children in his passport to enable them to spend holidays with my family. That the fact that they had never been home ever since I was detained might have a grave psychological effect on them in the long run. They are still too young and need the security of the family. I asked him to treat the matter as urgent. I also stated that the attorney and the guardian have to administer the Waterford[43] Bursary and certain forms to this effect have to be signed urgently. Brig reminded me that I was not to mention the note to anyone as he had been stopped from permitting correspondence between us. He was doing me a special favour!

MEDICAL REPORTS

I would like my defence to apply for all the medical reports which have been submitted to the Commissioner of Police. After all Mr Levin was furnished with fully detailed reports each time I saw a doctor, and he had not even asked for these reports. I suggest we ask for these reports from the very first one dating back to the 12 of June 1969, the first date on which I was seen by a cardiac specialist. I am naturally concerned about the fact that there seems to be a great deal of anxiety about my present state of health on the part of Brig and the prison senior staff. The day he left for Robben Island Brig told me they were awaiting further instructions on the various specialists' reports before I undergo further treatment.

---

43. Waterford Kamhlaba school in Swaziland.

Chapter 7

Interrogation

I was taken to Compol Building for interrogation. I was interrogated continuously day and night … I started answering their questions on the fifth day. Several other people whose connection with me was just their visits to my house were reported to be detained by Major Swanepoel until such time as I would answer their questions. I was told by Swanepoel that these people would be released as soon as I gave satisfactory answers which were in fact merely confirmation of everything they knew.

(FROM THE JOURNAL)

MAY 1970

INTERROGATION

(a) On the 1st of May 1970 I was taken to Compol Building for interrogation. Upon arrival I was taken to Major Swanepoel's office where he and Major Ferreira[44] interrogated me. The interrogation went as follows:

Major Swanepoel: 'I notice you look very cross and you have lost a great deal of weight. What's the matter? Why do you look so unhappy?'

Acc. No. 4:[45] 'I have nothing to be happy about.'

---

44. Petrus Ferreira of the security police's 'Sabotage Squad'.
45. Winnie Mandela.

M.S: 'Have you lost a lot of weight?'

Acc. No. 4: 'I am not in the habit of answering the obvious.'

M.S: 'Anyway you have been brought here for re-interrogation. We want a lot of details from you about your connections with the overseas group, especially about the correspondence you carried on with that Tanzania crowd. We have discovered that you know far more than you made us believe when we interrogated you. Now I am going to ask a lot of questions and you must answer them.'

Acc. No. 4: 'You kept me awake for five days and six nights to answer all your questions. In terms of the Terrorism Act you took me to court after you satisfied yourselves that I had made a satisfactory statement, otherwise you would not have stopped interrogating me. I am not answering any questions.'

M.S: 'That is where you are making a mistake; what we did then does not matter at all. We want new information from you and you have to answer the questions and you know we are very patient. Are you going to answer now or on the date of your choice?'

Acc. No. 4: 'I have told you already I am answering no questions and if you keep asking me the same thing I'm going to keep quiet that's all. There is only one place where you and I can talk to one another – that is in court – rotten as our country's courts are, they are my only platform even though the magistrates and the judges are your puppets. My only consolation is that I've got the world on my side and you are an isolated minority.'

Major Ferreira: 'You seem to have completely forgotten that you are a detainee and at our disposal at that. Look here, you are detained under the Terrorism Act, I'll bring you a copy to read, perhaps you do not know that we can interrogate you as long as we wish. If you do not want to answer now we will try again next year or in 1978. Let me go and get the Act and show you what I mean. (He left the office to fetch the Act.)

M.S: 'You talk of platforms Winnie, I am only a policeman, I have nothing to do with platforms. I am only concerned with State Security as you know. You have made serious allegations about the country's magistrates and you know I get as much help from them as anyone else whenever I appear before them.'

Acc. No. 4 interjected: 'Yes they give you utter hell! I particularly noticed the hell they gave you on the Lenkoe[46] case's two-minute judgement. At least you should have electrocuted the right man.'

He suddenly stood up and went to look through the window which is behind his desk giving me his back, both hands thrust into his trouser pockets. I could see him breathing heavily. I knew he was battling to control his temper. Just then Major Ferreira walked in and said he could only find the Afrikaans copies of the Act and wanted to know if I could read Afrikaans. I told him I speak the language of my first oppressors and that the raw and undeveloped so-called language of my second oppressors was not compulsory in the Cape where I was educated. Major Ferreira was furious with me over this and he threw the Act on the table. They both resumed their seats.

M.F: 'You are simply wasting your time anyway. You better know right now that you will talk whether you like it or not. No one is here to please you anyway. You are delaying your own case. You will determine when you want to go on trial. We discovered you merely confirmed what we said and you told us nothing of your own accord.'

Acc. No. 4: 'Brig Aucamp told me we are detained because we violated prison regulations. I have nothing whatsoever to do with you, I expect the Commissioner of Prisons to frame charges against me in any case, not you.'

M.F: 'And what is Brig Aucamp in this matter? We are concerned with interrogating you and we are going to use certain methods to induce information from you since your attitude is what it is. You are going to talk against your will for that matter.'

Acc. No. 4: 'You can use the Phillip Golding[47] method or the Caleb Mayekiso[48] method, whichever you please. We can go to the torture room now, I'm ready. My defence has my instructions on my prospective inquest.'

M.S: 'Now that is the real Winnie Mandela talking! Do you know where we are Major Ferreira? We are back in the early 60s, that's how wild she was. I thought

---

46. James Lenkoe died in detention and Joel Carlson acted for his widow at the inquest. The judgment referred to could be the inquest judgment, which pronounced it to have been suicide.
47. A British trade unionist who was tortured and forced to give evidence in the first trial in December 1969.
48. A detainee who died in detention eighteen days after his arrest in May 1969.

she had outgrown that. We disappointed her then, we knew she was dying to be picked up for 90 days but we decided not to. And you know what is so bad? She means what she says and no one can do anything about it. Alright Winnie we shall try again, next week, next month, next year etc. Won't you give us your nice smile before you go? (I kept quiet.) Please take her back Major, it's Friday, perhaps Fridays are not her best days or it's our unlucky day.'

I stood up and M.S. again said: 'By the way you'll find your lunch cold in prison, what can we buy you for lunch? Don't you also need some cosmetics, we will buy you anything just give me a list.' (I kept quiet.) He repeated the above question thrice with no response from me. He then ordered Major Ferreira and another officer to drive me back to Central Prison. Upon our arrival Acc. No. 7 was taken.

I have no knowledge of any additional evidence against me. I therefore assume that the case will be as before unless the charges in the new indictment date back prior to October 1967. In that event there may be new charges of recruiting for military training. There are two witnesses who gave evidence in the Rivonia[49] case and the Carneson trial who would give this evidence. The charges would then have to date back to 1962–1964 when such activities took place. None of the present accused were involved in my activities then. The last batch of 64 recruits were arrested on their way out. None of them revealed my name. Most of them served prison terms and others were released. They are almost all out now.

---

49. The Rivonia Trial for sabotage against Nelson Mandela and his comrades.

Chapter 8

Interrogation and Other Issues

After Winnie Mandela's husband was arrested on 5 August 1962, he was initially held at the prison in downtown Johannesburg known as The Fort or Number Four. While he was there he met a prisoner serving a sentence for fraud. This man, Moosa Dinath, was usually allowed to mix with him and was also occasionally allowed out of prison. He was married to a white woman named Maud Katzenellenbogen or Maud Kay. Dinath persuaded Nelson Mandela that their wives should meet. While they became friends, it later transpired that Maud was not to be trusted. She and her husband introduced Mrs Mandela to a way her husband could escape from jail.

* * *

In 1962 when my husband was at the Johannesburg Fort I visited him regularly. In one of my visits he told me to go to a certain flat in Twist Street where I had to meet his friend's wife, Maud Kay. He also told me about Moosa Dinath who was sharing the same cell with him, what a wonderful person he was and how well he looked after my husband. He also told me not to worry about bringing him food as there was too much food for Dinath who shared it with him.

Before I went to the flat I received a cheque from Mrs Kay just as a gift for the children. In a covering letter to the cheque she directed me to her flat in case I wanted to visit her. I went to the flat – that is how I met Maud, we immediately became very good friends. She literally clothed me and my children.

One day in November 1962 just after my husband was sentenced I received a telephone call from the officer who was in charge of the Fort. At this stage I had met Dinath several times in the company of my husband during my visits.

The officer received me in this office, he told me Dinath wanted to see me to convey an urgent message from my husband. Dinath later came into the office. He told me in a coded language that he had worked out a scheme with the officer in charge of the prison through which my husband could be smuggled out of prison. The officer wanted a lot of money for this as he was taking a serious risk. I was told to go and think about this. I reported this matter to some officials of the ANC.

A day after this discussion I received another telephone call from the same officer to report to his office. He told me that police had decided to transfer my husband on a Saturday that same week and that I had to act fast. My husband was later brought in. He spoke to me about the same matter in coded language. He said he was leaving everything to me to investigate. I was with him for a few minutes. Dinath was later brought in. He discussed this with me. He told me I would be given the details later that same day.

I again went to the same ANC official who told me the prison official would meet me on a Saturday night and I was to hand over to him a deposit and then a getaway car was to stop at a certain corner. I was to be given a certain sign which meant my husband had left the prison and was on the way to the getaway car. Then I have to hand over the rest of the money. I was also told that my husband was to be provided with material to saw the bars of his cells. As this was related to me a telephone call came through.

The call was for the person I was speaking to … the prison officer was on the phone. He had changed his mind, he wanted all the money in advance before my husband was handed over to me. I asked for time to go and think the matter over. I returned later in the day and was shown all the money wanted by the officer. I had made my decision then.

I explained that I feared that it might be a plot to murder my husband as he might be shot dead after escaping, and the excuse would be he was found trying to escape from custody. I refused to carry out the scheme and so my husband was transferred to Pretoria Local Prison.

*   *   *

Mrs Mandela was also interrogated about the funeral of her mother-in-law, who died on 26 September 1968 while Nelson Mandela was incarcerated on Robben Island. He was forbidden from attending her funeral. Winnie Mandela was granted a reprieve from her banning orders to leave Johannesburg to bury her mother-in-law.

Her prison journal details not only the funeral but demonstrates how the act of burying a member of the family had become part of the police investigation against her. Here she writes about it for her own notes and for her attorney's eyes after she had been questioned about it under security police interrogation.

MY MOTHER-IN-LAW'S FUNERAL

On the 6th of October I attended my mother-in-law's funeral in the Transkei. My family and myself were transported to the Transkei by Sikosana who took us down 'out of sympathy'. I did not have money to hire a car and was given four days. I furnished the Chief Magistrate with Sikosana's name and address. I got him through Mrs Ndala who furnished me with his telephone number which I entered in my little green diary which was produced in court as having been found by Major Viktor.

The following travelled together with me: Telia Mtirara,[50] Edna Mandela,[51] Olive Nomfundo Mandela, Tanduxolo Madikizela[52] and my two daughters.

At the funeral I met No. 20[53] who approached me on his own. He was covering the funeral for the *Daily Dispatch*. We discussed the general political situation. He told me he had been abroad to the offices of the ANC and also said he was a bit distressed by the lack of political activities. I told him I would communicate with him. He gave the address I should use. I met several other people with whom I made similar arrangements. I addressed several meetings at night. Both the Matanzima[54] Camp and the Dalindyebo[55] Regions were well represented.

I left Sikosana with my children at my father's quarters, the Dept of Agriculture and Forestry where they had a royal time. They attended the funeral and returned immediately to the government quarters.

Sikosana and my sister-in-law fetched me earlier than we had arranged from my mother-in-law's place because my small daughter (9 yrs) started performing and rebelling against staying in a government house, she wanted to return to Johannesburg. When the big one joined her in the performance we

---

50. Mrs Mandela's sister-in-law.
51. Nelson Mandela's cousin.
52. Mrs Mandela's brother.
53. Owen Vanqa.
54. The people supporting Kaiser Matanzima, a relative of Nelson Mandela. He co-operated with the apartheid authorities and agreed to establish the Bantustan called the Transkei.
55. Dalindyebo is the family name of the Thembu royal family, which raised Nelson Mandela. King Sabata Dalindyebo was opposed to the Bantustan system.

drove back to Joburg. I paid for the petrol only.

My children had to return to school which was already opened. We dropped Telia Mtirara at work. On our way to the Orlando Police Station where I had to report my return, my small daughter who is an embarrassing extrovert said to Sikosana, 'Uncle Sikosana you know my mummy is going to start running around looking for a car to take us to school,[56] you have a nice big car won't you take us?' I could not pinch her on time as I often do. And so Sikosana took them to school the following day after entering them in his travel document[57] with ease. Again I paid just for petrol. From then Sikosana became very friendly with my children and they were very fond of him. When they were on holiday he used to take them on drives to Maud, Alexandra[58] and places unknown to me.

Under interrogation I did not understand when Swanepoel and others kept on saying I was ungrateful and if there was anybody the police have assisted with transport and children it was me. They also said they will see to it that I pay dearly for this and there was someone who would not like it at all on Robben Island.

*   *   *

One afternoon without any prior arrangement with Mrs Costa[59] I asked Sikosana to drive me and the children to Mrs Costa's house which was unknown to me. When we got to the house we used the back entrance. Sikosana knocked at the kitchen door which was wide open. An African woman appeared and Sikosana said in Zulu, 'Hello, Grace how are you – meet Mrs Mandela.' Grace who was smiling at first quickly froze and appeared shocked. She called Sikosana aside whilst my children and I remained standing outside. After a minute or so Sikosana came over to me and whispered that 'Grace says she will give you anything if you say nothing about her father's affairs and if you are asked anything by Mrs Costa please, for Grace's sake confirm that her father is banned.' I laughed and told him that was not what I had come for and that Grace had her own conscience to worry about, that that was none of my business. Grace relaxed again after Sikosana had spoken to her.

She entered the house, within a short while she came back followed by Mrs

---

56. In Swaziland.
57. Africans were then forbidden from having passports.
58. Alexandra township.
59. Wife of activist Dr Costa Gazides, who was a political activist and one of the accused in the Bram Fischer trial. He had left the country and Mrs Mandela was visiting his wife.

Costa. Grace introduced me to her, Sikosana was standing next to me. Mrs Costa said, 'Good Lord! Are you really Winnie Mandela, yes you look like your photographs but I expected a much older person, well I never.' We shook hands and followed her inside the house. She shouted to Grace to give the children cakes and cold drink and we went into the lounge.

She was packing, there were suitcases all over, the curtains were pulled down and there were books all over. We sat talking for a while, she told me how distressing the whole business of packing was. Sikosana had remained in the kitchen with Grace. I told her how grateful I was for what her husband had done for my people and that I thought it was the best thing for him to do i.e. to leave the country since he could only do so little in this country. She was very pleased by this and said her husband will be very happy to learn I did not think he had run away, leaving the ship to sink.

She told me her husband had sent her a recording of his flight to amuse the children who were devoted and attached to him. She said she thought I would enjoy some parts of the recording so she played the tape for me. Some parts sounded as though he had recorded portions of a BBC programme, then somewhere there was an interview of an African head of state, it sounded like Nyerere who expressed his views on the situation in Southern Africa. President Kaunda also spoke, at this stage Sikosana walked in. I was looking at the books in the big bookshelf. Mrs Costa had interrupted the programme and told me to select some books for myself since she was giving away a large number of books.

I recall President Kaunda saying, 'We shall not rest until our thirst for freedom had been quenched in the whole of Africa ... the western powers must choose between Africa and South Africa.' Then there was the Zambian slogan repeated twice: 'One Zambia one nation'. Mrs Costa switched the tape off when some Congolese music was playing. In between the recordings Mrs Costa interrupted and told me when it was her husband's voice ... he announced, 'we are now flying over so many miles ... over Rome ... the scene is too beautiful boys ... what are you doing back home, darling?' (This is the terrorist recording Sikosana is supposed to have listened to.)[60] This fabrication is so shockingly absurd.

After this the agents who were selling the house for Mrs Costa arrived so I had to leave. I chose six books. Mrs Costa said she would also give me a lot of clothes to give to the poor. Both the books and the clothes were collected the following day by Sikosana who brought them to my house. My children

---

60. Referring to evidence against her.

played with Mrs Costa's children in the swimming pool. This was the first and last contact I ever had with Mrs Costa Gazides. For two days and two nights I was interrogated continuously on this.

LEGAL CONSULTATION OVER DR BRAUN

In the meeting held at Mrs Tsimo's place to discuss dissolution and No. 7's affair I made a report of the meeting with Dr Braun.[61] The general opinion was that it was a police trap but it was decided I should seek legal opinion as to how we could establish our suspicions and also to seek advice on the matter raised in our earlier meetings.

THE LAST TWO MEETINGS WITH DR BRAUN

Dr Braun called again at the office to make a second appointment. I told him for his own safety and mine I suggested he should meet my lawyer and produce his credentials to him (a suggestion made by my lawyer who assumed if Braun was a trap he would not have enough courage to meet him). Dr Braun said he would think about this. The following day he called, told me he was in touch with his superiors and they agreed that he should meet my attorney whose name and address I gave him. Dr Braun had to contact my lawyer direct.

I went to tell my lawyer of the developments. Dr B subsequently made an appointment with Mr Carlson. They arranged to meet in a certain hotel, this arrangement was made over the phone. Mr [crossed out] did not turn up. Dr Braun phoned me a day later, he was furious over his wasted time. He told me

---

61. Dr Braun claimed to be working for the Communist Party of the Soviet Union but they were never able to work out exactly who he was.

he would contact me again for another appointment. A few days later a German girl who looked like a student walked into my office, like Dr Braun she said, 'You must be Mrs Mandela – I have a note for you from your Dr friend.' I offered her a seat opposite my desk. Mxakeki Ntlantsi was sitting on the couch. He had visited me about the pass problems of his fellow men from the Transkei. I was typing letters to the Umtata Chief Magistrate for Mxakeki's friends.

This girl produced a letter from her handbag – it was in a sealed white envelope. She broke the envelope, took out the letter and held it for me to read and before I finished reading it for the second time to absorb the contents, she folded it. I told her I was not a fast reader, could she give me the letter to read again. She opened it once more for a few seconds and closed it again. She held it in one hand whilst she took a blank paper from her handbag. I grabbed the letter from her hand. There was a brief struggle as she tried to retain it and I pushed her onto the chair with one hand. She cried and begged me to return the letter. I told her it was mine and if she tried to get it once more she would have herself to blame. She asked what would she tell the doctor – I said to tell him I have received the letter thank you. She ran out. I took the letter to my attorney. The letter writer wanted an appointment at 12 midnight.

Two days later Dr Braun walked into the office full of smiles and said, 'I noticed we shall do very little physical training with you, congratulations for such caution, I hope you destroyed the letter.' I said the letter was destroyed. We made an appointment for the same evening at the USIS.[62] I picked up No. 1[63] who was to keep observation outside Shakespeare House and follow Dr Braun and take the car number plates. Although the appointment was for 8pm I learnt from Mohale he turned up at 7pm. On all occasions he wore dark glasses, at night as well.

We went to the storeroom again. He took off his glasses on this occasion because he wanted me to trust him. On the previous occasions he was struggling with English but this day he was very fluent although he spoke with a German accent. He produced his identity card which bore his name – and I noticed SA citizen – he quickly explained, 'You know why it bears SA citizen – it's easy to have things for this country.'

This day he said his government does not support violence at this stage but believes that the Africans should start training within the country on espionage, counter espionage, intelligence and some other training he could not mention at that stage. He personally felt I was the right person to undergo this

---

62. United States Information Service.
63. Samuel Ndou.

training and thereafter made suggestions as to how this would be imparted to the people gradually. He said his major task was to train me on the formation of a real underground movement and not another silly Rivonia. He again gave me two weeks to go and think it over. No. 1 followed him when he left but soon lost his trail amongst the pedestrians.

Our last meeting in 1968 was at the entrance of Shakespeare House where he picked me up at 8pm with No. 1 whom I introduced as an illiterate tribesman from the Transkei who does my garden sometimes. I had just brought him along so that I would have company when I drove back to Orlando. No. 1 played his part exceptionally well – he did not hear a word of English and spoke with signs with him. I had also enlisted Desmond Blow's[64] assistance in tracing Dr Braun. Des followed us to the venue arranged by Dr Braun. The venue was a dilapidated flat in De la Rey St, Newlands, but we drove to Bryanston, Randburg, Parktown North [where] Braun shook off Des near Zoo Lake but Des had managed to take the number plates.

The discussion was similar as before except that on this occasion he said I should name any figure of money I wanted. If I had an account it would be transferred to my account, if I wanted it cash I would get it in cash. He said his superiors are a bit concerned about his slow progress with me as they wanted results. He wanted me to commit myself about training. I told him he should give me time to find a job first because I had just lost a job. I claimed it would be easier to meet him in town. He was very sorry to learn of my plight, offered to get me a very good job on condition I kept quiet about it as he would be taking a serious risk by doing so. He gave me R20 pocket money and said I would hear from him. No. 1 sat right through this discussion as quiet as ever. We were then driven back to town where I picked up the car.

The meeting which was held in Makhene's house in Dec 1968 was to report the above affair. I remember this because the meeting took place before the leaflet distributed on the 16th of Dec and this money given to me by Dr Braun is the money I use[d] for buying my sister the ticket to Umtata. Our money was finished, we each financed our own trips to the areas of distribution. As I was unemployed I kept that money from Dr Braun. There was no discussion about blowing up a power station in Makhene's house.

The last time I saw Dr Braun was when he called at 10pm one January night in my house. He was dressed as an African clergy with the long black and white robes. He came to make an appointment with me to start training. He was carrying a Bible and a hymn book. When he walked out he forgot the

---

64. A journalist.

Bible, we both turned to fetch it. When he was picking it up the Bible fell and as he was bending down to pick it up I saw a revolver on the left side under the robes which opened up in that process and I said to him, 'I notice God is not enough protection in Mandela's house', he laughed and said, 'This is my baby brother'. All this was reported to Paul Joseph.[65]

Dr Braun gave me the name of a person in Lesotho with whom I could check his credentials. Later No. 6[66] brought to me a [crossed out] who desperately wanted to see me. He gave No. 6 some names of contacts. This student was in the West German group of students on an exchange programme. I did not use these contacts. I was interrogated on this German Dr Braun for three days and three nights continuously although the SBs had all this information from No. 1 who was interrogated before me plus Sikosana and the others.

*   *   *

Maud was already waiting for me and she gave me a letter which she told me she had received some time back but because she was busy with the Florida Supermarket she kept postponing telephoning. We drove back home.

This was the letter from No. 20 in which he was giving a report of the distribution in Umtata. In the same letter he also said he wanted to see someone from our end soon to pass on certain valuable information he claimed to be in possession of. He mentioned that the SBs were very busy on the Port St John's coast and they were said to be looking for one Makiwane whom they were just about to find. No. 20 believed this Makiwane to be vitally linked with our freedom fighters.

INFORMAL DISCUSSION ON NO. 20'S LETTER

A day after receiving No. 20's letter I sent Sikosana to pick up 1, 2 and 4.[67] I met them in my house – the front room. I read to them the letter from No. 20.

---

65. An anti-apartheid activist living in exile in London.
66. Elliot Shabangu or Joyce Sikakane.
67. Samuel Ndou, David Motau and Hlengani Jackson Mahlaule.

I complimented No. 20 for being conscientious and I remarked about the fact that we had not heard from PE.[68] I also said we should raise fare for someone to go down to visit our contact – meaning No. 20.

On this day the subject of positive action cropped up again. I do not remember how it started but someone said, 'What is the use of having such militant people like our contact as he will also soon tell he wants positive action and we discourage him?' I knew this was directed at my attitude towards single acts of violence. I said, 'Gentlemen, go and read *Rivonia Unmasked*[69] again, no one who had read that book can make comments such as these.' Swanepoel recited my words just as I have reproduced them. He maintained this statement was a communist bluff, that I was functioning with another group and did not want these men to take the glory or positive action!

In this discussion I again repeated that acts of sabotage would have to be committed nationally by trained people. I even said even if it means something like setting fire to the Afrikaner farmer's mealie fields all over the country we would achieve something better than blowing up telephone booths which would take five minutes to repair and went on to say this means trained manpower.

In the end they saw my point of view. They stood up to leave. When Sikosana was at the door, the other three were behind, No. 2 laughingly said, 'Well then, get me five hundred men, you'll see. I do not care whether I'll be killed in the process and I'll go to this man who is going to teach me bombs.' We all laughed. No. 1 said, 'And I'll also burn all the cars in Joburg.' No. 2 said, 'I would never support such nonsense.' They left, Sikosana still roaring with laughter.

INFORMAL DISCUSSION BETWEEN 1, 2 AND 3

Almost a week after this informal discussion on No. 20's letter at my house I spoke to No. 2 about a trip Charlotte Masinga intended undertaking during the long Easter weekend. Charlotte Masinga has been described already in these notes. She was more or less a member of my family. She had all her

---

68. Port Elizabeth.
69. Published in 1965; the apartheid regime's account of the Rivonia Trial.

meals in my house, bathed her children and herself in my house. She only went home to sleep and on most occasions she slept in my house. Whenever I went out to meetings at night I left her in my house with my niece Olive. She had to wait until I returned. She did not know where I used to go to. I used to just tell her when to expect me. She was known to my parents because I was nursed by her and my sister-in-law whenever I was ill. They often spoke to her over the phone and they were desirous to meet her.

She asked me to organise a car for her to go to my home. She was prepared to finance the trip. She had met my father once as our so-called Minister of Agriculture in Umtata and my father invited her home.

I suggest to 2 and 1 that the person who had to visit 20 could go along [in] the same car. We decided to collect fare. Father Rakale came as we were still talking, I left the two for a while and spoke to Father. He left soon. I joined them again.

I told No. 2 that I had been wanting to ask him for a long time who this expert on bomb making was but that I had not wanted to discuss this in the presence of many people. He was hesitant for a long time then he gave the name Gasago. I then asked him if this was not the same man who had given evidence against some of our people who are serving long terms of imprisonment on Robben Island. He said yes.

Both No. 1 and I were shocked by this. I asked him how he could possibly approach a man who was a state witness knowing full well that most of them end up as the SB informers. He said it did not matter because this man would 'sell' only him. I told him he forgot that anything he did affected all the activists who were actively involved with him. He said he had not realised the danger then. I told him to go and withdraw the request for assistance from this man and to try and find a way of pretending it was a joke. He said he would definitely do so.

WHAT I LEARNED UNDER INTERROGATION IN RELATION TO THE ABOVE

A statement was brought to me but was held at a distance. It was a statement made by No. 2 either in 1963 or 1964 in connection with explosives in his garage – these were dug out of the floor of the garage and the man Gasago was involved.

Under interrogation the police were trying to connect No. 2, 3, Mxakeki and Gasago with No. 2's trip and Mxakeki to Carletonville to find explosives. It is possible that Gasago may be a surprise witness to collaborate Mxakeki's false evidence.

The notes on Mxakeki already submitted were fully detailed – there is nothing to be added. (I find No. 2 very confused and incapable of recalling these things.)

On more than one occasion Major Swanepoel indicated to me that they were most annoyed about that nonsense of a right English gentleman who was supposed to have financed the SWA case.[70]

He also said to me that I must remember that contrary to what I think about my friends in SA I have been quite a nuisance to certain people and certain organisations abroad because of my frank criticism and my being too outspoken towards certain leaders who are leading wonderful lives in this most lavish hotels abroad, so it was in their interests too that I should be silenced.

He said the freedom fighters who were used in the first two incursions in August 1962 were trouble-makers in the training camp who had to be got rid of by the leadership.

He also suggested that if I could broadcast a statement against the communists there would be [no] trial, we would all be freed. He asked me why many banned people were working and not hindered in any way by the police. He said I must watch out and see who will be right, that he was convinced no funds would be forthcoming for Winnie Mandela because there are certain people who are convinced that I am not worth wasting money on, in the same way my husband was better behind bars.

He and Major Coetzee told me they would like to show goodwill to the African people but releasing the women for instance who are involved in this trial would hardly be expected of them if the case is conducted as a form of political propaganda as had been done in the past by English speaking attorneys who have no particular interest in us but mostly use us for as long as this perpetuates racial hatred.

Major Swanepoel said for as long as there are trials and incursions they would never recommend such release but if they only kept quiet like Mrs Sobukwe[71] we would have our husbands back if only my husband would

---

70. It could refer to 1967 when Carlson was instructed by London lawyers to defend 37 Namibians, including Andimba Toivo ja Toivo. It is therefore possible that the defence was paid for by a British benefactor.
71. Wife of Pan-Africanist Congress leader, Robert Sobukwe.

promise to be neutral. One thing I should know however is that it is the end of me in the urban area of Johannesburg. They will recommend that I should be repatriated if and when I leave prison.[72]

I must also mention that when Mr Levin came to see me in the cells on the date of the trial he informed me that Mrs Kay had decided to pay for our defence since I refused government money. I told him I could not go against my husband's wish that I be defended by Mr Carlson.

My husband and I have been banned from communicating with each other because according to Brig Aucamp they quarrelled the last time he saw him when my husband demanded to see Mr Brown[73] or Mr Carlson. After our appearance in court on the 28th of October Brig Aucamp called me to the office and told me that he would be visiting the Island and he would grant me permission to meet with my husband.

I asked him for permission to see Maud and told him that there are so many things I did not understand as a result of the confusion which arose in court and since she was present in court I assumed she was not a state witness. Brig Aucamp told me the matter would have to be discussed by the police first and that he would let me know the following day what there is. Today is the 10th of November and I have not heard from him.

*   *   *

Swanepoel [was furious] over the [use] of the Afrikaner newspaper's letterheads for the leaflets[74] and right through the interrogation he kept saying, 'Even the Communists have never played this one on us, Winnie Mandela, and it was a good one but your fun has not lasted.' He also said, 'I am shocked to learn a woman drew such a document. Yes, I must compliment you because your work is original unlike Lilian[75] whose speeches were drawn [up] by Ruth First[76] – that bitch who has been thrown out of the African independent states.' He later referred to No. 3[77] as the woman with strange organisation powers, who within a year had the whole police force running all over the country. He sarcastically wanted to know, 'What do you do with all your friends especially

72. Mrs Mandela was banished to the Free State town of Brandfort in May 1977.
73. An attorney.
74. In August 1968 one of her group of activists who had a friend who worked in the storeroom of the *Vaderland* newspaper managed to access some out-of-date *Vaderland* letterheads. They used this to roneo about 3 000 leaflets, which were distributed to both English and Afrikaans newspapers.
75. Lilian Ngoyi.
76. Political activist, then in exile.
77. Winnie Mandela.

your men who all end up doing your wish. Leave us some inheritance before that heart stops.'

My view is that the police would have arrested us on the spot and prevented the distribution of such an inflammatory leaflet. Since No. 9[78] and myself were banned it would have even been more dramatic to arrest us there and then.

*　*　*

In June 1969 whilst I was still under interrogation, Major Coetzee of Johannesburg told me that Mr Zwarenstein would appear for me and others if I should be charged because Mr Bizos[79] no longer wanted to appear for me as he had lost interest in political cases. Coetzee further went on to say Mr Zwarenstein is one of the greatest advocates the country has and that he was once listed but the police recommended the removal of his name from the list of Communists because he is such a good man. This recommendation is supposed to have been made by Ludi.[80]

During the 3rd week of October 1969 I was taken to Compol Building again and Swanepoel said to me, 'Winnie! My favourite freedom fighter. I do not want you to be defended by that Bizos, Soggot, Kuny crowd, then there'll be no convictions, is that our deal?' My experience with this type of mentality is that silence is the best weapon. I simply kept quiet and could not waste my time replying to this trash.

78. Rita Ndzanga.
79. Her advocate George Bizos.
80. Gerard Ludi, a police spy who had infiltrated the Communist Party.

Chapter 9

Attitude of the Interrogators

ACC. 4 25-6-70

MY IMPRESSIONS OF THE ATTITUDE OF THE INTERROGATORS

I got the impression that there was really no intention to interrogate one seriously. It seemed the idea was merely to test one's feelings perhaps to establish to what extent solitary confinement had affected one's emotion.

I also thought that if they (the SBs) had any 'plants' among us, the intention was perhaps to get reports from them without arousing the suspicion of others. Since we are locked up next to one another, it would be impossible for the police to communicate with one without the knowledge of the others.

Brig Aucamp on his visit of the 24th of February told me that the case was definitely withdrawn and there was no possibility of a retrial on the 'old' indictment. He assured me that if there was ever a case it would definitely be a new case.

The impression I got from Swanepoel was that we would be held indefinitely and later released. When he spoke to me on the 1st of May he remarked that they had been very kind to have withdrawn the case against us and that I had to co-operate as I know they are very patient; that they were in no particular hurry as there was no case pending. They could interrogate me until 1978.

On two of the visiting magistrate's visits I asked for the documents confiscated from us on the day of our re-detention. I explained that I had notes for my defence and records of the trial; I stated that the police had no right to take these documents as we still face the same case. The reply was brought by the magistrate on the third visit. He said he had had repeated requests from the men for these documents. He had made representations for us and he was assured that they would be given to us when we were released. He further said I need not have any fears as there would be no more case based on these records.

On each occasion when the Security Branch visited me in the cells (which was every week prior to my admission to hospital) they wanted to know how I felt, whether I didn't want to make special representations to be released. My reply was if I had committed no crime, and if their own court had found me not guilty there was no reason why I was in Central Prison at all, and under solitary confinement for that matter. It seemed they were very keen that the suggestion or the plea should come from me and I knew this would invite 'strings attached to our or my release'.

Even in hospital they paid me one visit during the second week accompanied by matron Zeelie and they asked me the same question. I reported this to my colleagues and told them I would not make any representations for our release but that any one of them could do so and we would see what the reaction would be. I also felt accused No. 9 should not do so if asked.

During the discussion held with Brig Aucamp a few days before my admission to hospital he gave me a definite impression 'certain things might happen within the next three or four weeks' before the hearing of an application by our attorney but that our fate would be decided after the application was heard. Were 'these certain things' perhaps the present case? And his comment as we left the office, 'I want you to ease your mind and can assure you, you have no cause to worry and lose any more weight.'

My informant mentioned in the smuggled note works in the staff office where she has replaced a girl who was released two months back on special parole and she works for the Minister of Justice Mr Pelser. On Sunday the 14th of June this girl visited my informant. She told that her 'Baas' was very upset, he had not even eaten his supper the previous night. She overheard him tell his wife that there were people who did not agree with him that the 'Terror people' should be released that weekend. That these people felt there should be a case first but he did not agree with that, he felt it was easier to (just let them go as there was too much talk). They had therefore quarrelled a lot.

The strange relaxation [of] Brig's strict security measures on notes for our attorney makes me feel very suspicious. Not once has the wardress in charge of me at the hospital ever asked to check my notes nor is the very diligent matron Zeelie bothered about my notes. She used to strip me naked before I saw my attorney. This makes me feel very suspicious that there is yet another plot. When Brig Aucamp visited me in hospital on the 24.6.70 when he brought my husband's letter he found me writing and he said, 'What are you writing Winnie.' I said, 'The usual stuff for my attorney.' He extended his hand quite impulsively to take the notes and perhaps have a look but he quickly withdrew his hand and seemed to have remembered something. He was accompanied by an officer with lots of rank stars and matron Zeelie. They were all so damned sulky you would have thought they were in a procession!

The day I screamed at Brig Aucamp about the suitcases and the conditions of our detention was the first time for him to ever attempt to whitewash himself – this suggested to me that there was something wrong somewhere. His comments inter alia were, 'What have I got to do with your being here? I am merely detaining you on a new police warrant, if they issue your warrant of release now it does not matter if I have sentenced you to twenty days. I have to let you go.'

The Brig Aucamp I know is the one who thumbs his chest and says, 'You will be here for as long as I want, your Soggot[81] will not have me transferred from here, nor will Winnie Mandela and I'll see to that – you and I will be together for a long time and your defence will not be there.'

To even go to the extent of calling Acc. No. 7 to prove to me that he had been 'very kind' and considerate by not charging her and Acc. 20 for the letter sounded so strange and so unlike him.

I am very puzzled about their sudden concern over my health. It is such a terrible inconvenience for all of them to keep me in hospital as it is locked day and night. I am so much better that normally they should have long discharged me back to the cell. I am checked thrice a day by the senior hospital orderly.

---

81. Advocate.

Chapter 10

May Diary

*Being held incommunicado was the most cruel thing the Nationalists ever did. I'd
communicate with the ants; anything that has life. If I had lice I would have even, I
would have even nursed them. That's what this solitary confinement [does]; there
is no worse punishment than that. I think you can stand imprisonment of 27 years.
You are mixing with the other prisoners, you get your three meals a day, the only
thing you have lost is your freedom of movement. Your mind isn't incarcerated that's
all but with solitary confinement you are not allowed to read, you are not allowed
to do anything, you have just yourself.* — WINNIE MADIKIZELA-MANDELA 2012

Late in the afternoon after my return from Compol Building Brig Aucamp
came to my cell with Matron Zeelie. I was still fuming with rage over the
morning incident. He said he was shocked to see how much weight I had lost
and wanted to know whether there was anything particularly troubling me.
In reply I said I should imagine he must be delighted to note the effect of the
brutal conditions to which he had subjected us. I wanted to know how else he
expected to find women whose clothes were wrapped in lice-riddled blankets,
eating half rations, with nothing to read, locked up for 24 hours each day with
ten minutes break thrice or twice a week, with lights on day and night to make
it impossible to sleep – at this stage I was screaming at him – he interrupted
and said, I [knew] very well that those were not his instructions – I interrupted
also and said I thought he was in charge of prison security – I therefore wondered how our suitcases were a security risk and went on to tell him that in
fact Major Ferreira and Swanepoel had said who is he to have told me we were
detained because we violated prison conditions. I also said I thought he was at
least a little more respected by his colleagues and was surprised to hear such
comments from ordinary majors. He became furious and wanted to know if

they had said anything else. I said they told me it's him who confiscated our suitcases and stripped us of everything. That it was him who gave specific instructions about our treatment. We hardly had toothpaste, face creams, etc.

He said, 'I am going to fix them up, how dare they lie, what have I to do with your suitcases. I am detaining you here on a new warrant from the Security Branch and if they issue an order that I should let you go it does not matter if I have sentenced you to twenty days for violating prison conditions I would be forced to let you go. You also know that all that about you being detained for breaking prison conditions was just a joke. I'll prove to you how I have ignored all those petty violations – at this stage he sent matron to fetch Acc. No. 7.

He said to her, 'Did I not catch a letter of yours from Magubane and what did I do about it?' No. 7 replied in the affirmative about the letter and said nothing was done about it. He then addressed me again saying I was accusing him of things he had not done just like my husband. He also said he would prove that he knew nothing about the suitcases – that he was going right away to speak to Swanepoel and Ferreira. He stormed away.

The following day our cells were opened and we were ordered out. We saw each other for the first time since the 16th of Feb. Brig Aucamp addressed us – he told us we could get our suitcases back, that those of us who had money could buy face creams, that he would discuss the question of reading matter with the police but that he was still too cross with Swanepoel, he was not prepared to speak to him yet – that if there was anything else we needed I should discuss it with him. I told him I wanted a further discussion with him on the conditions of our detention. He said he would find time to see me.

DISCUSSION BETWEEN ACCUSED NO. 4 AND BRIG A

I raised the following matters with him the following day when he called:

(a) That I deeply resented the underestimation of my intelligence by his men. That I saw through the Levin plot whilst I was under interrogation on the 26th May 1969. That even a fool knows when he is being fooled. That I decided to carry on with the fooling around to the end to see who would win the battle of wits. I therefore decided I would instruct my own defence publicly in court on behalf of my colleagues naturally as it was my responsibility. I therefore requested him to tell his men to stop interrogating my colleagues about the attorney – that there was no mystery about it. I instructed my attorney to appear for all of us. That the police have all my correspondence from abroad – that nowhere does it refer subversively to my attorney. That the police boast of having had one of their men amongst us – the so called Soweto Group – this man knows we were not involved with my attorney in our activities. That in any case it was also my husband's wish that Mr Carlson should defend me and I had in any event given instructions to my brother-in-law in front of Tucker to instruct Mr Carlson the day I was detained.

In reply to this he said he had discussed this whole matter with my husband who is a very understanding man. That they discussed this for two hours and he gave my husband his reasons for having objected to Mr Carlson. 'In any case Winnie let us be quite frank with each other – at the moment he is the only attorney who can get funds from overseas and is the best political attorney because he is handling all political cases – it is natural to want an experienced man when in trouble.' He promised to discuss the interrogation with his men.

(b) I then discussed the general horrible conditions of detention. How these conditions lead to quarrels between us and the prison staff who are merely carrying out instructions. That I was shocked to learn there was someone else giving instructions other than him because what we and our defence know was that the matrons are acting on his instructions. I said I felt there was some mischief within his own ranks because the matrons had never mentioned anyone else's name to our defence except his. (We had already been given our suitcases as proof that Swanepoel's crowd has given the instructions for their confiscation.) (But of course he knows about this though I pretended I was not aware of that.)

That I hoped he would sort out this confusion once and for all as we were under the impression that anything that concerned us within the prison premises was his responsibility. He quickly said, yes, indeed it was so, and no one else had any right to give any type of instruction concerning us.

I reminded him that Swanepoel and Coetzee had told me they were the ones who would decide when I would be flown in a military plane to visit my husband. He said there was no such a thing, he and he alone decides who should see my husband.

He told me that he fired matron Jacobs when he discovered that she was carrying out instructions from other people. This was discovered accidentally when my diary was impounded. He said he was shocked to notice we were not getting exercises, showers etc in my diary and an explanation was demanded from him – surely he was not expected to take us personally to the shower and for exercises. He then wanted to know whether everything I had written in the diary was really true. I replied in the affirmative, he apologised and said he thought I merely wanted propaganda to stir up trouble between my defence and himself but that he had also discovered that Jacobs was double-faced.

'I will do nothing for you Winnie through your lawyers, I have nothing to do with them, discuss matters with me and we can settle them where I can. Haven't I had a shower specially constructed for you – where are your lawyers now? I was not pleasing them.'

(c) He said there was very little else he could do about the other aspects of the conditions of our detention as he could not change the law but would do everything in his power to ease the conditions. He then referred to me and my lawyer again. He said just out of the blue, 'When you and Carlson flew down to Cape Town you were so busy with each other you did not even see me, I was on the same plane and I sat near you. You remember he walked with you on the non-European side after we landed. He wanted to take you down by car and had the audacity to make an application to that effect – and what would the people say Winnie about their leader's wife driving all the way to Cape Town with another man? Why do you think I talk to you and not to anyone of those others – it is because I acknowledge the fact that your people regard you as their leader in your husband's absence and there are very many things you cannot do no matter how innocent they may seem. Look at all that trouble about Xmas cards, who was the cause? Your headstrong attorney.

'We have got to understand each other Winnie. You people must understand my difficulties, as much as I try to understand you individually. Look how you screamed at me the other day for instance and it was not the first time you lost your temper with me but I have never lost mine with you. I even go so far as to say if I was in your position I might have even done more. I understand your difficult position and I appreciate it – a young woman with a husband doing life imprisonment. Look at Joyce, I've got to understand her too, I am a man Winnie, she does things so abruptly, she will scream and swear and in the same breath she bursts out laughing. You remember I once said I would never speak to her after she had insulted me but the following day did I not speak to her? Was she not as gay as if nothing had every happened? How can I punish a child like that? The other day it was reported to me that she was caught kissing No. 20, I could have cancelled your joint consultation if I was [as] small as you think. That nonsense they wrote to each other with Magubane, I did not even waste my time to ask Magubane, it was such childish nonsense they discussed I could have charged them and other officials were pressing for charges.'

(d) Without waiting for any further comment from me he continued: 'Look how thin you are, I do not rejoice seeing you in this condition. I want to ask you to ease your mind. Your attorney made a certain application which should be heard within the next three to four weeks. The discussion about your fate will be taken after that hearing. Please do not ask me any further details but I can assure you there is nothing to worry about.' I merely asked what nature of application it was and he said 'that you should not be ill-treated but do not ask me any more. I was not really supposed to discuss this with you.'

He then told me he had made arrangements for me to be examined by the prison doctor on the 6th of May. He told me he was going to Robben Island that weekend and that he would take a message to my husband if I wanted him [to]. I said I would be very grateful. That was the end of the discussion. As he walked out of the office he repeated that I should not worry about anything in between these four weeks, definitely a certain decision would be taken after the hearing of my attorney's application even if there are things that might upset one in between.

Chapter 11

June Diary

They destroyed your being; you were made to feel a nobody.

The sanitary bucket was made by the prisoners, it was something like a two, two-and-a-half-litre tin that you did everything in. It was emptied once in the morning and the wardress would come, open that door, those doors, those three doors; burglar proof door – the first one, your door, the cell door, the third one and she stands there, you know she never touched it.

The only thing you could do to keep sane was to use the blanket. I used to use the blanket to polish the cell; I polished the cell with my legs so much that if there was enough light you could; you could mirror yourself on the floor. There was nothing else to do. So she would stand at the door of that open cell and you put the, and then you put the, this thing, the pan at the door there to be taken. You never saw who actually took it because we were not allowed to be in contact with the black prisoners and then they would take your sanitary bucket; sometimes they did not even rinse it. And then they turned the lid and they put your plate on an unrinsed lid. So as a result you don't eat. For a month I didn't eat. The only time I had a meal was a bacon and egg toasted sandwich when I was under interrogation for seven days and seven nights. To this day I cannot stand that – bacon and egg.

And the prison food, the porridge sometimes had maggots and they gave us rotten porridge. Lunch was cooked mealies. I don't even think you have seen that, dried cooked mealies called inkobe. Dried cooked mealies. That was lunch. And dinner the same porridge and the days when you are supposed to have meat it would be pork then it would be – what do you call pork fat? They would put the pork fat and the porridge would actually swim in this fat so you can't eat it and it has got maggots.
— Winnie Madikizela-Mandela 2012

26.6.70

Saw our defence in the morning. Felt extremely happy after seeing the girls as well. I looked forward to seeing our defence as it's the only time I leave the locked hospital. There are three other patients now admitted on Thursday after seeing the doctor. I am still not allowed to communicate with them although I am now an awaiting-trial prisoner which means the hospital should not even be locked really, it's normally left open. After our consultation I was taken back to the hospital. Miss Nel, the wardress who was on duty, told me Matron Zeelie instructed her to take me to the others only at two o'clock.

At about 1pm Miss Nel brought a dixie with about 2 ozs[82] of biltong out of the packets, the slab of chocolate taken out of its wrapper and put on top of the biltong with two oranges on top. I was so fed up given my food in such an unhygienic manner. Last year when Jacobs did the same thing we protested to Brig Aucamp and he gave instructions in our presence that food like biscuits, raisins, biltong etc which is in any case packed in transparent paper should not be opened.

Miss Nel fetched me at 2 o'clock after I had just been given my injections. I picked up my notebooks and the newspapers, she promptly told me that I was not allowed to take anything with me. Fortunately I had just given all the notes to my defence Mr Carlson and Mr Soggot, otherwise they would definitely have been searched and that was the idea. I decided not to protest, I left.

We were taken to No. 9's cell where we sat almost on top of one another and not to my cell which is bigger. No. 7 picked up her notebooks and papers, her cell was the first to be opened, she was given the same instructions. I quickly told her not to protest as Miss Nel was carrying out instructions. I repeated this to all my colleagues and that this should be our attitude right through now that we have decided that all these matters must be handled by our defence. I was not given my cigarettes although I asked for them, I was told by matron Zeelie I do not smoke. I told her I do and I want them, she just ignored me. It must have been 3.30pm when I was fetched by matron [and taken] back to hospital.

On my return I noticed I started bleeding again. At about 8pm I had a series of black-outs each time I tried to stand up and go to the toilet. I became very dizzy, the other prisoners were still awake. I had to balance on the wall when I stood up. The two prisoners Mabel Kgosi and Elizabeth George remarked

82. 56 grams.

about this and wanted to know what was wrong. I took my night tablets and fell asleep soon.

Earlier I was told by my informant that Nondwe Mankahla and the other unidentified African woman were released this morning very early. They were picked up by the Security Branch with all their belongings and told they were going home.

27.6.70

Reported to the head hospital orderly Mr Rautenbach that I was bleeding once more and having black-outs. He gave me a mixture for the black-outs and said we must watch the bleeding. He could not give me more injections as I had received too many already. Later in the afternoon the bleeding stopped. I was in bed the whole day. I was not taken to the others. Miss Nel had told me the previous day that she would take me to the others today as yesterday. No explanation was given – Perhaps the excuse will be that I am not well again. I was locked up the whole day as usual. The other three prisoners are still patients – but I do not communicate with them on Brig Aucamp's instructions. My bed is still screed off. Matron Zeelie brought me two oranges at 3.30pm.

28.6.70

Locked up the whole day like yesterday, remained in bed the whole day. Black-outs continued especially in the morning. Not taken to the others again. Locked up since Friday. Both yesterday and today I was not even given water to wash. My informant tells me that Brig Aucamp had another hushed meeting with the matrons yesterday at 8am. I felt better than yesterday except the loss of appetite which is very bad again. Two senior members of the Prisons Department on their usual Sunday rounds came to the hospital to find out how I am. Told them I feel better. They were accompanied by matron Zeelie. We still have not been given the last *Rand Daily Mail* which carried a follow-up story on the second detainee. *The Star* was so heavily censored it's just pieces. I intend giving it back to our attorney to see what it looks like. If this continues there is no point in bringing us newspapers. What right have they to censor newspapers to this ridiculous extent?

29.6.70

For the first time I was given Pronutro[83] for breakfast this morning. The wardress told me matron Zeelie told her the new instructions were that I be given it for breakfast. Did not eat it, will find out from my colleagues if they were given the same breakfast, if they were not I will not eat it alone, ill as I am, we are all undernourished.

Had the usual black-outs this morning. Reported to Mr Rautenbach. He gave me the injections, took the pulse, told me I have to be seen by doctor again.

Showed Mr Soggot the copy of censored *Star* when he came this morning. Matron Zeelie removed the *Star*. After the consultation I was taken back to the hospital. The two prisoners discharged themselves this morning. They were moaning the whole weekend about being locked up. Am now left with one.

83. A type of porridge.

Chapter 12

July Diary

ACC. NO. 4: 1.7.70

Not feeling well again. Feeling nauseous all the time. Starting vomiting after lunch. Reported to Mr Rautenbach – given treatment – white tablets to take after meals. Continued vomiting even after supper.

2.7.70

Vomiting much worse than yesterday. Given more tablets by the newly employed nursing sister. She thinks I am reacting to too many drugs – I take twelve different drugs a day at the moment. Am told doctor will see me tomorrow.

In the afternoon my sister Iris Xaba called. She brought me food as usual. The parcel was taken away from her whilst we were talking. She left when we were told it was time up. Later during supper Miss Scott the wardress in charge of us brought me:

1 chicken leg
2 apples
2 oranges
Approx 1oz peanuts
2 bananas

She told me Matron Zeelie sent away the rest with my sister and that I am allowed just enough for one meal. I asked Miss Scott to tell matron Zeelie I would like to see her to discuss the matter with her. That I want to be treated as an ordinary awaiting-trial prisoner.

Discussed with Mr Rautenbach the question of my discharge from hospital. He is in charge of the hospital and is a trained nurse presently doing a doctorate in Nursing.

He told me that he does not think he will take the chance of discharging me from the hospital before the trial as the most important thing is that I should be fit to attend court. He further said I should think in terms of my discharge after the trial whatever the outcome will be.

He said he has withdrawn all the tablets except Inderal and the psychiatrist's prescription which he cannot withdraw, until the prison doctor has seen me. I asked him whether Dr Morgan's tablets are the anti-depressants. He kept quiet for some time and the laughingly said, 'You must take them so that you do not scream at me. You see the hospital is so small, where will I run to if you lose your temper with me?'

Later in the day I developed a running stomach, stopped eating – reported to the nursing sister my condition. She said she was afraid to give me anything without doctor's orders – that I will have to wait for the doctor.

Brig Aucamp came to see me with Matron Zeelie. He said he had heard that I am unwell and wanted to know how I feel. He said he hoped I would get better soon so that I should attend the trial. He wanted to know whether I have any complaints. I discussed the food question with him. As usual he said I know the law says he should permit enough food for one meal and no open food stuff is allowed into the cells anyhow.

I asked if there has been a change in the law since our detention last year as we had discussed the same thing last year and he had allowed us all the food brought by our relatives who can't really come all the way from Johannesburg to bring one meal. He laughed and said, 'Here we go again – even on the sick bed she can't stop talking – alright I'll discuss the matter with the matron, she will tell you my decision.'

Matron said, 'I think we should really leave it at that Brig because I haven't got time to keep the cats from their food in my office. You should see what these relatives bring, chickens, cakes, chocolates – food enough for ten people brought for one – I can't go through all that, I have work to do.' Brig again said they will discuss the matter.

I could not help but feel the malicious glee in Brig Aucamp. He was full of smiles – I suppose it's because in the letter to my husband I told him how unhappy I am in hospital and how much I look forward to my discharge so that I would join my colleagues. I knew he had read the letter today. If there is anything that thrills him it is the knowledge that we are unhappy. He left.

4.7.70

Severe stomach cramps continued with the running tummy. Still stopped eating. Mr Rautenbach is off duty and sister says she is afraid to give me anything as my condition is definitely a reaction to the tablets. Did not eat the whole day – had a cup of black coffee in the evening.

5.7.70

Cramps better, ate porridge in the evening – in bed the whole day, feeling very weak.

Mr Rautenbach still off duty.

6.7.70

Ate a little bit of porridge – stomach cramps bad again. Mr Rautenbach called from the men's quarters to see me. He withdrew the Inderal – says he will leave only Dr Morgan's tablets: [Tofranil] until I see Dr on Wednesday. Gave me two tablets each to take just before I eat. He says he will give me these only for today. Feeling nauseous at moment.

ACC. NO. 4: 21.7.70

THE VISIT AND FOOD

On 21.7.70 Mrs Gladys Masinga one of my relatives in the 'Maud Camp' visited me, brought by Maud of course. She brought with her tinned food. After the visit I was taken to No. 17's[84] cell to join my colleagues. Our attorney came during the visit and had to wait for about 20 minutes so the visit was long for a change to delay our attorney.

We had the legal consultation as usual outside. We were taken back after the consultation to No. 17's cell. Just before we entered the cell the wardress Bezuidenhout told us in Afrikaans to 'Trek Uit' – undress. We all took off our dresses and she repeated the same order again. I could not possibly condescend to this order, not only that but because of my state of health. I told Bezuidenhout to search me if she wanted to and that I wanted to dress up; (I took off only the dress). I also told her that I am not well and could not afford to stand outside naked. Besides I am bleeding profusely again I told her. She then searched me all over my body and told me to dress up. She ordered No. 7 to take off her underwear. No. 7 told her to search her as she had taken off her dress. The other three accused were taking off their underwear at this stage.

No. 7 had a severe altercation with this woman. Bezuidenhout was talking in Afrikaans so I did not understand her. She ordered No. 7 to go to her cell where she locked her up alone.

We were locked up in No. 17's cell. For the first time I was told to have lunch with the others. After 2, at about 3pm I was taken to the hospital. I was not given the morning and afternoon treatment.

AT THE HOSPITAL

I found my bed upside down, my creams scattered all over the floor, in fact only a few of them. All my clothes were gone, my suitcase which has the few clothes I am altering for the case as they are all too big, was gone. All my books were gone. The few tins of tinned food which were given to me by Wessels and Zeelie were gone, the rest of the creams gone.

---

84. Venus Thokozile Mngoma.

I had no panty to change with during the night, nor did I have any treatment for the whole day and night.

THE FOOD

Bezuidenhout brought me the following items: In one dixie there were a few glucose sweets, 2 halves, beef sticks, 2 rotten oranges (two pieces of cheese unwrapped). In the other dixie were the following tinned foods, all emptied in to the one dixie and spilling over:

1 tinned peas
1 tinned green beans
1 spaghetti in tomato sauce
1 biryani – curry and rice

The water from the tinned peas and beans was not drained, the whole things was a shocking mess. Even a dog could not possibly eat food served in this manner. As the food was handed to me by the prisoner who accompanied Bezuidenhout the latter burst out laughing. I was sitting on the bed staring at the creams scattered on the floor and the newspapers thrown all over around my bed. Bezuidenhout said, 'And that is the news for the day'. I kept quiet. If I had been alone I would have burst into tears and slapped Bezuidenhout, I was too provoked and found it hard to control myself – on the instructions of my attorney. I will not be able to control myself that much again.

PETTY BRUTALITY CONTINUED

This is a definite follow up to the letter I was instructed to write on the 12th of July asking for special permission to be discharged from hospital. I refused to write the letter so I should be intimidated and be subjected to this petty brutality a few days before the trial starts.

I am in hospital subjected to solitary confinement even though I am an awaiting-trial prisoner. All my books have been confiscated, my warm clothing which I put on when going to the consultation is confiscated. I was instructed by Zeelie through Scott not to take anything other than my file when leaving the hospital for the consultation or to my colleague's cell. All the items now confiscated from me were given to me by Zeelie and Wessels. I am entitled to all these, I cannot keep them anywhere else save where I am. These are of no inconvenience to anyone at all. In fact mine were neatly packed in a shopping bag and a small suitcase. Those I was busy altering were hung on hangers on the screen.

Underneath the beds of the other prisoners are cardboard boxes with their belongings which are untidier than mine. If I am to be discharged after or during the trial where else can I keep my belongings which I need for the trial.

How long can anyone go on like this? We have not had exercise from Saturday the 18th, today it is the 22nd.

THE OTHER FOOD

Zeelie is a compulsive liar. Whilst she told Scott to tell me she knew nothing about the food left by my sister on the 16th and that I had to wait for Wessels who was on duty last week – that Wessels would be back on Monday the 20th. She knew that Wessels would only [be] back on Friday the 24th.

I am told by our informant that Zeelie was given the food by Wessels, it is presently rotting in the office. Wessels gave her the list I signed, Zeelie intends giving the rotten food to my sister when she comes tomorrow the 23rd. Such cruelty is unheard of. The rotten oranges are possibly part of a bag brought by Father Rakale for the five of us on the 8th of this month. Zeelie would rather the food, our food rot than give it to us.

If I can I intend taking the tinned food mixed up in one dixie to my attorney to see for himself. I did not have supper or breakfast. I am too upset.

I have decided to go on a hunger strike until the application is made. I am not prepared to take this type of thing anymore. I barely have a jersey to wear in this weather when I have my clothes with me.

Our informant tells me that strict instructions have been given to the white staff to the effect that our attorney should be delayed as much as possible and no one should attend to him.

WHY SO MUCH CONFIDENCE

Not only is Zeelie acting on Aucamp's instructions, she does what she likes because she was put in this position by General Nel whom she was private secretary to for years. General Nel promoted her last year in September. She is also related to the captain who is one of the supervisors in this prison.

My informant told me yesterday evening that Zeelie says our defence can go to General Nel and get a shock of their lives, he will not listen to them and intends fixing us up with this silly lawyer, he has not had enough from [him] consulting with his clients outside her office.

One gets the impression that we are getting towards some other drama, perhaps we shall be re-detained on the 3rd of August. We were subjected to similar treatment a week before the trial in February 1970.

22.7.70

Got only half the medical treatment (Inderol and Valoid). Not given the white mixture I take three times a day. No [Tofranil], no injection. No exercise. No explanation given about my clothes, books, etc. Got the prison supply of milk and bread. Gave the milk away, kept the bread for my colleagues.

23.7.70

My informant tells me she has arranged to receive the parcel from my sister if she comes. My informant feels bad about the food which is rotting in Zeelie's office and will be given to my sister. She will try to see her before she comes in so that she should not be upset when she gets the food. She further says my sister should hand in clothes and cosmetics from now henceforth because Zeelie intends sending back all my food.

On 22.7.70 we did not have lunch together. Wardress Bezuidenhout was instructed by Zeelie in my presence to lock me up alone in hospital and the others in their single cells. We were put together after lunch. We obviously lunched together on 21.7.70 to enable Zeelie to strip me of all my possessions in hospital. I am told by the prisoner who was present during the search that Zeelie and Bezuidenhout went through each item thoroughly as if they were looking for something.

The success of my informant's plans will depend on her 'gate contact'. Bezuidenhout apologises for her actions privately. Says I should understand she is carrying out instructions.

THE QUESTION OF THE PRIVATE DOCTOR

My interest at the moment is to be discharged back to the cell to enable us to resume joint consultations. I think the arrangements for the doctor should be made then, otherwise they will deliberately keep me in hospital to separate me from my colleagues. There is one patient at the moment at the hospital – I am not allowed to communicate with her, my bed is screened to prevent any communication between us and that I should not even see the other prisoners. I am now an awaiting-trial prisoner and want to get back to my fellow accused to communicate with them. The hospital is still locked up and only opened when I got to see my defence.

Chapter 13

My Husband

APPLICATION TO COURT

If need be I want an application to be made in court on my instructions for my attorney to see my husband. Brig Aucamp has no right to choose which attorney should handle my domestic affairs. This has gone on long enough.

My brother-in-law told me he received a letter from Nelson last week. In the letter were messages for the children meant for last year. My husband stated in the letter to me (20.6.70) that he wrote the letter last year and another urgent one in March this year but has had no reply to both. We cannot possibly go on like this, we need urgent relief in these self-made problems. It is not enough that we are both in prison and our children deprived of both of us. It was enough of a blow to them to be without a father and all the struggle I've gone through trying to maintain them without employment. The said letter was obviously posted by Brig Aucamp last week when he visited Robben Island and after reading Nelson's letter to me.

My brother-in-law tells me his application to see Nelson was delayed because he was told there were already people who had applied before him, their applications had to be considered first according to the Robben Island commanding officer – and who are these people? Makgatho's aunt's children – useless visits which Nelson can do without.

On the other hand Nelson says he cannot understand why it is so difficult for Xaba[85] to visit him when he expected him to be the first member of

---

85. Marshall Xaba, the husband of Mrs Mandela's sister Niki Iris Xaba.

the family to see him to discuss family matters. All this is Aucamp's mischief to break down completely family relationships. Nelson although very understanding is naturally deeply hurt about all this and so am I. What can Nelson and I do about this? Nothing. We can only rely on our defence! If Nelson knew he would have refused any other visitor until he has seen Xaba.

He states in his letter that he has had no news of the children since September last year, this is a bitter blow to him he says. The string of useless visitors know nothing about the very urgent matters he is so worried about.

I am sure of a very long sentence, I want these things settled now once and for all. I would like my mind eased to enable me to prepare for the case which is presumably even more serious than the last one.

Nelson also wanted to know if Chief Vulindlela Mtirara – Telia's brother got his letter and why he has not replied to the urgent matters he raised. Mr Carlson should please get the address from Telia and check on this. Chief Vulindlela is in the Transkei. It's possible he never got the letter of course!

MY NEW INSTRUCTIONS

For Urgent Attention: Mr Carlson

(a) I was alarmed to discover from my husband's letter of 20.6.70 that all his attempts to see our attorney had failed and that he had been battling with this application since May 1969 when I was detained.

(b) I am not aware of any law that prevents me from instructing an attorney of my choice to handle my family affairs. I do not know what new story my husband was told by Brig Aucamp for him to have resorted to instructing Mr Brown to handle our domestic affairs. Such instructions are completely inconvenient – Mr Brown whom I have great confidence in knows nothing about my personal and domestic problems which have been handled by Mr Carlson for years. I am now instructing Mr Carlson to make an urgent application to see my husband to sort out urgent family matters which weigh heavily upon my shoulders at the moment and are a continued source of extreme anxiety on my part.

(c) I want my attorney appointed by my husband as a caretaker for the house in view of the present family feud to which I see no solution

·at the moment as long as we are both in prison. The City Council of Johannesburg is just waiting for me to be convicted, it will repossess the house. Of all blows, that we cannot afford. The last thing that should ever happen is that our children should be deprived of a home because of our views. They have suffered enough as it is, at a very tender age for that matter.

(d) I was shocked to note that although Brig Aucamp has seen my husband on several occasions since my admission to hospital he failed just to tell him that I was in hospital. Nelson wants to see all the medical reports which he expected the Prisons Department to have furnished him with, of their own accord in view of the circumstances – the fact that I could not communicate with him to tell him personally. I am instructing my attorney to get all the medical reports and take them to my husband.

(e) Although my husband is entitled to write and receive one letter per month, his letters never reach their destinations. Enquiries made by him under difficult circumstances revealed that the letters never even leave the Island. I am instructing my attorney to conduct a full investigation into this matter and to see Nelson about it.

(f) The most important of all these matters is the appointment of a guardian for the children. I have repeated this a million times and am extremely worried about it. Mr Brown has had no dealings with all the people who are involved with the maintenance of the children at the moment. They only know my attorney and I am convinced they will never co-operate with a strange attorney who is suddenly introduced into these matters at this stage.

(g) Both my husband and I are very upset about the fact that Makgatho[86] has not gone to Fort Hare as arranged although he assured his father in his last visit to the Island that he was leaving for Fort Hare on the 14th of February. The lousy excuse he gave was that there was nobody to remain in the house when in fact my sister told me that Makgatho locked out of the house a couple they got to live in my house as a result of Telia's influence. If there had been a legal caretaker for the house all this would have been avoided and who is sitting back and having a good laugh at all our problems? The Security Branch who have successfully drawn a wedge between members of my family and my in-laws through Maud. There must be an end to this!

---

86. Nelson Mandela's second son.

(h) Why has Marshall Xaba or one of my sisters not been to visit Nelson?
     Is it still the old story of no permit for them?

A few minutes after writing the above sentence my sister[87] and her husband
Xaba arrived. I was thrilled. My sister looked upset about my loss of weight.
We had a lengthy discussion about the house. Makgatho seems to be quite
impossible. He has done everything to prevent anyone else from settling in the
house and actually got *tsotsis*[88] to threaten them. I told them to rather leave
the whole matter, I'll discuss it with my attorney. Both of them also felt that
there is only one way of solving this matter – Mr Carlson should discuss the
matter with Nelson or act on his own from my instructions. In his letter my
husband said Makgatho suggested Lulu and her husband, his aunt's daughter
who has been to visit him. He and Telia decided on this. My husband said to
Telia, Lulu could move into the house on the condition I approved of this, I
prefer a completely neutral couple. If Lulu moved into the house this would
drive the two families more and more apart. It is in the interests of all of us that
the families should settle their differences. I naturally love both families and
am torn in between. I also told my brother-in-law about our decision about
the three, Father Rakala, Uncle Mzaidume[89] and himself acting as guardians
of the children.

(i) Please write to Telia and find out from her what the position is about
     my clothes. Was Maud speaking the truth when she said she handed
     everything to her?

---

87. Nikiwe Iris Jane Xaba.
88. Thugs or gangsters.
89. Winnie Mandela's uncle, Paul Mzaidume.

Chapter 14

New Trial

New charges were put to the accused at their appearance in court on 3 August 1970. The charges, this time under the Terrorism Act, were very similar to the charges under which they were charged in 1969. Three of the original group of 22 were no longer on trial and a new accused was added, an MK operative, Benjamin Ramotse. This case became known as the State vs Benjamin Ramotse and 19 others.

*   *   *

WHAT I THINK OF THE LATEST TRIAL

I think they ultimately decided to go on with Swanepoel and Coetzee's original plans. Coetzee felt that we should be found guilty and sentenced to very long terms of imprisonment but that a large number of the political prisoners would be released on the 31st of May 1971 when they celebrate 10 years of the Republic. In this way they hoped to show 'good will' to the 'Bantu' in their own words. The Security Branch recently remarked to Martha Dlamini No. 18 when she said she wants to go home, 'Not when you are still going to spend another year in prison'. Although they lie so much, I am inclined to believe that.

WHAT I THOUGHT OF THE SUDDEN STATE WITHDRAWAL OF THE CASE

When I wanted to state in my plea on the 1st of Dec 1969 that it was a mock trial I sincerely believed that the State could not afford an ANC trial which might backfire just before the general elections. I told my colleagues that I expected a dramatic withdrawal of the case by the state.

When I suggested this to Mr Soggot he said, 'I am sure you have suffered brain damage – these further particulars are the best I've ever had from a prosecutor.' Later when I heard him 'interrogate' No. 10[90] in the last trial I agreed with him that I must have suffered brain damage – especially when I heard what the present Acc. No. 7 had told the 'boys' about sabotage and military training. But I still believed that even then the State could not afford a trial which would give the impression that the ANC was not completely destroyed as they had made the country believe.

During the short trial I thought if there was anyone who furthered the aims of a banned organisation it was 'comrade' Rothwell.[91] The trial simply served as the best ANC propaganda the movement had had since the Rivonia Trial.

If Swanepoel and Co had suspected my intentions about Levin there would have never been a trial. In the interests of the ANC it would have been most destructive if we had simply been released without any trial after our detention. The masses would have immediately thought we had 'sold' out the people especially in view of my informer's rumours which the Security Branch had managed to circulate through my people for years. I still sincerely believe that when a lie is repeated too often the tendency is to believe it.

I would not be surprised if my own defence had doubts about me at the beginning of the trial before they had a full explanation about Levin. I have been accused of being an individualist who always thinks she can outwit everybody. It is perhaps this aspect of my personality that always creates doubts about me to those who have not worked closely with me. Looking back at some of my actions I do not think it is a wrong accusation perhaps. Even Nelson used to thunder at me, 'Zami! You are undisciplined.'

Swanepoel was fully convinced that I believed every word he told me about the possibility of Mr Carlson giving evidence although he knew I would still get him to defend me if there was the slightest opportunity.

If the Swanepoel crowd had known that we would have our present defence

90. Joseph Zikalala.
91. One of the prosecutors.

after all they would have rather released us and face the wrath of their elector-
ate than our defence. Their fear of our defence team is almost neurotic and
pathetic. They were prepared to bargain with me to the extent of saying, 'If you
do not get the Bizos, Soggot, Kuny[92] crowd for your defence Winnie there will
be no convictions,' when they had so much evidence against us especially after
the arrest of No. 20 with all my documents and witness Mohale's evidence.

What still puzzles me however is their exclusion of the whites in our trial
when on the other hand they want to prove that we are a group of 'misled
Bantu, misled by white Communists'. It is possible they wanted to prove to us
that 'the whites are not prepared to face imprisonment' which statement was
often repeated during interrogation to me. They might have hoped that we
would then lose confidence in those whites we have been working with.

The Security Branch seems to be working under serious strains. On the 1st
of May when Swanepoel spoke to me he was too furious when I made reference to the Lenkoe case but he battled to control his temper and he remained
as calm and polite as ever. The Swanepoel I know is the one who said to me
during interrogation last year, 'The bloody bitch has sucked the saliva of all the
white communists, look at her! Cool, calm and collected. Nothing shocks her
at all, just does not react. The last time I ever interrogated a similar communist
is when I went through that Goldberg, he is just like this one – I should have
taken tape recordings of your love making and play them for your husband.'
On that day his partner said, 'Winnie would [have] seduced the Pope if she
wanted to use him politically,' they roared with laughter! I expected a similar
reaction when I hurled my replies at them on the 1st of May. Often when they
are furious they say a lot they normally did not intend saying.

ACC. NO. 4: 20/7/70

Draft notes on 'we seek relief in these matters'

Continued.

---

92. Lawyer Michael Kuny.

WASHING

The detainees do their washing in the cells usually over the weekends. We do the washing in these washing buckets, i.e. the same buckets we use for washing our bodies. We ask for rinsing water, if you are lucky it is brought in a separate bucket but usually you are advised that the prisoners will rinse the clothes for you because there aren't enough buckets because the same are used for scrubbing the floors, the yards and also for night soil. Sometimes the buckets stink so much that it is impossible to use them. On such days I used my drinking water for washing my body ... The prisoners never rinse the clothes, they just hang them on the wall with all the soapy water and there is nothing you can do about this as the clothes will be brought to you already dry when next the warders bring your food.

The position with awaiting-trial prisoners is that they are taken to the laundry yard where they spend the whole day washing their clothes under proper laundry facilities. The shower room which we also used originally is in the same exercise yard and laundry yard. Those who wish to shower do so freely. There is a hot and cold water system. This is in the yard Aucamp prohibited us from because it has convenient facilities. The awaiting-trial prisoners wait for their clothes to dry up. They spend the rest of the time leisurely in this yard.

NB. Since Zeelie took over the prison from Britz the awaiting-trial prisoners work in the laundry. They take towels from the washing machines and hang them on the lines, when these are dry they fold them up. Should they mess up this they are subjected to the same brutal corporal punishment as any other convicted prisoner. Wessels inflicts the corporal punishment with Zeelie. When the awaiting-trial prisoners are through with the towels they do their own washing, showering etc. They do not iron.

The buckets used by us detainees are rusty, filthy and they leak badly. The prison floors are black so the buckets are full of black polish. They have no handles anymore because they are old.

WHAT THE POSITION WAS LAST YEAR

In May 1969 I was taken to the laundry yard daily for about half an hour. If I had any washing to do I did it during this half hour, that meant no exercise as this time was for exercise. This was even a better arrangement than the present set up.

When I was very ill in June my washing was done by the prisoners in the laundry. This continued until September 1969 when Zeelie joined the staff. She put a stop to this and I did the washing in my cell. Sometime in Sept Aucamp got the note I wrote to my sister, that same week I asked for permission from Zeelie to do my washing in the laundry yard which has sinks where I could do my washing standing because of my condition. She told me to put my bucket on the bed which I was given in August and Sept. 1969 per the prison doctor's instructions. I told Zeelie I could not do washing on the bed as my blankets and the mattress would be wet, she said that was not her business.

I then asked her for permission to see Aucamp. She said in any case Aucamp would have to be consulted. The following day I was taken to Aucamp in Britz's office. I told him of my request, he said he would not allow me to do my washing in the exercise yard because of the note I wrote to my sister. That was that. In any case the other detainees who had nothing to do with my sister's note were no longer using the laundry yard on Aucamp's instructions.

DISCUSSION WITH AUCAMP ON FOOD QUESTION

I have had discussions with this man on the above question time without number from 1969.

When we were charged in October 1969 the relatives brought us food, quite a lot of food besides the food we got weekly from the church. At first there was a misunderstanding on the question of sharing food which climaxed in a letter written by Accused No. 7 to Aucamp. Our attorney has a copy of this letter.

On this occasion Aucamp called us all to Britz's office. I told him that we wanted to be given the right to share our food with who we pleased among ourselves. Jacobs used to bring our food already dished onto the dixies, exposed to all the germs and all mixed up. I objected to the exposure of food, transparent items for that matter like biscuits, dried fruit etc all emptied onto dixies. I told him our relatives come all the way from Johannesburg and they

bring non-perishable food to last us until the next visit. That we had been subjected to a long spell of solitary confinement and starvation, we needed food
to build our strength, because we were all generally run down. I told him our
relatives brought us vitamin foods like Complan, Milo, condensed milk and
other tinned foodstuffs.

From that day onwards until our re-detention on the 16th of Feb. 1970 we
got all the food our relatives brought, whatever quantity it was.

Since we have been charged now I have discussed exactly along the lines
above with Aucamp the same question of food. On both occasions he first said
I am aware of the prison regulations – that we are entitled to one meal a day –
I told him he had said the same thing last year but had allowed food because
our relatives live so far and that in any case he could use his discretion in such
matters if he wanted to. On both occasions he said he would discuss the matter
with the matrons and they would all decide what's to be done. The position has
not changed at all.

We made numerous representations to our defence, instead matters deteri-
orated, we continued starving to an extent that although I am an awaiting-trial
prisoner entitled to food from my relatives the prison doctor had to prescribe
milk and bread because my anaemia was getting worse and loss of weight continued. The last time I was seen by the doctor was on the 15th of this month
when he declared me unfit to be discharged from the hospital. It is not the
prison bed and prison hospital which will improve my health, it is a proper
balanced diet, not bread and milk either.

I am at Aucamp's mercy even when I have access to my defence. What will
happen when I am convicted if this is what this man does to me now. Must
I go and serve my sentence in this physical condition? Who else would take
this type of treatment for so long. How much longer should any human being
be expected to have patience without exhausting it? We have now reached the
saturation point.

THE PRESENT FOOD POSITION

A week before the last long week I asked Zeelie for permission to see Aucamp
to discuss the food question once more. On both occasions Zeelie told me she
would convey the message to Aucamp … We are still given enough food for
one meal.

During my sister's last visit on Thursday the 16th I told her to keep a list of what was given back to her and hand this to my attorney. I would also do the same. I was later given a list of what was given to me and a list of what 'should have been returned to my sister but that she left before this was in fact handed back'. I signed and dated the list in Wessels' handwriting. Obviously Scott[93] reported what I said to my sister but my sister left as usual when Scott took me back to the cells. Over the weekend I asked for his food, I was told Wessels would be on duty on Monday the 20th but I know Wessels will be on Friday the 24th according to my informant. The food disappeared.

THE FOOD QUESTION AS APPLICABLE TO OTHER AWAITING-TRIAL PRISONERS

Ordinary awaiting-trial prisoners bring with them from court as much food as they can possibly carry whilst on trial, usually loaves of bread, fruit and cooked food which I have seen with my own eyes. I have also been taken to the visiting room whilst these prisoners had their relatives visiting them. I have seen them taking food from relatives, I actually saw one prisoner with three dixies carrying two loaves of bread, fruit, meat and potatoes, enough food to last her a whole week.

There were also packets (unopened) of biscuits, and cigarettes. Ours are opened, emptied, the containers thrown away for spite, as a result the cigarettes dry up and are rendered unhealthy. Our biscuits are thrown on these cigarettes, with toilet soap and all, this is done in our absence and we are expected to eat food served in this condition.

I have seen awaiting-trial prisoners being given food, it's taken by the wardresses on duty from the relative, searched in the presence of the prisoner and handed to the prisoner. She takes the food straight from the visit to the cell. Our food remains with the matrons and wardresses and the long time prisoners amongst whom it is divided whilst enough food for one meal is taken to the cell at supper time so that it should be impossible for the detainee to share even this with her colleague.

We normally hide even this little bit, take it with us in the morning when

---

93. A wardress.

we go to crowd in Number 17's cell where we share as if we are stealing our own food. I have been moved to tears when my colleagues grab the bread I have – prescribed by the doctor – I give this to them every morning if I can, I can do with the pint of milk a day. The bread is hardly enough for one person.

A whole [*sic*] Brig concerns himself with this petty brutality of giving such instructions about food – of what security risk is food for detainees? How is the security of the state at stake because No. 17 smokes twenty cigarettes a day? How is the state security similarly affected if my sister gives me vitamin food? Or a chicken?

GAMES, HANDKERCHIEFS AND BOOKS

On 8.7.70 our attorney brought us the above articles which have not been given to us on Aucamp's instructions. I have asked for these on numerous occasions from Scott and I get one reply on all occasions. Zeelie says she will find out whether she can now give us some – up to date. Zeelie is acting on instructions. I have explained that the handkerchiefs are mine, what I do with them is my business. Surely there is nothing illegal about my relatives giving me handkerchiefs to my attorney who sees me every day. I have told my sister in the presence of the wardress on duty that if she can't visit me for some reason she could take my parcel to my attorney.

HEALTH QUESTION CONTINUED

In December and January 1970 I made an application to see a dentist. Jacobs told me Aucamp said I should submit this in writing to him. I was most surprised, I expected the doctor who treats me to refer me to the dentist. I submitted the said application in writing about this application. I followed this application with oral enquiries until my re-detention.

To this date I have not seen the dentist because 'the Brig has not granted the permission yet'. I am aware than No. 9 made a similar application also with no success. Even after detention I pursued this application with no success.

FOOD IN HOSPITAL

The hospital has the same diet as the ordinary diet in prison. When I was very ill from the 6th of May this year I started bringing up all solids. I reported this to Zeelie and asked for porridge instead of cooked mealies for supper. She said she would inform Aucamp. For a week I did not have any supper because I could not be given porridge which I have up to date.

When I was discharged for a few days on the 10th of June I was given cooked mealies in the cell. The same complications arose with bronchitis, I did not have supper for the four days in the cell. I got the porridge again when I was re-admitted to hospital.

SUNDAY THE 12TH OF JULY

I forgot to tell my defence that on Sunday the 12th of May wardress Nel came to tell me whilst I was exercising that Wessels says I should write a letter and say I request permission to be discharged from hospital. I do not know what plot was behind this. I told Nel that I will write such an application as soon as I become mad but that whilst I am sane I would do no such a thing. The doctor is there to discharge me.

No. 18 overheard Wessels giving the report of my refusal to write the letter to the visiting 'Super' on Sunday the same day. This was of course Aucamp's underhand instruction. I suppose the doctor refuses to discharge me from the hospital.

DOCTOR'S VISITS

The doctor visits the prison once a week, the dentist once every two weeks. On such days those who wish to see the doctor submit their prison tickets to the wardress who does not even ask them what they suffer from. Then the prisoners, including the awaiting-trial prisoners, come to the consulting room without even an escort.

The detainees are subjected to scrutiny before they see the doctor. You report to the wardress on duty that [you] are not well, you give details of your complaint. These she take[s] to the matron, matron reports to Aucamp.

MEDICAL DIARY

3 attacks 24.12.69
Description of attacks[94]

1. Sharp pain in the middle of the chest – last approx 5 mins.
2. Complete loss of control of muscle function.
3. Breathlessness, choked, tongue as if full in the mouth, could not swallow or move at all. Half consc.
4. With a spasm body jerked into function.
5. Palpitations – burning pain beneath left breast.
6. Unable to estimate length of time each attack took, it seemed quite long – soaking wet – excess sweat.
7. Eyes bloodshot whole day foll[owing] attacks – persistent headache and loss of appetite – bitter taste in mouth.

MEDICAL DIARY[95]

3 attacks 24.12.69 midnight
Monday 29-12-69
(1) Did not see doctor (2) Shower (3) Consultation (4) Isolation (5) No exercise

Tues 30.12.69
(1) No shower (2) Consultation (3) Isolation (4) No exercise (5) Treatment incomplete (Whi T) (6) Brig

---

94. These few scraps of paper were found in Mrs Mandela's file at the National Archives of South Africa.
95. Found in Mrs Mandela's file in the National Archives of South Africa.

Wednesday 31.12.69
>   (1) Shower (2) Consultation (3) Together – supper (4) No exercise
>   (5) Saw doctor (6) BP under control

Thurs 1.1.70
>   (1) No shower (2) No exercise (3) Together

Frid 2.1.70
(2 attacks midnight) V. scream

Monday 5.1.70
>   (1) Shower noon (2) No morning tablet. Afternoon treat (3) Consultation
>   (4) No exer

Tuesday 6.1.70
>   (1) No shower (2) Morn, Tabl. (3) Consult. (4) Inc: De Bruyn. M Wes –
>   unilat dec sol. Approx 10–15 threats. (5) No exer (6) Our matr bus

Wednesday 7.1.70
>   (1) Shower (2) No tablets (3) Solitary till lunch – no tabl (4) No tabl
>   whole day – Hosp closed – after enquiries Matron (5) No exercise

Thursd. 8.1.70
>   (1) Minor attack 40m breathlessness. Sweating, palpitations burning
>   pain beneath left breast (2) Reported Matr J. (3) MJ sorted tabl will
>   give herself as from today

Friday 9.1.70
>   (1) Diahrr 3am till morning break (2) Drank Compl no other breakf
>   (3) Shower (4) Tablets morning (5) Tablets – told to take the whole
>   lot – usually for afternoon and night. Expl to Miss V how I have
>   [been] taking them – told that was wrong – had to take whole lot at
>   once – were together (6) Felt tired and unusually drowsy thereafter.

Saturday 10.1.70
>   (1) No shower (2) Solitary again (3) Lunch asked wardress why we were
>   subj to sol conf; she said she had asked Matron Wes. As one of us had
>   already asked same question; I asked what Matr Wes said – wardress
>   states she could not get any reply from MW further explained she

works upstairs (3) Told wardress to tell Wess we are supposed to be together and that we also have work to do for the lawyers

Sunday 11.1.70 (continued)

Until 3 pm – no explanation given about yesterday (4) Loss of appetite (5) Palpitations 6 pm (6) Excess sweat

Monday 12.1.70

(1) No shower (2) Consult (3) Together (4) Got all my tablets (5) No excer (6) Rot C sat

Tuesday 13.1.70

(1) No shower (2) Consult (3) Together (4) Consult JC (5) No exerc (6) Got all my tabl (7) Request B refused

Wednesday 14.1.70

(1) Shower at noon (2) Tablets given at lunch (3) Solitary till lunch (4) Clothes brought by MJ (5) 10 mins consult … Choked, breathlessness – body jerked in painful spasm into functions

(2) State of semi-consciousness until body jerked into funct

(3) Unable to estimate how long this lasted – seemed long

(4) Shortly after the last bell rang. Looked at the mirror – eyes bloodshot – pupils seemed dilated

(5) Took last tablets for the night – afraid to sleep as if I'll have an attack again – sat up and wrote diary
Prior to the attack had been thinking a great deal of my husb and the children. Also thought about my clothes with Maud and my husband's clothes with Maud. Thought about family quarrel – Telia reported ill.

(6) No preceeding aura – I now feel burning pain beneath left breast as I write. Sweating excessively. Have been dbbr since morning when we were locked up

Thursday 15.1.70

(1) Report Matron J not feeling well – requested to see hospital man re blood press (2) Shower (3) No morning tablets given Rep again MJ request to see hospit man – he never came (4) Got morning treatment at lunchtime (5) Consult 10 mins JC (6) Visit my younger sister food and blouse (7) Afternoon and night treat. All given at supp

(8) Mugs put out early – upside down – 'phuzamandla' (9) Together

Friday 16.1.70
   (1) 4 or 5 am woken up by severe stomach cramp – diarrhoea – feel
       like bringing up. Report to Matron and request to see the doctor (2)
       Shortly af. break told by matron Z doctor not available today – given
       something for diarrh and my usual treatment – tabl
   (2) Dizzy

26.7.70

BRIEF MEMORANDUM ON NATURE OF COMPLAINTS[96]

(a) Cells:
   We, the detainees occupy a block of cells originally designed for punishment. It has been explained to us that this is the best accommoda-
   tion available for us at the moment. We quite appreciate this problem. Due to the size of these cells movement is highly restricted. We
   are locked up in one of these during the day, we almost sit on top of
   each other. As awaiting-trial prisoners we request that the cell doors
   be left open to allow us free movement like the other awaiting-trial
   prisoners who move freely within a specific yard. We understand
   that the gate would be kept locked to separate us from the other prisoners. For hygiene reasons it is necessary in any case to keep the cells
   opened during the day, especially in view of their size and the fact
   that we are confined to them day and night.
(b) Food and clothing:
   There has been a great deal of misunderstanding between us and
   members of the staff as a result of new instructions concerning our
   food from relatives. These instructions are completely different from
   those which were applicable under Lieutenant Britz, matron Wessels
   and matron Jacobs.
       We are aware of the prison regulation with regard to food. Last
   year we made special representation to Brig Aucamp to allow us to

---

96. Found in Mrs Mandela's file in the National Archives of South Africa.

receive all the food brought by our relatives in view of the fact that our relatives come all the way from Johannesburg and we needed the food to augment the prison diet until the next visit. We share the food normally and there has never been any danger of us keeping excess food because we seldom all get visitors on one day. Brig Aucamp then authorised us to receive all the food our relatives brought. He further instructed that food such as sweets, biscuits, dried fruit, cigarettes, cheese etc. which is often in transparent paper should not be opened. Thus we received our food hygienically wrapped with no danger of germs contaminating our food.

The present set-up is as follows:
 (1) We are allowed only one meal's worth, the rest has to be taken back by our relatives.
 (2) The food is taken out of clean containers, if it is tinned food it is opened and mixed up into one dixie, cheese is unwrapped, cigarette containers thrown away and these given to us loose, often cosmetics and soap are put on top of the food thus rendering even this little one meal's worth inedible.
 (3) The food is kept until supper time thus making it difficult for the individual to share, if she so wishes, with the others.
 (4) The parcel of food and clothing from the relative is not shown to the detainee during the visit, this means we only know after the relatives have left what they brought. If there are items of clothing the detainee perhaps wanted to send back this waits for the next visit whereas this could be eliminated by the relative simply showing the detainee and the wardress on duty what has been brought as is the case with the other awaiting-trial prisoners. There would be no need to keep the lists of what the detainee was given, what was returned etc. We request that we be treated like last year on this question of food and clothing. This has been raised with Brig Aucamp.
 (c) Shower:
   A special shower was made for us just behind our cells and this we appreciated very much. The shower is however unsuitable for us in winter as it is just an enclosure outside. As a result we have declined to go for a shower in this weather. We request the use of the ordinary prison shower which we used originally until warmer weather. I personally last had a shower in April 1970 due to this weather problem.
 (d) Exercise:

We do not get sufficient exercise. For instance this week ending on the 15th we had exercise only once on Thursday the 23rd. We are often locked up from Friday to Monday without a breath of fresh air. I have noticed however that when matron Wessels is on duty over weekends we get our exercises as usual.

(e) Sanitary buckets:

Our pons are emptied once a day. This means keeping a dirty pon right through the day and night, this is terribly unhygienic. We request that these be emptied twice a day.

(f) Weekend detention:

We request to be allowed to be together over weekends especially because these weekend days are the longest in prison. Because of the situation of the cells it does not take the wardress on duty five minutes to put us together. In fact it is less work to open one cell instead of five. We do understand that it may be difficult to give us exercise during the weekend as the prison has skeleton staff.

(g) Basins:

We request an extra basin in which we may wash our spoons, mugs and dixies after supper especially. At the moment after each meal we wash our spoons onto the sanitary bucket and this is very unhealthy.

(h) Washing facilities:

We have insufficient washing facilities for our clothes. We wash our clothes in the buckets which we use for washing our bodies. These buckets are rusty and some are used for scrubbing floors so they are full of black floor polish whilst others leak badly. Very often it's difficult to get rinsing water in a separate bucket because there aren't enough buckets as they are used for scrubbing.

Could we be rather taken to the laundry yard at least once a week to do our washing properly. We would be prepared to forego our exercise time on such days. This was the case on our arrival in prison during our first detention. Then we were taken individually, it would be far better now that we are awaiting-trial prisoners as we can wash together.

(i) Lunch:

We are at a loss as to what the actual position is with lunching together. Sometimes we are locked up individually, at other times we are left together. As we are now awaiting-trial prisoners could we kindly be left to lunch together.

(j) Visitors time:

We request the extension of other visitors time. We do not know actually how much time we are allowed to speak to our relatives but at the moment it is rather too short.

(k) Games, books and hankies:

On the 8.7.70 the above items were brought for us. Could we be granted permission to receive them now please?

(l) Newspaper censorship:

We are of the impression that whoever carries out Brig Aucamp's instructions to censor newspapers is either suffering from gross ignorance or deliberately exceeds Brig Aucamp's instructions. We accept the fact that we may not be allowed to read all the news but what is going on now has reached alarming proportions. So much is cut out that we sometimes get half a paper with whole pages missing or articles cut out in the middle.

Newspapers are kept for such long periods that for instance on the 26th we got newspapers dated the 13th. If newspapers are left to accumulate naturally the work for whoever censors is doubled.

(m) Ironing facilities:

Lieutenant Britz made arrangements for us last year to have our clothes ironed once a week when we were attending court. We handed our clothes to whoever was on duty and they were ironed for us. If we had ironing facilities we would not mind doing this on our own. We request the resumption of same. She also furnished us with nails on the wall on which we hung our clothes as we have no clothes [*sic*] and cannot possibly take clothes from the suitcase and wear them. These were removed on our detention. Could we kindly be furnished with these?

(n) Dispensary:

It is often a struggle to get proper medical care. We do not know what the actual problem is as we report to whoever is on duty if we are not well and we wish either to see the doctor or the hospital orderly. We have to keep reporting for days on end before we get even ordinary tablets for headaches etc.

In conclusion we would like to point out that it is our desire to have a peaceful atmosphere between ourselves and members of the staff. We have adhered to Brig Aucamp's suggestion that we should concern ourselves with defence matters only. It is our sincere wish that these matters be solved without going any further. In this way there shall be a harmonious relationship for all concerned.

6-8-70

FOR ATTENTION: MATRON WESSELS[97]

1. For the past three weeks I have been getting my tablets meant to be taken three times a day, once a day in the evening only. I am aware that this is the hospital's responsibility. Would you please attend to this.
2. Please check up what happened to our games – we would like to have them. They were brought on 8/7/70 with handkerchiefs – the latter we got. The games are: Drafts, Snakes and Ladders & Solitaire.
3. There is also two weeks supply of our weekly biscuits which we did not get. The only supply we got is the one received by you which you gave to us. As you know the packets have sweets and cigarettes like the one you gave us and have our names marked on them.

Matron Zeelie told us to check these with you yesterday.

With thanks

[Signed] W Mandela

31-8-70[98]

FOR MATRON ZEELIE'S ATTENTION (A)

In June 1969 I was given the following clothes by Matron Wessels which had been sent by my relatives in a cardboard box:

1 brown pr slacks
2 pairs black pantyhose
1 pr winter socks (black)
1 brown corduroy jacket

---

97. Found in Winnie Mandela's file in the National Archives of South Africa.
98. Found in Winnie Mandela's file at the National Archives of South Africa.

(B)

In the same parcel were the following items which were not given to me:

1 pr brand new boots size 8 (long)
1 pr brand new gloves
1 black twin set jersey (new)
2 winter panties (they were 4 originally. I was given two on the 6th May
1970, a whole year later)
1 fawn jersey (washed once) new
4 tubes Weleda toothpaste
1 black pr fishnet stockings

In January 1970 I was given dresses by Matron Jacobs nothing was said about the above clothes. Brig Aucamp has a copy of a letter acknowledging the said clothes, the other copy is with my defence as I wished to keep a record of these clothes. On the 6th of May 1970 I was given a travelling leather bag with some of my winter clothes which have been at this prison from May 1969 although I had been writing letters to my relatives requesting that I be furnished with clothes. In the leather bag the clothes marked B above were missing. Please note that I was in solitary confinement when these clothes were brought to me by the Security Branch.

I kindly request that these clothes be given to me at your earliest convenience together with the two doeks[99] removed from my bed during a search in my cell.

[Signed] W Mandela

[undated note]

In the leather bag the following items were contained:

2 skirts, 1 brown, 1 check
1 navy twin set (new)
1 red skipper
1 new winter night dress
1 new winter pyjamas
2 new winter panties

99. Head scarves.

1 blue dress
1 yellow jersey

The leather bag was given to the Security Branch on the 16th of May 1969 and given to me on the 6th of May 1970 upon my admission to hospital.

[Signed] W Mandela

* * *

On 14 September 1970 the accused appeared in the Old Synagogue in Pretoria for the last time. On behalf of the defence team, Advocate Sydney Kentridge had applied to have Ramotse's prosecution set aside as he had been kidnapped from a foreign territory and unlawfully handed to the South African authorities. Kentridge had also applied to have the charges against the other clients withdrawn on the basis that they were similar to the charges in the first case.

Judge Gerrit Viljoen declared the Ramotse capture lawful. Then he said: 'In the final result, therefore, the special plea for accused 1 fails but the special plea of accused 2-20 succeeds'. It meant that all but Ramotse were free to go. He was eventually sentenced to fifteen years in prison. Joel Carlson hosted a celebration at his house for his jubilant nineteen clients. Winnie Mandela was reunited with her children but she was again placed under house arrest and her banning order was re-imposed on 20 September 1970 for another five years. According to a report in the *Rand Daily Mail* she was given two weeks of freedom from restriction in error. Justice Minister Pelser had signed the order on 18 September. After her release, she travelled to see her father, Mr Columbus Madikizela, and on her return she was served with the orders.

The day after her release she applied to visit her husband on Robben Island and permission was granted on 23 September. She was prevented from going when the new banning order was imposed. After intervention by Joel Carlson, she was finally allowed to see him on 3 November 1970. They had last seen each other on 21 December 1968.

Part Two

Letters

Background

Nelson Mandela was arrested on 5 August 1962 after being underground for seventeen months, mostly on a trip around Africa to raise support for the armed struggle against apartheid. On 7 November 1962, he was sentenced to five years in prison for leaving the country illegally and inciting workers to strike. He was a sentenced prisoner when his colleagues were arrested in the Rivonia raid on 11 July 1963 and stood trial with them for sabotage. On 12 June 1964, he and seven others were sentenced to life imprisonment.

The first time his wife was allowed to visit him on Robben Island was 28 August 1964 but it was through thick glass and for a mere 30 minutes. They had eight more visits in the next four years. The last time, before she was detained on 12 May 1969 was on 21 December 1968. The next time they saw each other was on 7 November 1970.

He was informed of her detention by a letter from his lawyer, Joel Carlson, and responded in a telegram, which, it appears, was never received.

During this period of her detention Nelson Mandela's eldest child and son, Thembi,[100] by his first wife Evelyn Mase, was killed in a car accident.

Mrs Mandela was informed in this way: 'One day she was taken to see him [Swanepoel] and he asked her abruptly, "Who is Thembi Mandela?" When she explained this was her eldest stepson, he said, "He is dead. He was killed in a car accident." And he walked off. She lost all control and broke down and wept.'[101]

---

100. Madiba Thembekile 'Thembi' Mandela.
101. From Joel Carlson, *No Neutral Ground* (London: Davis-Poynter Ltd, 1973). It refers to the way in which she received the news that her stepson was killed in a car accident on 13 July.

LETTER TO NELSON MANDELA
FROM JOEL CARLSON INFORMING HIM OF HIS WIFE'S ARREST

Mr Nelson Mandela,
No. 466/64[102]
c/o Officer Commanding,
ROBBEN ISLAND
16 May 1969
Registered

Dear Sir,
re: YOUR WIFE

This serves to advise you that Mrs. Winnie Mandela was arrested by Police early on Monday morning and is at present in custody. I am unable to advise you whether she has been arrested on any particular charge, or whether she is at present detained as I have been unable to obtain this information from the Head of the Security Police Brigadier Venter.

However the children are being cared for by the relatives in Johannesburg, and Mr. Ludumo Xaba[103] was present when Mrs Mandela was removed by the police.

I understand that the Security Police have also allowed Mrs. Mandela to receive a change of clothing. I shall advise you further as soon as further information comes to hand.

Yours faithfully
J. Carlson[104]

---

102. Nelson Mandela's prison number.
103. Her brother-in-law.
104. Joel Carlson, Nelson Mandela's attorney.

LETTER FROM NELSON MANDELA
TO THE COMMANDING OFFICER OF ROBBEN ISLAND

18th May 1969

I have received information that my wife has been arrested and I should be pleased if you would kindly authorise the dispatch of the following telegram to attorney Carlson of Johannesburg at my own cost.

[Signed] Nelson Mandela

JOEL CARLSON. 'LAWCARLSON' JOHANNESBURG.

re. Arrest Winnie stop require full details of date of arrest charge names and addresses of her co-detainees and bail. Did she receive letter of fourth April.

Nelson Mandela

LETTER FROM JOEL CARLSON
TO THE COMMANDING OFFICER OF ROBBEN ISLAND

19th May 1969

Dear Sir,

RE: <u>LETTER TO MR. NELSON MANDELA NO. 466/64.</u>

On the 16th of May I wrote a letter reading as follows:

to Nelson Mandela: –

'This serves to advise you that Mrs. Winnie Mandela was arrested by Police early on Monday morning and is at present in custody. I am unable to advise you whether she has been arrested on any charge, or whether she is at present detained as I have been unable to obtain this information from the Head of the Security Police Brigadier Venter.

However the children are being cared for by the relatives in Johannesburg, and Mr. Ludomo Xaba was present when Mrs. Mandela was removed by the Police.

I understand that the Security Police had also allowed Mrs. Mandela to receive a change of clothing. I shall advise you further as soon as further information comes to hand.

Please acknowledge receipt hereof.'

Although the letter was sent by registered post, it has not been acknowledged by the Postal Authorities. I have received no acknowledgements or reply to this letter which was addressed to your office. I shall be pleased to have your acknowledgement and receipt of same.

Yours faithfully,
[Signed] J. Carlson

LETTER TO JOEL CARLSON
FROM THE COMMANDING OFFICER OF ROBBEN ISLAND·

11th June 69

Dear Sir,

Re: <u>LETTER TO PRISONER MANDELA.</u>

In acknowledging receipt of your letter of the 5th instant, I have to inform you that your letter of the 16th ultimo addressed to the above-named, was received at this office on the 19th of May and transmitted to my head office on the same date.

Any further correspondence in regard to the matter should be address to the Commissioner of Prisons, Private Bag 136, Pretoria for attention Brigadier Aucamp.

Yours faithfully,
J.J. VAN AARDE
COMMANDING OFFICER

LETTER FROM NELSON MANDELA
TO WINNIE MANDELA

23.6.69

My Darling,

One of my precious possessions here is the first letter you wrote me on Dec 20, 1962 shortly after my first conviction. During the last 6½ years I have read it over and over again and the sentiments it expresses are as golden and fresh now as they were the day I received it. With the aspirations and views that you hold and the role you are playing in the current battle of ideas, I have always known that you would be arrested sooner or later. But considering all that I have gone through, I had somehow vaguely hoped that such a calamity would be deferred and that you would be spared the misfortune and misery of prison life. Accordingly when the news of your arrest reached me on May 17, in the midst of feverish preparations for my finals[105] then only 25 days away, I was quite unprepared and felt cold and lonely. That you were free and able within limits to move about meant much to me. I looked forward to all your visits and to those of members of the family and friends which you organised with your characteristic ability and enthusiasm, to the lovely birthday, wedding anniversary and Xmas cards which you never failed to send, and to the funds which in spite of difficulties you managed to raise. What made the disaster even more shattering was the fact that you had last visited me on Dec 21 and I was actually expecting you to come down last month or in June. I was also awaiting your reply to my letter of April 2 in which I discussed your illness and made suggestions.

For some time after receiving the news my faculties seemed to have ceased functioning and I turned almost instinctively to your letter as I have always done in the past whenever my resolution flagged or whenever I wanted to take away my mind from nagging problems:

> *Most people do not realise that your physical presence would have meant nothing to me if the ideals for which you have dedicated your life have not been realised. I find living in hope the most wonderful thing. Our short lives together, my love, have always been full of expectation … In these hectic and violent years I have grown to love you more than I ever did before … Nothing can be as valuable as being part and parcel of the formation of the history of a country.*

105. University exams. He was studying law by correspondence.

These are some of the gems this marvellous letter contains and after going through it on May 17 I felt once more on top of the world. Disasters will always come and go, leaving their victims either completely broken or steeled and seasoned and better able to face the next crop of challenges that may occur. It is precisely at the present moment that you should remember that hope is a powerful weapon and one no power on earth can deprive you of; and that nothing can be as valuable as being part and parcel of the history of a country. Permanent values in social life and thought cannot be created by people who are indifferent or hostile to the true aspirations of a nation. For one thing, those who have no soul, no sense of national pride and no ideals to win can suffer neither humiliation nor defeat; they can evolve no national heritage, are inspired by no sacred mission and can produce no martyrs or national heroes. A new world will be won not by those who stand at a distance with their arms folded, but by those who are in the arena, whose garments are torn by storms and whose bodies are maimed in the course of contest. Honour belongs to those who never forsake the truth even when things seem dark and grim who try over and over again, who are never discouraged by insults, humiliation and even defeat. Since the dawn of history, mankind has honoured and respected brave and honest people, men and women like you darling – an ordinary girl who hails from a country village hardly shown in most maps, wife of a kraal which is the humblest even by peasant standards.

My sense of devotion to you precludes me from saying more in public than I have already done in this note which must pass through many hands. One day we will have the privacy which will enable us to share the tender thoughts which we have kept buried in our hearts during the past eight years.

In due course you will be charged and probably convicted. I suggest that you discuss matters with Niki[106] immediately you are charged and make the necessary arrangements for funds for purposes of study, toilet, Xmas groceries and other personal expenses. You must also arrange for her to send you as soon as you are convicted photos with suitable leather picture frames. From experience I have found that a family photo is everything in prison and you must have it right from the beginning. From this side you will have all my monthly letters, darling. I have written a long letter to Zeni and Zindzi[107] care of Niki explaining the position in an attempt to keep them informed and cheerful. I only hope they received my earlier letter of Feb. 4. Last month I wrote to Mummy[108] at Bizana and to Sidumo. This month I will write to Telli

---

106. Winnie Mandela's sister.
107. Their daughters.
108. Winnie Mandela's stepmother in her home town of Bizana.

and to Uncle Marsh. I have heard neither from Kgatho, Maki, Wonga, Sef,[109] Gibson,[110] Lily, Mthetho and Amina[111] to whom I wrote between Dec. and April.

It has been possible to write this letter by kind permission of Brig. Aucamp and I am sure he will be anxious to help you should you desire to reply to this letter whilst you are still under detention. If you succeed please confirm whether you received my April letter. Meanwhile I should like you to know that I am thinking of you every moment of the day. Good luck, my darling. A million kisses and tons and tons of love.

Devotedly,
Dalibunga[112]

109. Sefton Vutela, the husband of Winnie Mandela's sister Nali.
110. Gibson Kente.
111. Various friends and relatives.
112. Nelson Mandela's initiation name.

LETTER FROM NELSON MANDELA
TO HIS DAUGHTERS ZENANI AND ZINDZI MANDELA

23.6.69

My Darlings,

Once again our beloved Mummy has been arrested and now she and Daddy are away in jail. My heart bleeds as I think of her sitting in some police cell far away from home, perhaps alone and without anybody to talk to, and with nothing to read. Twenty four hours of the day longing for her little ones. It may be many months or even years before you see her again. For long you may live like orphans without your own home and parents, without the natural love, affection and protection Mummy used to give you. Now you will get no birthday or Christmas parties, no presents or new dresses, no shoes or toys. Gone are the days when, after having a warm bath in the evening, you would sit at table with Mummy and enjoy her good and simple food. Gone are the comfortable beds, the warm blankets and clean linen she used to provide. She will not be there to arrange for friends to take you to bioscopes, concerts and plays, or to tell you nice stories in the evening, help you read difficult books and to answer the many questions you would like to ask. She will be unable to give you the help and guidance you need as you grow older and as new problems arise. Perhaps never again will Mummy and Daddy join you in House no. 8115 Orlando West,[113] the one place in the whole world that is so dear to our hearts.

This is not the first time Mummy goes to jail. In October 1958, only four months after our wedding, she was arrested with 2000 other women when they protested against passes in Johannesburg and spent two weeks in jail. Last year she served four days, but now she has gone back again and I cannot tell you how long she will be away this time. All that I wish you always to bear in mind is that we have a brave and determined Mummy who loves her people with all her heart. She gave up pleasure and comfort for a life full of hardship and misery because of the deep love she has for her people and country. When you become adults and think carefully of the unpleasant experiences Mummy has gone through, and the stubbornness with which she has held to her beliefs, you will begin to realise the importance of her contribution in the battle for truth and justice and to the extent to which she has sacrificed her own personal interests and happiness.

---

113. The family home in Soweto.

Mummy comes from a rich and respected family. She is a qualified Social Worker and at the time of our marriage in June 1958 she had a good and comfortable job at the Baragwanath Hospital. She was working there when she was arrested for the first time and at the end of 1958 she lost that job. Later she worked for the Child Welfare Society in town, a post she liked very much. It was whilst working there that the Government ordered her not to leave Johannesburg, to remain at home from 6pm to 6am, and not to attend meetings, nor enter any hospital, school, university, courtroom, compound or hostel, or any African township save Orlando where she lived.[114] This order made it difficult for her to continue with her work at the Child Welfare Society and she lost this particular job as well.

Since then Mummy has lived a painful life and had to try to run a home without a fixed income. Yet she somehow managed to buy you food and clothing, pay your school fees, rent for the house and to send me money regularly.

I left home in April 1961 when Zeni was two years and Zindzi three months. Early in January 1962 I toured Africa and visited London for ten days, and returned to South Africa towards the end of July the same year. I was terribly shaken when I met Mummy. I had left her in good health with a lot of flesh and colour. But she had suddenly lost weight and was now a shadow of her former self. I realised at once the strain my absence had caused her. I look forward to some time when I would be able to tell her about my journey, the countries I visited and the people I met. But my arrest on August 5 put an end to that dream.

When Mummy was arrested in 1958 I visited her daily and brought her food and fruits. I felt proud of her especially because the decision to join the other women in demonstrating against the passes was taken by her freely [and] without any suggestion from me. But her attitude to my own arrest made me know Mummy better and more fully. Immediately I was arrested our friends here and abroad offered her scholarships and suggested that she leave the country to study overseas. I welcomed these suggestions as I felt that studies would keep her mind away from her troubles. I discussed the matter with her when she visited me in Pretoria Jail in October 1962. She told me that although she would most probably be arrested and sent to jail, as every politician fighting for freedom must expect, she would nevertheless remain in the country and suffer with her people. Do you see now what a brave Mummy we have?

Do not worry, my darlings, we have a lot of friends; they will look after you, and one day Mummy and Daddy will return and you will no longer be

---

114. The conditions of her banning order.

orphans without a home. Then we will also live peacefully and happily as all normal families do. In the meantime you must study hard and pass your examinations, and behave like good girls. Mummy and I will write to you many letters. I hope you got the Christmas card I sent you in December and the letter I wrote both of you on February 4 this year.

With lots of love and a million kisses.

Yours affectionately,
Daddy

LETTER FROM NELSON MANDELA
TO HIS SISTER-IN-LAW NIKI IRIS XABA

15.7.69

My dear Niki,

I had originally planned to write this letter to Uncle Marsh. But I consider you mother to Zami and not just her eldest sister, and when I received the news of the detention of Nyanya,[115] in addition to that of Zami,[116] I realised just how much the whole affair must have disturbed you. In the circumstances I decided to send the letter to you instead.

In the letter I wrote to Ma at Bizana on May 4, I told her I spent a lot of time thinking of Zami, the painful experiences she was having and the numerous problems that face her as a result of my absence. I pointed out that my confidence and regard for her had risen considerably, and that my only hope was that one day I might be able to give her the peace, comfort and happiness that would compensate for her dreadful hardships. Little did I know at the time that only 8 days thereafter Zami would be back in jail. Her arrest is a real disaster for the family and I must confess that I am very concerned. She is unwell and prison might worsen her condition. When I was arrested I had the fortune that she was outside and free. Before I was convicted she saw me on every visiting day without exception, brought me delicious provisions and clean clothes, and wrote me sweet and charming letters, and never missed a single day of my 2 trials to which she brought many friends and relatives, including my mother. I will never forget the day of sentence in the Rivonia Case for, besides the immense crowds of supporters and well-wishers that turned up, there sat behind us Zami, Ma, Nali[117] and Nyanya. It was a rare moment which comes seldom in a man's career and it deepened my love and respect for Zami and drew me closer to my relatives – to Ma, Nali, Nyanya and to all of you. During my 5 years on this island Zami has visited me no less than 9 times and organised 10 other visits which brought me into contact with relations and friends I much value and respect. Even when difficulties on her side were growing, when she was without a job and her health was giving trouble, she thought first and foremost of me and my happiness and never failed to send me funds, wonderful letters, birthday and wedding anniversary cards. All these things have meant

---

115. Winnie Mandela's youngest sister Nonyaniso, who was detained at the same time.
116. An affectionate name for Winnie Mandela – an abbreviation of her first name Nomzamo.
117. Winnie Mandela's sister Nali Nancy Vutela, who was married to Sefton Vutela.

much to me. One has to be a prisoner to appreciate fully the true value of many things we take much for granted in life outside prison. During the nearly 7 years of my imprisonment Zami has been truly at my side. Now it is her turn and she needs all my love and affection, all my sympathy and help, and yet I can do absolutely nothing for her. She can look forward to no visit from me that would bring some welcome change from the depressing routine to which she is now subjected, tasty provisions that would suit her indifferent health, no warm and affectionate letters that would bring back happy memories. If she should ultimately be charged, it will not be possible for me to show solidarity through physical presence, and none of the countless things she did for me as prisoner shall I be able to do for her.

The tender faces of small children, distorted by fear and drowsiness, seeing their dear mother escorted away in the dead of night, and unable to understand the issues involved is a memory that could haunt the most fearless mother. Add to this picture the fact that for years her children may live like orphans and that she may be completely deprived of the opportunity of giving her children the help and guidance which they would need in the most critical years of their lives. I know Zami is devoted to the children and if there is one thing that would do further harm to her health it is the uncertainty and insecurity that now threatens them.

These are the reasons why I regard her arrest as a family disaster, Niki. I am not in a position to make any predictions as to how she will face up to the situation and I shall certainly not risk any prophecy. But her record up to now has shown her as a woman of great courage who has stuck to her principles in spite of severe trials.

My only hope is that she will find it possible to survive even this one in spite of her indifferent health. I am equally proud of Nyanya and have grown to love her much more than I ever did in the past. I sometimes think that if I were at home these last 8 years she would have made good progress both in her studies and ideas in life. In my last letter to Bawo I expressed my concern over the fact that she was idling at home and suggested that she should at least be given some vocational training. I hope she will also benefit from this experience.

At the time of writing to Ma I was actually expecting a visit from Zami as I had last seen her in December and I had had no visit since then. Our friend Radebe (Mgulwa)[118] was due to visit me in February but for reasons unknown to me he did not come. I had looked forward to that visit because it offered me the only opportunity of hearing something about Zami and the kids as

---

118. A cousin of Nelson Mandela.

apparently none of the letters I have written monthly since December last has reached its destination.

On June 28 another good friend, Moosa Dinath,[119] who was coming down from Johannesburg for the express purpose of discussing family problems caused by Zami's detention, also failed to turn up and again the prison authorities were unable to give me an explanation for this mysterious behaviour on the part of my visitors. I now know that before May 12 Zami had applied for a visiting permit for Kgatho[120] for May 24. The authorities never even told me of this particular visit. The result is that I have been completely cut off from my family and friends at a time when such contact has been absolutely essential. On June 23 I wrote Zeni and Zindzi a long letter which I sent to Brig. Aucamp of the Headquarters, Pretoria, and asked him to forward it to you. I hope at least this one has reached you. In December I wrote to Nali, February to Zeni, Zindzi, Marsh, to my nephew Gibson[121] and to Lilian.[122] All these letters were addressed to 8115 Orlando West. The fact that I received no acknowledgement compels me to infer that the letters were not received and perhaps Uncle Marsh will make the investigations and let you know. I have also written to Tellie requesting her to find out about the letters to Kgatho and Maki in January and February. I was sorry to hear that you were involved in a car accident in which you fractured a leg. I hope you are recovering and am anxious to get some details in your next letter. How are the children getting on and what are their names? How old are they? How many children has Bantu? Love and fondest regards to Marsh, Bantu and hubby, Tellie, Mfundo, etc.

Sincerely,
Nel

---

119. In 1962 Nelson Mandela had met Moosa Dinath, who was in jail for fraud. Nelson had Winnie Mandela meet his wife Maud Katzenellenbogen and they became friends. However, they were both later disillusioned with them.
120. Mandela's second eldest son Makgatho with his first wife Evelyn Mase.
121. Gibson Kente.
122. Activist and friend Lilian Ngoyi.

LETTER FROM NELSON MANDELA
TO HIS SISTER-IN-LAW TELLIE MTIRARA

15.7.69

My dear Nkosazana,

There is hardly a single person I know who welcomes problems. This is understandable since problems often interfere with one's plans, pleasure and happiness. Worse still, they may bring a lot of hardship and suffering. The detention of Nobandla[123] has really disturbed me precisely because it carries just these dangers. She may be kept in jail for years without trial. If she is at last charged she may be given a heavy sentence. In either case this would mean many years of forced separation from the children, relations and friends, many years of toiling and sweating and the denial to her of the privileges of a free person. This is a heavy price to pay. But though always painful and unpleasant, problems may have the advantage of reminding one of those trustworthy and devoted members of the family to whom one instinctively turns when hard times come. Ever since I saw you in court during the Rivonia Case, and especially after you accompanied Nobandla to Cape Town in Aug, '64,[124] it has been my intention to write and thank you for the ready and unfailing assistance that you have given at home. But the very fact that you are a member of the family induced me to take it for granted that you will always know that I have the highest regard for you and that I am fully conscious of the important role you are playing at home in my absence. This in turn gave me the excuse of postponing writing to you until I had attended to what appeared to be the more urgent cases. But Nobandla's arrest has now cut me off from home, my friends and relatives and now I must rely on you and Niki. The two of you will have to arrange my visits as well as those of Nobandla when she becomes entitled to them.

I have already written and requested Niki to investigate whether the letters I wrote to Zeni and Zindzi, Nali, Gibson and to Lilian were received. I should like you to give me a report on whether Kgatho, Maki and Mrs Amina Cachalia got their letters which were written in January, February and April respectively. I require the following additional information on Kgatho: How is his health? Did he go for circumcision? Did he pass the supplementary examinations which he wrote in March? What work is he doing at present and

---

123. A name for Winnie Mandela.
124. For her first visit to her husband on Robben Island since his conviction in the Rivonia Trial.

what are his future plans? Perhaps it would be advisable for him to come down so that we could discuss the whole matter. I should also like to know whether Nobandla still possessed the car and the house telephone, as well as what arrangements, if any, have been made for the payment of the accounts? As you know we have a family attorney who has handled all Nobandla's matters in the past and I should be pleased if you would kindly let me have the name of the lawyer or lawyers who are watching her interests at present and who will appear for her when she is charged. In my letter to Niki I mentioned that this year I expected visits from Kgatho, Moosa Dinath and Alfred Mgulwa and none of them turned up and I should be glad to be informed why they failed to come. Last December I wrote to Dr Wonga Mbekeni,[125] P.O. Tsolo, thanking him for attending my late mother's funeral and for his contribution towards the expenses of the ceremony. I also gave him my condolences on the death of Nkosazana Nozipho[126] and asked him to send me some information which I indicated. As he did not reply I assume he never received this important letter. You must, however, answer this particular one immediately without waiting for Wonga's answer. This can be sent later when you hear from him.

Do you happen to know where Nyanya[127] is being kept? If you are able to communicate with her, do give her my love and let her know I am very proud of her indeed. You should also give my love and fondest regards to Amakhosazana Nombulelo[128]and Nobatembu[129] and let me know whether Nombulelo is still working at the eiderdown factory in Selby. Then there is Nkosazana Nqonqi[130] for whom I have the greatest admiration and respect. She has always been a tower of strength to me. Way back in 1942 she stayed next to the power station in Orlando East. Then she moved next to the Communal Hall, later to Jabavu and finally to Killarney. I frequented these places and she always treated me very warmly as she has frequently done to members of the family. When I married Nobandla she lived with her at her Killarney home. One of my wishes is that she may live long until I am released so that I can have the opportunity of thanking her for what she has done for me and Nobandla. You will of course tell me everything about the child who must be very big now.

Last year I received very inspiring letters from Jonguhlanga,[131] Nkosikazi

---

125. Nelson Mandela's cousin, a chief who negotiated his marriage to Winnie Madikizela.
126. Wonga Mbekeni's sister.
127. Winnie Mandela's younger sister was detained around the same time.
128. Nombulelo Mtirara, a sister of Sabata.
129. Nelson's Mandela's cousin's daughter.
130. Nqonqoloza Mtirara, Nelson Mandela's aunt.
131. Chief Jonguhlanga, Nelson Mandela's cousin.

NoEngland,[132] and from Chief Vulindlela.[133] In the course of the nearly 7 years that I have spent in prison I have received several letters from friends in various parts of the country, all of which I value. But letters from the family have special significance for me, particularly when they come from people such as the Abahlekazi and Nkosikazi above, who have made tremendous sacrifices on my behalf and whom I trust completely. As for you Nkosana I need only mention that I have lived with you since the early fifties and one of the striking qualities you possess in full measure is honesty, love and devotion to the family. The free and open manner in which you discussed problems with me and the valuable and constructive criticisms you made of myself, all created a deep impression which I have not forgotten up to the present day. With people like you and Niki round the house I have little cause to worry. I am fully confident that both of you will do your best to keep things steady and even. Love and fondest regards to Nkosazana Samela and husband, to Nomfundo and Mtsobise.[134]

Very sincerely,
Tat'omncinci

---

132. NoEngland was the wife of the Regent Jongintaba.
133. Nelson Mandela's relative.
134. Cousins of Nelson Mandela.

LETTER FROM NELSON MANDELA
TO HIS WIFE WINNIE MANDELA

Special Letter to Zami

16.7.69

My Darling,

This afternoon the Commanding Officer received the following telegram from attorney, Mendel Levin:[135]

> 'Please advise Nelson Mandela his son Thembekile passed away 13th instant result motor accident in Cape Town.'

I find it difficult to believe that I will never see Thembi again. On February 23 this year he turned 24. I had seen him towards the end of July 1962 a few days after I had returned from the trip abroad. Then he was a lusty lad of 17 that I could never associate with death. He wore one of my trousers which was a shade too big and long for him. The incident was significant and set me thinking. As you know he had a lot of clothing, was particular about his dress and had no reason whatsoever for using my clothes. I was deeply touched for the emotional factors underlying his action were too obvious. For days thereafter my mind and feelings were agitated to realise the psychological strains and stresses my absence from home had imposed on the children. I recalled an incident in December 1956 when I was an awaiting-trial prisoner at the Johannesburg Fort. At that time Kgatho was 6 and lived in Orlando East. Although he well knew that I was in jail he went over to Orlando West and told Ma that he longed for me. That night he slept in my bed.

But let me return to my meeting with Thembi. He had come to bid me fare-well on his way to boarding school. On his arrival he greeted me very warmly, holding my hand firmly and for some time. Thereafter we sat down and con-versed. Somehow the conversation drifted to his studies, and he gave me what I considered, in the light of his age at the time, to be an interesting apprecia-tion of Shakespeare's *Julius Caesar* which I very much enjoyed. We had been corresponding regularly ever since he went to school at Matatiele and when he later changed to Wodehouse. In December 1960 I travelled some distance

---

135. Mendel Levin was an attorney suggested by Maud Katzenellenbogen. He planned to defend Winnie Mandela in her trial but she ultimately chose Joel Carlson.

by car to meet him. Throughout this period I regarded him as a child and I approached him mainly from this angle. But our conversation in July 1962 reminded me I was no longer speaking to a child but to one who was beginning to have a settled attitude in life. He had suddenly raised himself from a son to a friend. I was indeed a bit sad when we ultimately parted. I could neither accompany him to a bus stop nor see him off at the station, for an outlaw, such as I was at the time, must be ready to give up even important parental duties. So it was that my son, no! my friend, stepped out alone to fend for himself in a world where I could only meet him secretly and once in a while. I knew you had bought him clothing and given him some cash, but nevertheless I emptied my pockets and transferred to him all the copper and silver that a wretched fugitive could afford. During the Rivonia Case he sat behind me one day. I kept looking back, nodding to him and giving him a broad smile. At the time it was generally believed that we would certainly be given the supreme penalty and this was clearly written across his face. Though he nodded back as many times as I did to him, not once did he return the smile. I never dreamt that I would never see him again. That was 5 years ago.

During the intervening period, you gave me many interesting reports on him in your letters and during your visits. I was particularly pleased to note his attachment to the family and the personal interest he took in matters affecting his relations. This attachment and interest is demonstrated by the warm letter he wrote you in June 1967, meeting you at the airport when you visited me the same month, looking after Ma[136] in Cape Town and bringing her to the Docks to board the Island boat, visiting you when he recently came up to Johannesburg with his family and taking Zeni and Zindzi out. I do not know whether he managed to go down to see Ma's grave. He has sent messages through Kgatho and gave me the parental honour of asking me to name his baby. Maki also told me that he bought Kgatho and herself clothing and all the other things they need. I know what a shattering blow his death is to you darling and I write to give you my deepest sympathy. I have sent Ntoko[137] our condolences. Though taken away so early in his life, he will rest in peace for he has done his duty to his parents, brothers and sisters and to his relations. We will all miss him. It is a pity that neither you nor I could pay him the last respects that are due from parents to a beloved son who has departed. To lose a mother and a first-born, and to have your life partner incarcerated for an indefinite period, and all within a period of ten months, is a burden too heavy

---

136. Nelson Mandela's mother who died in September 1968.
137. Thembi's widow.

for one man to carry even in the best of time. But I do not at all complain my darling. All I wish you to know is that you are my pride and that of our wide family.

Never before have I longed for you than at the present moment. It is good to remember this in this day of bitter misfortunes and bitter reverses. The writer, PJ Schoeman, told the story of an African Commander-in-Chief who took his army of magnificent black warriors for a hunt. During the chase the son of the Commander was killed by a lioness and the Commander himself was badly mauled by the beast. The wound was then sterilised with a red-hot spear and the wounded dignitary wreathed with pain as the wound was being treated. Later Schoeman asked how he felt and he replied that the invisible wound was more painful than the visible one. I now know what the commander meant. I think of you every moment of the day. Tons and tons of love and a million kisses, Mhlope.[138]

Devotedly,
Dalibunga

---

138. Mhlope is a nickname for Winnie Mandela.

LETTER FROM NELSON MANDELA
TO HIS DAUGHTERS ZENANI AND ZINDZI MANDELA

August 3, 1969

My Darlings,

On July 17 I received a telegram from Kgatho in which he told me that Buti
Thembi, your beloved brother, had died in a car accident. The accident occurred in Touws River, near Cape Town, on July 13. I am told that apart from
him two Europeans, who recently came to this country from Italy, also died.
Your brother will be buried in Johannesburg today. In this telegram Kgatho
informed me that he was sending the full details of how Thembi died. But my
letters take a very long time to reach me and, at the time of writing Kgatho's
letter had not arrived, and I am thus not in a position to give you more particulars on the matter.

I write on behalf of Mummy and myself to give you our deepest sympathy.
All of us were very fond and proud of Thembi and he, in turn, was devoted
to us, and it is indeed very sad to think that we will never see him again. I
know just how he loved you. Mummy wrote to me on March 1 and advised
me that he spent his holidays with his family in Johannesburg, and that during that period he took you out several times and gave you much pleasure
and joy. Mummy has also informed me that he had invited you to spend the
forthcoming December holidays with him in Cape Town and that you were
looking forward to a lot of fun. There you would have seen the sea; places like
Muizenberg and the Strand where you could swim. You would also have seen
the Castle, a large stone fort which was completed about the year 1679. Here
the Governors of the early Cape lived. It was also here that the famous African
king, Cetywayo, was kept for a while after the Battle of Isandhlwana in January
1879 where the Zulu army defeated the English. In Cape Town you would also
have seen Table Mountain which is about 3,549 feet high. From the top of
the mountain you would see Robben Island across the waves. Thembi's death
means that you will not be able to spend your December holidays down there,
and you will also miss the pleasures and beautiful places I have mentioned
above, and we are all very sorry that our Thembi is really gone. He meant
much to us and we will miss him.

It was not possible for Mummy and myself to attend his funeral. Both of us
are in jail and our request for permission to go to the funeral was not granted.
You also did not attend, but when you return from school Kgatho will arrange

for you to be taken to see the grave and bid your departed brother farewell. Perhaps one day Mummy and I will be able also to visit the grave. But now that he is gone, we must forget about the painful fact of his death. Now he sleeps in peace, my darlings, free from troubles, worries, sickness or need; he can feel neither pain nor hunger. You must continue with your schoolwork, play games and sing songs.

This time I have written you a sad letter. On June 23 I had written you another letter which was just as sad, because it dealt with the arrest of Mummy. This year has been a bad one indeed for us, but happy days will come when we will be full of joy and laughter. What is even more important is that one day Mummy and I will come back and live happily together with you in one house, sit at table together, help you with the many problems you will experience as you grow. But until then Mummy and I will write to you regularly.

Tons and tons of love, my darlings.

Affectionately,
Tata

LETTER FROM NELSON MANDELA
TO IRENE BUTHELEZI[139]

3-8-69

Our dear Mndhlunkulu,

I was moved by the message of condolence contained in the telegram sent by my chief, Mangosuthu,[140] on behalf of the family and which I received on July 18 (my birthday), and I should like him to know that I deeply appreciate it. 1968 and 1969 had been difficult and trying years for me. I lost my mother only 10 months ago. On May 12 my wife was detained indefinitely under the Terrorist Act, leaving behind small children as virtual orphans, and now my eldest son is gone never to return. Death is a frightful disaster no matter what the cause and the age of the person affected. Where it approaches gradually as in the case of normal illness, the next-of-kin are at least forewarned and the blow may not be so shattering when it ultimately lands. But when you learn that death has claimed a strapping and healthy person in the prime of his life, then one must actually live through the experience to realise how completely paralysing it can be. This was my experience on July 16 when I was first ad- vised of my son's death. I was shaken from top to bottom and for some seconds I did not know exactly how to react. I ought to have been better prepared for Thembi was not the first child I lost. Way back in the forties I lost a nine months baby girl. She had been hospitalised and had been making good pro- gress when suddenly her condition took a grave turn and she died the same night. I managed to see her during the critical moments when she was strug- gling desperately to hold within her tender body the last sparks of life which were flickering away. I have never known whether or not I was fortunate to witness that grievous scene. It haunted me for many days thereafter and still provokes painful memories right up to the present day; but it should have hardened me for similar catastrophes. Then came Sept. 26 (my wife's birthday) when I was advised of my mother's death. I had last seen her the previous Sept. when she visited me on the Island at the ripe age of 76, having travelled all alone from Umtata. Her appearance had much distressed me. She had lost weight and although cheerful and charming, she looked ill and tired. At the end of the visit I was able to watch her as she walked slowly towards the boat which would take her back to the mainland, and somehow the thought flashed

---

139. Mangosuthu Buthelezi's wife.
140. Chief Mangosuthu Buthelezi.

across my mind that I had seen her for the last time. But as the months rolled by, the picture I had formed of her last visit began to fade away and was altogether dispelled by the exciting letter she wrote thereafter testifying to her good health. The result was that when the fatal hour struck on Sept. 26 I was again quite unprepared and for a few days I spent moments in my cell which I never want to remember. But nothing I experienced in the forties and in Sept. last year can be likened to what I went through on July 16. The news was broken to me about 2.30pm. Suddenly my heart seemed to have stopped beating and the warm blood that had freely flown in my veins for the last 51 years froze into ice. For some time I could neither think nor talk and my strength appeared to be draining out. Eventually, I found my way back to my cell with a heavy load on my shoulders and the last place where a man stricken with sorrow should be. As usual my friends here were kind and helpful and they did what they could to keep me in good spirits. My second son, Kgatho, sent me a telegram on July 17 and I felt even much better. The telegram from the Chief created a deep impression on me and greatly contributed to my complete recovery from the shock. I should like to assure him that I will always remember his inspiring message of sympathy, as well as the one he sent on the occasion of my mother's death. I feel mighty and strong and confident because of the good wishes and messages of solidarity that have come from my trusted friends, among whom I am privileged to include you and the Chief.

My thoughts very often go back to the forties when I lived at Mzilikazi where I first met your parents. Your father, the son of Mzila, was really a grand old man I admired and respected in all sincerity. He was dignified, courteous and confident and throughout the 4 years of my stay at Mzilikazi we were on friendly terms. The conversations I had with him indicated a man who was proud of the traditions and achievements of his people, and this aspect, more than anything else fascinated me.

But though he loved and respected his own history and culture he was sensitive to modern and progressive ideas and valued education. In this respect you and your brother should be witnesses. He was often seen at the Bantu Men's Social Centre[141] in his black and gold regalia, decorated with medals and ribbons, playing drafts [sic] and other games with remarkable skill against distinguished sportsmen of that city. I will always remember him as a man who gave me much encouragement and help in my struggling days. I have not forgotten the Old Lady and the warm smile with which she always greeted me. I valued it even then, but you have to be behind bars for at least 7 years to appreciate

---

141. In Johannesburg.

fully just how precious human kindness can be. It gave me much pleasure to be able to act on her behalf when the Old Man's estate was wound up. Always remember that I highly value my association with your family and that I hold the Chief in esteem. My fondest regards to you all and to Dr Dotwane and your sister-in-law.

Once again many thanks to the Chief for his inspiring message.

Yours sincerely,
Nelson

LETTER FROM NELSON MANDELA
TO BRIGADIER AUCAMP CARE OF THE COMMANDING OFFICER OF
ROBBEN ISLAND

August 5, 1969

The Commanding Officer
Robben Island

Attention: Col Van Aarde.

Kindly approve of the enclosed urgent letter to Brig. Aucamp.

[Signed] Nelson Mandela 466/64[142]

August 5, 1969[143]

The Commissioner of Prisons EXTREMELY URGENT
Private Bag, Pretoria

Attention: Brig Aucamp

I should be please if you would approve of the attached letter to my wife, which
[discusses] the important and urgent question of legal representation. Kindly
arrange with the [security police] staff for delivering to her at the earliest possible convenience.

I should further be pleased if you would now grant me the permission
I have been seeking since May 20 to communicate with the firm of Messrs
Frank, Bernadt and Joffe.[144] I should like to remind you that since the arrest
of my wife, none of the 12 letters I have written up to last June had reached its
destination. Four successive visits which had been arranged for me for [the]
past six months failed to materialise. Even letters addressed [to me] were delayed unreasonably, a discriminatory practice which contrasts sharply with
the treatment afforded my fellow prisoners. A letter that arrived on the island
on Apr 24 was only delivered to me 44 days thereafter on June 7. Another one
which was received by the Post Office on June 17 was handed to me 39 days

---

142. Handwritten note at the bottom: 'Send in the ordinary way to Brig Aucamp.' – signed and dated 5/8/69.
143. Handwritten note at the top in Afrikaans: 'Nelson Mandela 466/64 Letter to Brig Aucamp.'
144. His attorneys.

later on July 26. I should add that at the time of writing I have received no authentic information on the death of my son. My younger son telegraphed to me on July 17 – four days after the fateful accident – and advised that he was sending me the full particulars. But in accordance with previous practice, I probably will not be allowed to receive it timeously not withstanding its nature. By way of contrast I refer to a letter that was written to a fellow prisoner on June 16 and which reached him 6 days thereafter. Another one which was [sent to] the same man on July 13 reached him again 6 days after it had been written. In the circumstances it is reasonable for me to urge you to grant my application without further delay. It is undesirable that I should be kept ignorant about [questions] which are so important to me and the family, and I appeal to you to expedite the matter. In this connection, I should like you to know that I deeply appreciate the opportunity you are giving me to communicate with my wife. The approval of the permission sought above will enable me to deal with all domestic problems caused by my wife's detention, and will be an appropriate and logical complement to the help you have already granted me and my wife.

[Signed] Nelson Mandela 466/64

LETTER FROM NELSON MANDELA
TO WINNIE MANDELA

EXTREMELY URGENT August 5 1969[145]

My Darling,

I have been thinking about the question of the firm of attorneys that should act for you in the event of you being charged at the end of your period of detention.

I have no information as to how the services of Mr Mendel Levin were engaged in the matter, and have nothing against his firm, but I would strongly advise that we immediately instruct Mr Joel Carlson to represent you and to handle our affairs. I do not have to remind you of the invaluable services Mr Carlson has rendered to us in the past and the personal interest that he takes in our affairs, as well as his wide experience in matters of this nature. All I wish to stress is that it would be most unwise not to avail yourself of his services.

You rightly point out that there are problems about him, and the prison authorities have informed me that he is prohibited from entering any South African prison. The authorities may be acting within their rights in imposing these restrictions and we cannot interfere. But they cannot claim, nor do they have the right to interfere in any way with the exercise of your right to be defended by a firm of your own choice. If Mr Carlson is not allowed to interview you in jail, then the South African Police are obliged to take you to his office or to one of the courtrooms for purposes of consultation ... Although I was a detainee during the 1960 State of Emergency on several occasions the police took me from prison to my office in Johannesburg to work on the firm's books with my accountant. Again the accused in the Treason Trial, all of whom were detainees during the period of the Emergency, had numerous consultations with counsel ... during recess. I suggest you communicate immediately with Mr Carlson by registered post and give him formal instructions to represent you as soon as you are charged. Mr Levin could be informed that you are acting on my advice.

I would not advise you to take this course unless it was absolutely necessary for you to do so. I might mention that since May 20 I have made repeated representations for leave to communicate with Mr Carlson or his Cape Town representatives on the position of your arrest and its implications ... In the

---

145. Handwritten note at top in Afrikaans: 'Nelson Mandela 466/64 Special letter to his wife'.

meantime keep well and strong darling. I think of you all the time. Tons and tons of love and a millions kisses.

Devotedly

LETTER FROM NELSON MANDELA
TO HIS NIECE NOMFUNDO MANDELA

8.9.69

My dear Mtshana,

I was indeed very shocked to hear that you, a little girl in her teens, in a rough and cruel city like Johannesburg, have for the past four months lived all alone, exposed to all kinds of danger, and that those who took away your Auntie[146] from home did not even take the simple and reasonable steps of making sure that you will at least be safe by arranging for some elderly person to look after you and the home. How you get your food, buy your clothing and soap, travel to and from school, pay for your school fees and books, and all the many things a child of your age needs, is regarded by them as something which is no concern of theirs. I can well imagine just how hard and difficult things must be for you these days. All domestic work such as cooking, cleaning the house and polishing the stoep must now be done by you alone, leaving you hardly any time to attend to your school work. Add to this the strain caused by many hours of loneliness, uncertainty as to how long Auntie will be away from home, and fear of the unknown. Perhaps some days you wake up in the morning and go to school without having eaten, or drank tea, because there is no money to buy meat, milk, eggs, sugar, bread, butter, mealie meal, coal or paraffin.

It is possible that you have sat for long moments wondering why you are so unfortunate, comparing yourself with the happy and well-fed children you meet at school, and in Soweto, children who live with their parents, who are always full of laughter, who have never suffered in their lives and who have none of the problems that now worry you. May be that at times you doubt whether you will ever see Auntie and myself again, and that it is even diffi-, cult to understand why all this human suffering should occur in the Christian world of the 20th century. There have been moments in my life when in spite of my old age I have had these doubts and difficulties too. The little education that I have, enables me to follow with real interest the progress which man has made over the one million years of his history on earth, developing from a backward and superstitious savage to the cultured individual he now is supposed to be. Yet the cruel experiences you and other members of the family

146. Winnie Mandela.

have had, and their suffering and misery, make me wonder whether it is correct to talk of any human being as being Christian or cultured. Today you are an orphan living in the greater part of the day in loneliness, sadness and fear, because your Auntie and myself, who are alive and well, and who would have given you the chances in life that you deserve, have been jailed by other human beings, by our countrymen who, like true Christians and civilised beings, should treat us with love and kindness. We were seized and thrown into prison not because we have killed, stolen or committed some other crime, but because we stand for truth, justice, honour and principle and because we will never agree that any human being is superior to us. If my whole life and that of Aunt Nobandla should be spent here and we should never see you again; if we should never have the chance of sending you to university as we had hoped, of giving you a decent wedding when the time comes for you to get married, and of helping you to start your own home, then dear Mtshana, you will at least know the true story about us. It will not be because we did not love you, Kgatho, Maki, Zeni and Zindzi, or that we were not conscious of our duties as parents. That will be due to the fact that we loved you so much that we could never allow that you should be denied in your own country the rights and opportunities which human beings elsewhere have enjoyed for many centuries. This is the real truth that explains why we are prisoners, why we are away from home, and why you now sit alone in 8115 Orlando West.

Whatever difficulties you may be having now, Mtshana, do not be discouraged and leave your studies. Though in jail, we will do everything in our power to keep you in school and send you to varsity. Make sure that you pass at the end of the year. Though you may be living under great difficulties at the present moment, you will not die of starvation or loneliness. Sisi Tellie, Uncle Marsh and Aunt Niki will always be ready to help you. Besides, we have many good and trusted friends, like Aunt Gladys[147] on whom you may rely for advice and assistance. One day we will be back home and you, just as the other children at school and [in] Soweto do, will live happily with us. Gone will be your loneliness, miserable life and fear of the unknown, and the dangers to which you are now exposed will be no more. You will struggle less than you do now, eat better food and be able to laugh with joy. In the meantime, we should like you to know that we are very proud to have you as our Mtshana, a brave and clever girl like you, and nothing will please us more than to know that you have passed your examinations.

---

147. Winnie Mandela's maternal aunt.

My love and fondest regards to Kgatho, Maki, Zeni, Zindzi, Matsobiyane,[148] and to Sisi Tellie, Uncle Marsh, Aunt Niki and Aunt Gladys.

Good luck!
Tons and tons of love, Mtshana.

Your Malume[149]

---

148. Nobatembu Mtirara's daughter.
149. Uncle in the isiXhosa language.

LETTER FROM NELSON MANDELA
TO IRENE MKWAYI[150]

29.9.69

Our dear Nolusapho,

I was indeed encouraged by the touching message of sympathy you sent me on the occasion of the death of my eldest son, Thembi. Both the printed text of the condolence card, as well as the soothing sentiments you scribbled down next to the text, were singularly appropriate and they did much to inspire me.

I received the tragic news on July 16, and six days thereafter I applied to the Commanding Officer for leave to attend the funeral, at my own cost, and with or without escort. I added that, if Thembi would have been buried by the time my application was received, I should in that event be allowed to visit his grave for the purpose of 'laying the stone' (ukubek'ilitye) – the traditional ceremony that is reserved for those who miss the actual burial.

Ten months before this I had made a similar application when my mother passed away, and though the authorities had then adopted a hard line in refusing what I considered in all the circumstances to be a reasonable request, I nonetheless vaguely hoped that this time the death of two members of the family occurring so soon after the other would probably induce the authorities to give me the one opportunity I had in life of paying my last respects to Thembi. In the letter of application I expressly referred to the fact that I had been refused leave to be present at the graveside when my mother was laid to rest, pointing out at the same time, that approval of that application would have been a generous act on their part and one that would have made a deep impression on me. I drew attention to the fact that I had seen Thembi five years ago, and expressed the hope that they would appreciate how anxious I was to attend the funeral.

I was of course aware that 30 years ago the British had imprisoned a famous freedom fighter in one of the colonies, a man who later became Prime Minister when his country gained full independence in 1947.[151] He was in jail when his wife's health worsened, and when it became necessary for him to accompany her to Europe for medical treatment. British imperialism has brought untold misery and suffering to millions of people throughout the world, and when the English withdrew they left behind them countries which

---

150. The wife of his comrade, Wilton Mkwayi, who was sentenced to life imprisonment in the Little Rivonia Trial.
151. Jawaharlal Nehru of India.

had been plundered, and whose people were condemned to many years of poverty, famine, disease and illiteracy.

This period forms the black chapter of British history and many historians have justly censured Britain. On the other hand the English are widely known by friend and foe for their broad outlook and sensible approach to human problems, and for their deep respect for men who are ready to give up their lives for a worthy cause. Often in the course of political conflicts with leaders of national movements in their former colonies, they were able to treat political offenders humanely, and to render them genuine and substantial help whenever necessary. So it was that when the politician referred to above was faced with the problem of the illness of his wife, the English released him to travel abroad, Unfortunately, the wife died after reaching Europe and thereafter the bereaved man returned to his country to serve the balance of his sentence. This is how an enlightened government is expected to treat its citizens, and this is how the British Government responded to an application made on compassionate grounds by political opponents a little more than 30 years ago.

In the case of both my late mother and Thembi I was faced not with the problem of illness but that of death. I asked for permission not to travel abroad, but to another part of my own country which was under the constant surveillance of a strong and experienced Security Force. In Thembi's case my application was simply ignored and I was not even favoured with the courtesy of an acknowledgement. A further request for permission to obtain copies of press reports on the fatal accident was turned down, and up to now I have no authentic information whatsoever as to how Thembi died. All my efforts to obtain the services of an attorney to investigate the question of legal responsibility for the accident, any claims arising thereout and the estate generally, have been unsuccessful. Not only was I deprived of the opportunity of seeing for the last time my eldest son and friend, and the pride of my heart; I am kept in the dark on everything relating to him and his affairs. On Sept. 6 I received a report on my household affairs which greatly disturbed me. My niece, Nomfundo, who is still in her teens, lives in the house virtually alone, and I believe the lady who stayed there after Zami's arrest was frightened away. This indifference completely astonished me and kept wide open the painful wounds which the dreadful hands of death had made in my heart.

Your message must be seen in the light of these facts; of the obstacles and frustrations that surround me. Fortunately, my numerous friends here and outside prison have showered me with messages of sympathy and encouragement and the worst is now over. Among these is your own message; you, Nolusapho, the wife of the Amagqunukhwebe, the children of Khwane,

Cungwa, Pato and Kama. I should like you to know that I deeply appreciate your wonderful message. Though I have not yet had the privilege of meeting you, I have the picture of one who genuinely loves her people and who always places the welfare and happiness of others above hers. That you were able to send me this message in spite of your own illness and personal problems says a lot more in your favour than language can express. I sincerely wish you a speedy and complete recovery. Many thanks for the lovely Xmas cards you and Nomazotsho sent me. Love and fondest regards to Georgina, Nondyebo, Beauty, Squire, and Vuyo.[152]

Yours sincerely,
Nelson

---

152. Children of Nelson Mandela's cousin.

LETTER FROM WINNIE MANDELA
TO ATTORNEY MENDEL LEVIN

11.11.69

Dear Sir,

Re: My Affairs

I have today been given your account and note that the letters you wrote on my behalf have been to the value of R500. Since the 28th of October, the date on which it was publicly announced in court that my husband had instructed Mr Carlson to act for me. I wish to inform you that there had been no miraculous change in my financial position since the last three consultations which were arranged for you to meet me by the prison authorities for the specific purpose of discussing funds which I did not have, hence your solemn promise which you repeated time without number in Major Swanepoel's presence to the effect that you were prepared to continue acting for nothing but that advocates required fees.

I have had reason to mention this latter statement even to my present lawyer and have also had to hint to him without giving details that as a result of information given to me in confidence by the same Major I do not think there will be any funds for my case and I mentioned this in my last note to you even before I signed a power of attorney in your favour.

I must however point out that the events of the 28th Oct have raised serious puzzling questions in my mind. You will agree with me as a legal man that it is extremely difficult for a person behind bars in solitary confinement to understand people's motives. If there was so much confusion within a period of five and half months of my detention, what would not be going through the mind of a woman who has spent seven years in prison? It was because I wanted clarification of this situation that I made a request to see Mrs Kay[153] on the 19th of October and have had no reply, and it was also for the same reason of wishing to avoid such situations that I had been battling for the past six months to see my husband. This also did not materialise.

I find even more puzzling the fact that all the people who have visited my husband are in fact closer to you and have had more contact with you than me. I assumed from this that my husband must have surely discussed this matter

---

153. Maud Katzenellenbogen.

with them and yet my sister-in-law Telia, my step-son and my sister all took messages to Mr Carlson from my husband who had earlier been even visited by Mr Dinath to whom you are well known. Although this is now irrelevant I fail to understand why this was not drawn to my attention when I could still have tried more to communicate with my husband to clarify this set-up.

I regret to advise you that I do not have R500 and am not likely to have it even in the next ten years if I live up to that, nor would there by any point in me adding more worries on my husband by even informing him about this. It is not only enough that he is serving a sentence of life imprisonment but also in his own words he has found the past eleven months too much of a burden on one man's shoulders even under the best of times. We are also human beings.

I can assure you that I meant my gratitude which I tried to express and was cut short in court. I looked forward to meeting Mr Zwarenstein whom I was advised as long ago as June that he would be appearing for me. Needless to say I shall always remember Major Swanepoel's words for a long time to come, one of these incidentally was his advice on my ineradicable and irredeemable error of trusting too much.

Your faithfully,
Winnie Mandela

LETTER FROM WINNIE MANDELA
TO NELSON MANDELA

12-11-69

My Darling,

It is wonderful to be able to write to you once more. I gather from the numerous messages you endeavoured to send to me that you must have spent
anxious moments in the last few months of silence. Thank you my love I got
them all on the day I led my 'crusade' to their last journey into captivity on
the 28th of October. It's a band of Christians with the same spirit which drove
Christians into caves two thousand years ago in defence of the gospel. My
glorious surprise was the lovely anniversary card which was given to me on
the 26 of October,[154] quite appropriately two days before I was to be charged.
Words are too shabby to describe the sentiments it evoked in me. I have been
re-reading it since in the solitude of my cell and each time I get a new meaning
[of] life. The battered and torn envelope in a way told many tales and is the
very symbol of the harsh reality of the past eleven years, with no regrets.

It is irrelevant now to tell you how sorry I am that my attempts to see you
have not materialised. The case is set down for the 1st of Dec. The progress we
have made so far with Mr Carlson is infinitesimal. There have been no proper
consultations yet due to so many odds. As you are a co-conspirator I suppose
I can tell you that we are 22 accused and we are charged under the Suppr of
Comm.[155] Act. There are 21 main charges some of which concern me alone
really. It is absolutely imperative that you be acquainted with the full details by
a legal man though as this affects us to a large extent.

I had a serious relapse in September but was again seen by the specialist
who has since increased the treatment. The prison doctor has been almost fa-
therly in his medical care of me. He has explained just like the Joburg specialist
that the condition is permanent and will continue to deteriorate for as long
as we have our problems. I have failed him in one thing, my inability to stop
thinking. This is of course impossible darling for as long as one is held incommunicado. Perhaps things will be better when we are together. There are five
charged women altogether. If only the girls were a little older things would not
be so bad. I must tell you that in the past three months when I was quite ill Brig
and the doctor arranged for me to have a bed, I can no longer lie flat I have to

---

154. Their anniversary is on 14 June, she received it four months late.
155. Suppression of Communism.

be propped up due to the condition. I am feeling better darling you should not worry. If you want more details I do not suppose there would be any objection to your being furnished with the full specialists reports.

We have to plan for the children. By the way both my sisters and their husbands, Maud and friends were in court. After six months in solitary confinement I could not describe the feeling I had in seeing them. Niki has visited me already. It is amazing how different people can be when you look at them through the spectacles of prison life. I saw a completely different Niki. She has brought me a new wardrobe of clothes, the old ones are too big. The girls did not return because her husband's travel document was withdrawn. They spent the holidays with Uncle Allan Nxumalo.[156] Niki says Marshall has been promised that he will get the travel document back. The little souls must have been so hurt but they are very understanding. Uncle Mashumi has been to see them at school and says they are very well. I wrote to Kgatho and gave him messages [for] you only to find that he must have already seen you. The best news of the year was when Niki told me Kgatho is back at home with Nomfundo. Mr Levin told me he has lost interest in education, I found it hard to believe this although I have secretly nursed such a fear after all the emotional upheaval we have all suffered. Is this correct? What did you arrange with him with regard to next year or should I continue with what I had in mind?

One of the most moving in sympathetic messages came from Dad and has instructed Niki to cheer you up. He is sending our sister-in-law to represent the family because my brother will be at school for some time correcting papers as he is now the principal. By the way dad could not get the licence for the bottle store nor the loan from the Bantu Investment Corp presumably because of his children.

Have you got the examination results yet? I will be the most surprised if you did well and how are your funds?

I do not know how we shall discuss the question of the legal guardian of the children. Its seems to me it would be too late if we leave this matter until the end of the case. There are already so many difficulties. I plan [on] speaking to Major Coetzee of Johannesburg about the travel documents, it is already a few weeks before they close. He has assisted us before with correspondence to the school now during my detention and he said I should raise such problems with him.

I can well imagine your state of anxiety about these matters. I have learnt a lot darling and am still able even more so now to analyse situations even under

---

156. A friend in Swaziland who often looked after Zeni and Zindzi in the school holidays.

the best disguise. What a pity I was unable to see you before you were charged. I have developed a liking for studying human behaviour and human relationships. It has been a sense of rude awakening to me to realise the various categories under which we fall. Some of us see relationships between objects whilst others see objects between objects, does one watch and despair thereby committing physical suicide or does one despair and watch thereby committing moral suicide? No, both of these are undignified, so one must find a middle course, because there is a certain species in man that is beyond reason the immalleable. I am always reminded of a childhood story of my grandfather who is reported to have said to someone, 'What kind of men are these we are dealing with? They buy a cow from you and pay you with your own horse.'

How I laughed when you recalled the medical student. My wandering mind collapsed back the gates of 76 Hans Street[157] when the horrible green car refused to start at the wrong time and someone saw it and fainted. Do you remember the day MaMhlophe was driven back from Orlando on a trivial first misunderstanding and the following morning she collided with Mhlekazi at the office. They both went to wait for each other without any previous arrangement. Let alone the 'Cigarette'[158] and the famous statement, 'Lo mfana ondisusc kuwc unzima'. He must now be saying that was good riddance. Then there was MaMhlophe and Tshezi one day in that office at Bara[159] and how they could not stand each other.

The girls and I have shared moments of amusement too. One day two old ladies and the Methodist evangelist came to hold prayers, I was ill but we were in the front room. Unfortunately they chose the hour which usually belongs to the law on routine check.[160] Whilst the evangelist was in the middle of a very emotional prayer there was a violent knock and it persisted. I went to open and when I returned to my seat there was no sign of anybody. That was a year ago and that was the last I saw of them! How I miss you at such moments.

Keep well my love, tons of love and a million kisses

Yours forever,
Zami

PS: Have you heard from Sabata?[161] He is coming up at the end of the year to

---

157. The hostel in Jeppe in which Winnie Mandela stayed while she was studying at the Jan Hofmeyr School of Social Work in Johannesburg.
158. Winnie Mandela's nickname for Kaiser Matanzima.
159. Baragwanath Hospital.
160. The police would check if she was at home as stipulated in her banning order.
161. King of the Thembus.

settle the question of our late Thembi's estate. The property at Qunu was transferred to him just before his death. I do not know if I will be granted permission to see him but I'll apply.

LETTER FROM NELSON MANDELA
TO WINNIE MANDELA

16.11.69

Dade Wethu,[162]

I believe that on Dec. 21 you and 21 others will appear in the Pretoria Supreme Court under the Sabotage Act, alternatively, for contravening the provisions of the Suppression of Communism Act. I am informed that you have all in- structed Mr Joel Carlson to act in the matter.

From the particulars of the charge it would seem that you would require me to give evidence on your behalf and I look forward to an early consultation with you and Counsel. I would certainly consider it irregular and unjust and contrary to the elementary principles of natural justice to force you to start a long and protracted trial on a serious charge without arrangements having first been made for us to meet. We have not seen each other since Dec. last year and a meeting between us would go a long way towards easing the strains and stresses of the last 5 months and putting you in a better physical condition and frame of mind. Only after such a meeting could you have something ap- proximating a fair trial, and I sincerely hope it will be possible to arrange it. I am also keen to discuss the question of how you should conduct your defence and to anticipate the tactics the state will most certainly use. Since our wed- ding day in June 1958, you have, under some pretext or other, been dragged 3 times before the criminal courts and once before a civil one. The issues in- volved, at least in part of this litigation, are better forgotten than recalled. They caused much grief and concern. This will be the 5th occasion, and I suspect that here there is much that lies beneath the surface, and the proceedings are likely to be the bitterest experience of your entire life to date. There will be those whose chief interest will be to seek to destroy the image we have built over the last decade. Attempts may be made to do now what they have repeat- edly failed to achieve in former cases. I write to warn you in time of what lies ahead to enable you to prepare yourself both physically and spiritually to take the full force of the merciless blows that I feel certain will be directed system- atically at you from the beginning to the end of the trial. In fact, the trial, and the circumstances surrounding it, may so far influence your thoughts and ac- tions that it might well constitute an important landmark in your entire career,

---

162. An isiXhosa term meaning 'sister'.

compelling you to re-examine very carefully values you once fondly cherished and to give up pleasures that once delighted your heart.

Already the months you spent in detention have been a severe test for you and when you come to the end of the case, you will have got a deeper understanding of human nature and its frailties and what human beings can do to others once their privileged position is endangered. When this threat emerges all the lofty virtues of western democracy about which we read so much in books are brushed aside. Neither the moral standards of modern civilisation, the teachings of the Christian faith, the universal idea of the common brotherhood of men, nor pure sense of honour will deter the privileged circles from applying the multitudinous pressures at their disposal on those who fight for human dignity. Those who are on the front-line should be willing and ready to draw the fire onto themselves in order to inspire their colleagues and make things easier for them. In the battle of ideas the true fighter who strives to free public thinking from the social evils of his age, need never be discouraged if, at one and the same time, he is praised and condemned, honoured and degraded, acclaimed as saint and cursed as an irredeemable sinner. In the course of your short but lively political career you have been the object of all these contradictory labels, but you have never wavered; instead you held firmly to your convictions. Today even a bigger test faces you for a conviction will certainly entail many years of sorrow and suffering behind iron doors. But I have not the slightest doubt whatsoever that you will fight to the bitter end with all the tenacity and earnestness that you have shown on previous occasions, for you know only too well that substantial victories will be won by those who stand on their feet and not by those who crawl on their bellies.

In planning your own case and working out your strategy it will be important to bear in mind that you are engaged in a contest with an adversary who possesses vast resources in wealth and means of propaganda and who will be able to give facts any twist which he considers expedient. In such a situation your best defence, and one no power on earth can penetrate, is truth, honesty and courage of conviction. Nothing must be done or said which might imply directly or indirectly a repudiation of your principles and beliefs. The rest I propose discussing with you if and when I see you. That moment may or may never come. I do hope it will. If it doesn't, then I know you will, nevertheless, be in good hands and that you will be able to manage even without my help and advice. For the present, I send you all my good wishes and fondest regards.

I will keep my fist clenched, and will do anything to assist you, Ngutyana.[163] How is our dear Nyanya? Do tell me something about her.

I have just received the tragic news that Cameron[164] in Botswana had a stroke which resulted in paralysis and the amputation of a leg. To be struck down by such a fatal illness far away from your country and people is a disaster that may well make recovery difficult. I think of just how helpful he has been to you in my absence and regret it very much that we are not in a position to assist him. As far as I know, as an awaiting-trial prisoner, you can write as many letters as you please and I suggest that you immediately write to tell him that we wish him speedy recovery. Kgatho visited me on Oct. 25, following upon Nkosazana Tellie who was here on Sept. 6.

On Nov. 8 I received a disturbing letter from her in which she bitterly complains of having been left behind when relatives visited you on Oct. 28. She is very good to us, and is receiving wrong treatment from certain quarters. I hope it will be possible for you to let her know that she means much to us.

I received a stimulating letter from Amina[165] and she paid you flattering compliments. I am sure you will be happy to know that our friends have not forgotten you. I believe Lily[166] had at last got my letter. In July she sent me a warm and moving message of sympathy. I also received an equally inspiring condolence card from Irene. She seems to be a wonderful girl and has built up an impressive image. This month I wrote to Mrs Adelaide Mase, the wife of Mamqwati's[167] brother at Engcobo, thanking them for the letter they wrote me in August. Mamqwati also wrote in Oct. in reply to the message I sent to her on behalf of you and I.

The salutation to this letter will not surprise you. In the past I have addressed you in affectionate terms for then I was speaking to Nobandla, wife of Ama-Dlomo. But on this occasion, I can claim no such prerogatives because in the freedom struggle we are all equals and your responsibility is as great as mine. We stand in the relationship, not of husband and wife, but of sister and brother. Until you return to 8115, or some other appointed place, this is how I will address you, O.K? Perhaps this arrangement will provide room for the legions of students, medical or otherwise, that have crossed the life of one or other of us.

Finally, Mhlope, I do wish you to know that you are the pride of my heart, and with you on my side, I always feel I am part of an invincible force that is

---

163. A name for Winnie Mandela.
164. Madikizela.
165. Amina Cachalia.
166. Lilian Ngoyi.
167. Nelson Mandela's first wife, Evelyn Mase.

ready to win new worlds. I am confident that, however dark and difficult times might seem to be now, one day you will be free and able to see the beautiful birds and lovely fields of our country, bath in its marvellous sunshine and breathe its sweet air. You will again see the picturesque scenery of the land of Faku where your childhood was spent, and the kingdom of Ngubengcuka where the ruins of your own kraal are to be found.

I miss you badly! Tons and tons of love and a million kisses.

Devotedly,
Dalibunga

LETTER FROM NELSON MANDELA
TO MASHUMI PAUL MZAIDUME[168]

19.11.69

My dear Radebe,

I have received disturbing reports that my son, Makgatho, 8115 Orlando West, is not keen to go to Fort Hare next year. He should have registered at the beginning of this year, but he had to write a supplementary examination in March and apparently thought he could not be admitted for a degree course. It would be tragic if he were to miss yet another year and I should be glad if you would do everything in your power to get him to College in February at all costs.

He visited me on Oct. 25 and assured me that he had already filled in and forwarded to the Registrar the relevant application forms. We also discussed the question of fees and allowance whilst at College, and gave him the names of two friends in Johannesburg who, I believe, will be keen to help in this connection. Kgatho will be able to give you their names and addresses, and I would advise that you see them in person and thrash out the whole matter with them.

You may indicate to Kgatho that in appealing to you to assist on this question, I do not in any way wish to suggest that I doubt the assurance he gave me. I have complete confidence in his personal integrity and sense of honour and do not believe that he would ever deliberately wish to mislead me on matters relating to his future career. I am, however, a thousand miles away from Johannesburg, and it is natural and reasonable that I should feel concerned about any information which tends to indicate that he is not acting with the prudence and diligence that I expect from him. I also make allowance for the fact that he may have special problems which, because of my present circumstances, he is not keen to confide to me. I have even wondered whether he does not find it humiliating or embarrassing to discuss financial assistance with persons who are strangers to him, and I am asking you to take a personal interest in the matter, as I believe that the intervention of a relative, who will negotiate on his behalf on these delicate questions, will at least save him this embarrassment.

At present he has a good job and earns a steady income which enables him to assist in the maintenance of the family and in paying for the education of his

---

168. Winnie Mandela's uncle.

sisters. He may consequently doubt the wisdom of throwing away a lucrative post which makes it possible for him to shoulder important family responsibilities, only to start again from scratch some years later. Add to this his age. At 19 any young man in his position may not find it at all easy to resist the glittering attractions of a golden city. I mention all these things because I believe that you should be fully informed on the sort of problems that may be influencing the trend of his thinking and actions, and to enable you to know how to handle the situation. Anyway I leave the whole matter to you and to Mzala, Khathi.[169]

Incidentally last Saturday I received a sweet letter from my eldest daughter, Maki, who is doing J.C. at the Orlando High School. She had been keen on science but the death of her eldest brother, Thembi, to whom she looked for financial support, has clearly affected her plans. She now informs me that she is no longer keen to be a scientist because funds will not be available for this purpose. When I left home in April '61 we had made arrangements for the education of all the children and things went very well until the end of 1967. Even after that date, Zami, with all her formidable difficulties, just managed to keep things fairly even. But now that she is away things seem to be going into pieces. You may mention this aspect to my friends as well.

I never like to allow my thoughts to dwell much on Zeni and Zindzi. It was hard enough for them that I should be away from home. It should even be more so now that Zami has followed. I cannot be sure that this disruption of our family life may not have seriously affected them. I wrote to them in June and July but I learn that neither letter reached. I hear very little about them and this increases my anxiety and concern. But I am always consoled by the fact that you, Khathi, Marsh, Niki and many of our friends are there to give them all the warm love and affection that they need. If there is one thing that contributed to Zami's deteriorating health, it is precisely the plight of the children at the present moment, to whom she is deeply attached. But you will be happy to know that she counts you amongst those who will spare no efforts in making the children forget that they are orphans.

I hear from her now and again and it is a pleasure for me to be able to tell you that in spite of her indifferent health, she is in a grand mood. What a girl! She was brave enough to drag me to the altar, but I never once suspected that her courage would take her so far. I feel very humble indeed when I compare my own insignificant efforts with the heavy sacrifices she is making. My only worry is to know how C.K.[170] and Niki have taken the whole thing. Radebe,

---

169. Mzala is a name for cousin and Khati is Kathaza, Mandela's cousin's daughter.
170. Winnie Mandela's father, Columbus Madikizela.

it was a real pleasure for me to receive your moving letter exactly 12 months ago, and to hear something about abazala[171] and Granny. It's amazing how fast children go [*sic*]. I found it difficult to believe that Khathi was going to varsity. As a matter of fact I had planned to write to her and hear something about Fort Hare, but Kgatho's case compelled me to write to you instead. Love and fondest regards to all.

Sincerely,
Madiba

171. An isiXhosa word meaning 'cousins'.

LETTER FROM WINNIE MANDELA
TO HER SISTER-IN-LAW TELLIE MTIRARA

3/12/69

My dear Nkosazana,

I must say I have been quite unhappy since I saw you when you visited me. I was shocked to see you just a shadow of your old self and looking so run-down. A week thereafter I was allowed to read a portion of a letter from my husband in which he stated how disturbed he was over the letter you wrote to him complaining bitterly about certain family matters. I looked forward to seeing you in court as you had promised and I thought I might have got an opportunity of discussing some of these family problems with my sisters and yourself. I would have made special representations to be allowed to see you too.

I would like you to visit me as soon as you can. I wrote the letter you told Kgatho to tell me about although it was just a note authorising a member of my family to collect my clothes. I needed a few changing clothes from the light crimpelene summer wear and shoes, the pair I have is the one I brought along with me in May and it's getting quite worn out. I have had to borrow slippers from one of my friends and have promised to buy her a pair. Secondly I would like to send back some of the winter clothes. I did not even have something to hold my stockings with, and even the stockings were also given to me by another friend. I find this terribly embarrassing, to be so stranded when at least I've got clothes I've worked hard for with your assistance. We were cut off that [time] before we had discussed anything sensible.

Please make it a point to call soon. Thanks a million for the visit you arranged for Kgatho. I was thrilled to see my boy. He is a real man now and he spoke like an adult. I must discuss him with you too, his schooling next year and it's already so late in the year. I would like to say so much to you, about all what you have done for your brother and I, not to say anything about the children. Your holiday falls this month and I wondered whether you could fit in a visit to the girls. I understand you made them wonderful provisions after my detention when they returned to school. I had always known that in you they have more than an aunt.

How is sis'Thoko? I was told you see her very frequently, by my sister. I do hope as a Christian she has taken the bitter tragedy well. Do tell her how much I appreciate the sacred gesture of letting Kgatho take his responsibility.

I look forward to seeing you soon. Where is Nomaphelo?[172] Greet Mfundo and tell her I dreamt she does not scrub the floors on Fridays! Do eat a little more than you do. Love to my boy.

Fondest regards,
Nobandla

---

172. Nelson Mandela's sister Leabie.

LETTER FROM NELSON MANDELA TO WINNIE MANDELA

January 1, 1970
Sent 20.1.70

Dade Wethu,

A novel by Langenhoven, *Skaduwees van Nasaret* (*Shadows of Nazareth*), depicts the trial of Christ by Pontius Pilate when Israel was a Roman dependency and when Pilate was its military governor. I read the novel in 1964 and now speak purely from memory. Yet though the incident described in the book occurred about 2000 years ago, the story contains a moral whose truth is universal and which is as fresh and meaningful today as it was at the height of the Roman Empire. After the trial Pilate writes to a friend in Rome to whom he makes remarkable confessions. Briefly this is the story as told by him, and for convenience I have put it in the first person:

> *As governor of a Roman province I have tried many cases involving all types of rebels. But this trial of Christ I shall never forget. One day a huge crowd of Jewish priests and followers, literally shivering with rage and excitement assembled just outside my palace and demanded that I crucify Christ for claiming to be king of the Jews, at the same time pointing to a man whose arms and feet were heavily chained. I looked at the prisoner and our eyes met. In the midst of all the excitement and noise he remained perfectly calm, quiet and confident as if he had millions of people on his side. I told the priests that the prisoner had broken Jewish and not Roman law and that they were the rightful people to try him. But in spite of my explanation they stubbornly persisted in demanding his crucifixion. I immediately realised their dilemma. Christ had become a mighty force in the land and the masses of the people were fully behind him. In this situation the priests felt powerless and did not want to take the responsibility of sentencing and condemning him. The only solution was to induce imperial Rome to do what they were powerless to do.*
>
> *At festival time it has always been the practice to release some prisoner and as the festival was now due I suggested that this prisoner be set free. But instead the priests asked that Barabas, a notorious prisoner, be released and that Christ be executed. At this stage I went*

into court and ordered the prisoner to be brought in. My wife and that of other Roman officials occupied the bay reserved for distinguished guests. As the prisoner walked in my wife and her companions instinctively got up as a mark of respect for Christ but soon realised that this man was a Jew and prisoner whereupon they resumed their seats. For the first time in my experience I faced a man whose eyes appeared to see right through me, whereas I was unable to fathom him. Written across his face was a gleam of love and hope; but at the same time he bore the expression of one who was deeply pained by the folly and suffering of mankind as a whole. He gazed upwards and his eyes seemed to pierce through the roof and to see right beyond the stars. It became clear that authority was not in me as a judge, but was down below in the dock where the prisoner was.

My wife passed me a note in which she informed me that the previous night she had dreamt that I had sentenced an innocent man whose only crime was that of messiah to his people. 'There before you Pilate is the man of my dream; let justice be done.' I knew that what my wife said was quite true, but my duty demanded that I should sentence this man irrespective of his innocence. I put the note in my pocket and proceeded with the case. I informed the prisoner what the charge was against him and asked him to indicate whether or not he was guilty. Several times he completely ignored me and it was clear he considered the proceedings an utter fuss, as I had already made up my mind on the question of sentence. I repeated the question and assured him that I had authority to save his life. The prisoner's gleam dissolved into a smile and for the first time he spoke. He admitted that he was [a] king and with that single and simple answer he totally destroyed me. I had expected that he would deny the charge as all prisoners do, and his admission brought things to a head.

You know, dear friend, that when a Roman judge tries a case in Rome, he is guided simply by the charge, the law and the evidence before the court, and his decision will be determined solely by these factors. But here in the provinces far away from Rome we are at war. A man who is in the field of battle is interested only in results; in victory and not in justice, and the judge is himself on trial. So it was, that even though I knew that this man was innocent, my duty demanded that I give him the death sentence and so I did. The last time I saw him, he was struggling towards Calvary amidst jeers, insults and blows, under the crushing weight of the heavy cross on *which he was to die. I have decided to write you this personal letter because I believe that this confession to a friend will at least salve my uneasy conscience.*

This in brief is the story of the trial of Jesus and comment is unnecessary, save to say that Langenhoven wrote this story in the twenties to arouse the political consciousness of his people in a South Africa where and at a time when, in spite of formal independence his people enjoyed, the organs of government including the judiciary were monopolised by Englishmen.

To the Afrikaner this story may recall unpleasant experiences and open up old wounds, but it belongs to a phase that has passed. To you and I it raises issues of a contemporary nature. I hope you will find it significant and useful and trust it will bring you some measure of happiness.

Molokazana[173] paid me a visit this Saturday. She is a charming girl and I was really pleased to see her. On 14.1.70 she will be in Johannesburg for the '*Kulula*' ceremony. I am writing to Ntambozenqanawa[174] to ask him and Jongintaba Mdingi[175] to help in this task. Last month I wrote to her and to Vuyo Masondo, and gave our condolences on the death of her brother at Umtata.

May good luck be on your side.

Tons and tons of love, Mhlope, and a million kisses.

Devotedly,
Dalibunga

---

173. Thembi's widow, Thoko.
174. Chief Ntambozenqanawa Mtirara, Nelson Mandela's cousin.
175. Chief Jongintaba Mdingi, who had the right to name Nelson Mandela's children.

LETTER FROM WINNIE MANDELA
TO BRIGADIER AUCAMP[176]

15.1.70

Dear Sir,

I want to thank you for arranging for me to get my clothes which were given to the Security Branch by my sister-in-law Telia Mtirara in September 1969. I got these on 14.1.70.

I wish to make an application to have one of my teeth filled … I understand that I have to make such an application to you to see a dentist.

Thanking you,

Yours faithfully,
[Signed] W Mandela

176. Letter from the National Archives.

LETTER FROM JOEL CARLSON
TO THE COMMISSIONER OF PRISONS

20th January 1970

Dear Sir,

Re: Awaiting-trial prisoners held at the women's section, Pretoria Central Prison, in the matter of the State versus Samson Ratshivande Ndou & 21 others

Futher difficulties have arisen with regard to the treatment of the five awaiting-trial women prisoners in the above matter. These prisoners are Mrs Winnie Mandela, Joyce Nomafa Sikakane, Rita Anita Ndzanga, Venus Thokozile Mngoma and Martha Dlamini.

1. I am instructed that on Friday, the 16th instant, Matron Jacobz [*sic*] removed and read and then impounded certain notes and instructions written by Mrs Mandela, which she wished to bring to my attention as the defence attorney. This was done before the women prisoners left the women's gaol and were transported to the men's gaol, where the consultations are held. As soon as the report was made to me, I telephoned Matron Jacobz from the men's section of the prison, advised her of the nature of the report made, and asked her to hand over to me immediately the notes made. She refused to do this and said that she was referring the notes to Brigadier Aucamp and would then return the notes to Mrs Mandela on her return to the women's section of the prison later that day. She said that these notes had been removed on the instructions of Brigadier Aucamp. The notes were not returned to Mrs Mandela and are still impounded and in the possession of the prison authorities. The seizure of these notes by Matron Jacobz was unlawful and I am instructed to call upon you to take the necessary action to ensure that the notes are returned to Mrs Mandela immediately.

2. In addition, I am advised by these women prisoners that Matron Jacobz has demanded that they surrender all their statements and memoranda for their defence to her in order that she read them and that she insists on this being done before the women are permissed to leave the women's section of the prison for the purpose of consultation with their defence lawyers. Not only has Matron Jacobz read these prison notes in detail, but she has made comments on them

to the women prisoners. This practice has apparently been adopted by the said matron in regard to the written instructions given by the women prisoners to the defence lawyers since the 15th December, 1969. At an early stage the question of the reading of the statements by prison staff was raised and strong objection was taken to the demand which had been made to read prisoners' written instructions to their lawyer. I was subsequently assured that the prison authorities would not read or remove such documents from the prisoners, either in their presence or in their absence, and the women prisoners were then instructed by me to prepare written statements on certain issues. I have now learned that during my absence on holiday the undertaking given to me was not carried out, and that matron Jacobz has made a practice of reading these privileged documents in detail. If Matron Jacobz persists in this conduct, it will no longer be possible to ask the women prisoners to prepare written statements necessary for the preparation of the defence case, nor will it be possible to leave statements with them to read on their own.

3. The said women prisoners have advised me that in breach of the regulations, they have not been allowed exercise since the adjournment of the case in Court and that this applied throughout the week and over the weekends and holidays. This cannot be accepted and my clients must be permitted the exercise periods to which they are, in law, entitled.

In the circumstances, I have been instructed to request from you, as I hereby do, an assurance that there will be no repetition of the acts complained of.

Yours faithfully,
J Carlson

LETTER FROM JOEL CARLSON
TO THE COMMISSIONER OF PRISONS

20th January 1970

Dear Sirs,

Re: The State verus S.R. Ndou and 21 others – interview with Nelson Mandela – Robben Island Prison

I refer to the letter dated the 22nd December which was addressed to the box number of my Pretoria correspondent. The letter was received by my correspondent while I was on holiday in Cape Town and a copy of the letter was given to me after I had returned to Johannesburg.

I cannot accept your ruling that another attorney must be instructed to interview Mr Mandela. Apart from the fact that the ruling embodies discrimination against myself, it is wholly impracticable to instruct another attorney in view of the following considerations.

1. There are 22 accused for whom I am appearing.
2. The indictment alleges a conspiracy between the 22 accused and 7 co-conspirators, including Mr Mandela, involving activity for a period of over 1 and a half years.
3. The indictment and further particulars thereto covered 29 pages and alleged 21 allegations against each accused.
4. The State proposes to call a large number of witnesses and the trial, which has already gone on for some weeks, is expected to last several months.
5. I have already spent a considerable amount of time consulting the accused, and have also been present during the conduct of the trial and am accordingly fully acquainted with the nature of the defence and the full background thereto.
6. Some of the statements minuted are very long, and, together, the statements cover several hundreds of pages.

As a result of the consultations I have held, and my knowledge of the case, which I have acquired from studying the indictment, the further particulars and the preliminary statements, I will be able to discuss the relevant issues with Mr Mandela and establish whether or not he is able to give evidence or furnish me with information which will be of assistance to the persons whom I represent.

In the light of the aforegoing, it will be appreciated that it is impossible to instruct another attorney and that the refusal to allow me to consult with Mr Mandela is, in all the circumstances, wholly unreasonable and may result in grave prejudice to my clients. My clients see no reason why they should be prejudiced in this way and require me to undertake this task myself.

In the circumstances, I have been instructed to call upon you to reconsider your ruling and to grant permission for me to interview Mr Mandela. Should you persist in your refusal, I will be obliged to place these facts before the court and ask it to take appropriate action to ensure that my clients are not prejudiced.

Yours faithfully
J Carlson

LETTER FROM NELSON MANDELA
TO THE COMMANDING OFFICER OF ROBBEN ISLAND

January 29, 1970

Attention: Lt Nel.

Please investigate the following matters:

1. Prior to October 28, 1969, Mrs Jane Xaba,[177] from Johannesburg wrote to me a letter which I have not received.
2. At the beginning of December 1969 Mrs Rebecca Kotane, also from Johannesburg, sent me a Xmas card and a letter in which she advised me of the death of her husband's uncle. These did not reach me.
3. During the first week of December 1969 I sent six Xmas cards to members of the family and to friends. One of these was addressed to my daughter-in-law Lydia Thoko Mandela who lives in Cape Town. She visited me on December 27 and informed me that she had not received a card from me.
4. On April 4, 1969, I wrote to Mrs Amina Cachalia, Johannesburg, and the letter reached her only during the first week of September. In this connection I should be pleased if you would give me an explanation, if any, for the five months delay.
5. On May 4 I wrote to my mother-in-law, in lieu of [a] visit for April 1969, and my monthly letter went to Sidumo Mandela. These two letters are shown in your records as having been posted on May 7. In this connection I should be please if you would advise me whether they were sent by registered post as I had requested?
6. On November 19 I wrote to Mrs Nolusapho Mkwayi and should be pleased to be advised of the date when the letter was posted to her.

Apart from the specific enquiries made above I should be grateful if you would supply me with a record of letters received on my behalf as from January 1, 1969, to January 29, 1970, as well as my outgoing letters as from June 1, 1969 to January 29, 1970.

Finally my next monthly letter will be addressed to Miss Matlala Tshukudu,[178] in England and I should be pleased if you would allow me to send it by registered airmail.

[Signed] Nelson Mandela

---

177. Jane Xaba is the sister of Marshall Xaba.
178. A pseudonym for Adelaide Tambo.

LETTER FROM NELSON MANDELA
TO MARSHALL XABA

February 3, 1970
Sent 18.2.70
Registered airmail

My dear Uncle Marsh,

Please avoid any arrangement about House no 8115 Orlando West, which would have the effect of depriving Kgatho and sisters of a home during our absence.

Kgatho saw me last Saturday and appeared terribly upset over the fact that someone, who is not a relative and who is not acceptable to him and Tellie should be given charge of the house. He prefers my niece Lulu, who paid me a visit on November 29. I am in favour of Kgatho's suggestion provided that it is acceptable to Zami, and I should be pleased if you would kindly acquaint her with my views. I must confess that Kgatho's anxiety over the whole affair has worried me ever since he raised the matter on January 31, and I consider it most undesirable that he should at any time feel wronged and insecure. He told me that the matter might be finalised with the municipal authorities this week, and I hope that this letter will reach you in time and before you commit yourself to a decision which may cause ill-feeling. I should like you to draw this letter to Kgatho and put his mind at rest before he leaves for Fort Hare.

It is not necessary for me, Uncle Marsh, to assure you that I am fully aware that you and Niki have no ulterior motive in this matter and that your sole purpose is to safeguard our interests, and I am sure that now that you are aware of my views on the matter, you will do everything in your power to settle it amicably and satisfactorily.

The time was so short when I saw Kgatho that I forgot to ask about Zeni and Zindzi's school reports and health. Please give me some information when you reply. In her September letter, Niki indicated that you had applied to come down and I have been hoping that I would see you. I am also anxious to know whether Ma of Bizana received my letter of May last. Let Bantu know that she is free to visit me, and I would indeed be happy to see her. I hope Nali's letter, which I wrote in July last year, was received. I will write to my dear friends, the Ngakane's at the earliest opportunity, and add to your explanation.

Fondest regards and much love to you, Niki and family.

Yours very sincerely
Nel

LETTER FROM NELSON MANDELA
TO THE COMMANDING OFFICER OF ROBBEN ISLAND

February 23, 1970

Attention: Lt Nel.

The Commanding Officer
Robben Island

On the 11th of February warder Van der Westhuizen showed me the register of outgoing and incoming post and I must accept that the letters from Jane Xaba and Rebecca Kotane[179] and a Christmas card from the latter were not received by the Censor's Office. I believe that the persons mentioned above would not have given me the assurance if they had not actually written to me.

You will understand how important it is for a prisoner to be in regular contact with his friends and family. However most of the letters I have written in the last eight months did not reach their destination. Even the special and urgent letter that Colonel Van Aarde gave me personal support for and which I gave to the censors on 19 November 1969 had not reached its destination by 31 January.

My normal monthly letter of the same date (19.11.69) to Nolusapho Mkwayi, which was previously refused but which Brigadier Aucamp gave permission for on 16 November, did not appear in the above-mentioned register.

I would like to ask you to give your personal attention [to this matter]. [Before] all contact with family and friends is cut off.

[Signed] Nelson Mandela 466/64

---

179. The wife of political activist Moses Kotane.

LETTER FROM NELSON MANDELA
TO HIS SISTER-IN-LAW TELLIE MANDELA

March 6, 1970
Sent 17.3.70

My dear Nkosazana,

I received your letter which was posted in Johannesburg on October 22 and in which you reported that Joel had agreed to appear for Nobandla.

I also received your second letter written on October 28 in which you informed me that Joel had actually appeared when the case was remanded the same day. I am very grateful for all the efforts that you are making to straighten out our domestic problems, and more particularly for the important role that you have played in obtaining the services of Joel. Whatever may be the final outcome of the painful episodes in which Nobandla is now engaged, nothing pleases me more than the fact that the case and our affairs are handled by a man in whom I have the fullest confidence; and for this I am greatly indebted to you, Nkosazana.

I was very disturbed to hear that you were unable to see her in the court cells when she and her friends appeared for remand. In my present circumstances, Madiba, problems which I could have otherwise easily solved become extremely difficult to handle. You, Uncle Marsh and Niki, are all very close to Nobandla and me, and all of you are trying your very best to help us in every possible way. I feel sure that if Nobandla and I were free your differences with my in-laws would have been amicably composed. I hope to see Marsh soon and will certainly discuss all your complaints with him. I will advise that the three of you should come together and try to thrash out all issues that have spoilt your relations and that make harmonious co-operation difficult.

As you know, Kgatho saw me on January 31 and mentioned the problem of who should look after the home when he goes to Fort Hare, stressing at the same time that the matter was extremely urgent. I had hoped that the visit would, as usual, last an hour but, unfortunately, we were given only 30 minutes and the interview was terminated before I had given my views. I would have preferred to send a telegram to Kgatho and Marsh setting out my views but these things are not always possible here, and notwithstanding the urgency of the matter, I had to be content with an airmail letter to Marsh only and which I am not even so sure whether it ever reached its destination.

In this letter I asked Marsh to avoid any arrangement about the house which would have the effect of depriving Kgatho and sisters of a home during our absence. I informed him that I considered Lulu to be the most suitable person for this purpose, provided Nobandla approved of the arrangement. I hope this matter has now been satisfactorily settled.

In your letter of October 28 you report that the house was owing R34 and that you made means to have the money paid. Kgatho also told me that you had also bought dresses for Zeni and Zindzi. No words that I may write here can adequately give expression to our gratitude to you. Perhaps one day we may be privileged with the opportunity of returning your kindness, however humble our own act of reciprocity may be.

Incidentally, I should like you to know that it gave me much joy to hear that you felt quite different after you had seen me in October last year, that the cloud of depression had cleared, and that you were now looking at the brighter side of things. That is the correct spirit. It has been rightly said that when you laugh the whole world laughs with you, but when you weep you do so alone. Remember that!

On January 1, I wrote to Vulindlela straight to Umtata and to Ntambozenqanawa, care of Kgatho. On November 19 I had written to Nobandla's uncle, Mr Paul Mzaidume, 7012 Orlando West. I am anxious to establish whether any of my letters do reach their destination and I should be pleased if you would kindly check whether Ntambozenqanawa and Nobandla's uncle received theirs.

Finally I should like Joel to know that I urgently need R100 for purposes of studies and I should be pleased if he will kindly raise the amount on my behalf. There is nothing else that I can do with Nobandla away.

Once again I thank you for all that you are doing and more especially for having made it possible for Joel to act for Nobandla. Fondest regards to all and with much love to you.

Yours sincerely,
Buti[180] Nel

---

180. Brother.

LETTER FROM NELSON MANDELA
TO THE COMMANDING OFFICER OF ROBBEN ISLAND[181]

Attention: Col Van Aarde.

I am greatly disturbed and shocked by the way the Censor's office is handling my visits, and I would ask you to investigate the matter personally, at your earliest possible convenience, and put a stop to these unwarranted irregularities.

Molly de Jager,[182] my daughter-in-law, 'Hillbrow', 7th Avenue, Retreat, Cape Town, has for almost three months been battling to obtain a permit to visit me. She made the first application at the very beginning of February and advised me of this fact in a letter which was received by the Censor's Office on the 12th of the same month. Last month I was informed by the Censor's Office that her letter of application had not been 'received'. She applied again at the beginning of this month and I was warned to expect a visit from her on Saturday 18th April. She did not turn up.

But Beryl Lockman who visited her uncle, Walter Sisulu, last Saturday and who lives at the same address as my daughter-in-law, informed her uncle that she and my daughter-in-law had applied for visiting permits the same day. She received her own permit which did not contain the only essential information a permit should have, namely, the date for which the visit had been arranged. Beryl informed the uncle that my daughter-in-law had not come because her permit had not arrived. I am expecting her to come on the 25th instant and I ask you to ensure that the visit is not obstructed again.

I need hardly give you the assurance that this letter is not intended to be a reflection against Lt. Nel, the officer who is directly in charge of the Censor's Office and who treats every one of my requests sympathetically.

[Signed]

---

181. Date unknown.
182. Also known as Thoko.

LETTER FROM NELSON MANDELA
TO THE COMMANDING OFFICER OF ROBBEN ISLAND[183]

29th May 1970

Attention: Col Van Aarde

Yesterday, I advised you that on the 4th May I wrote you two letters, one relating to matters which are being handled by Brigadier Aucamp, and the second dealt with issues of a local nature, most of which have already received your attention.

There are, however, two matters which were mentioned in the second letter on the 4th May and which are still outstanding.

In June I expect my daughter, Makaziwe, to pay me a visit for the first time in her life since I was arrested, and I am anxious that the visit should be arranged for next month when she will be on vacation.

The second matter that is still outstanding is the special letter to Marshall Xaba which I handed in for posting on 3rd February with a request that it should be sent by ordinary post on February 18th notwithstanding the importance of its contents and urgency. You will recall that during the interview on 24th May, I informed you that by the 10th March the letter had not reached its destination, from which fact I inferred that it had probably gone astray.

[Signed]

---

183. A handwritten note, presumbley by a prison official, reads 'Censors kindly discuss 3.6.70'.

LETTER FROM NELSON MANDELA
TO HIS DAUGHTERS ZENANI AND ZINDZI MANDELA

1st June, 1970

My Darlings,

It is now more than 8 years since I last saw you, and just over 12 months since Mummy was suddenly taken away from you.

Last year I wrote two letters – one on the 23rd June and the other on 3rd August. I now know that you never received them. As both of you are still under 18, and as you are not allowed to visit me until that age, writing letters is the only means I have of keeping in touch with you and of hearing something about the state of your health, your schoolwork and your school progress generally. Although these precious letters do not reach, I shall nevertheless keep on trying by writing whenever that is possible. I am particularly worried by the fact that for more than a year I received no clear and first-hand information as to who looks after you during school holidays and where you spend such holidays, who feeds you and buys you clothing, who pays your school fees, board and lodging, and on the progress that you are making at school. To continue writing holds out the possibility that one day luck may be on our side in that you may receive these letters. In the meantime the mere fact of writing down my thoughts and expressing my feelings gives me a measure of pleasure and satisfaction. It is some means of passing on to you my warmest love and good wishes, and tends to calm down the shooting pains that hit me whenever I think of you.

In the first letter I told you that Mummy was a brave woman who is suffering today because she deeply loves her people and her country. She had chosen the life of misery and sorrow in order that you, Zeni and Zindzi, Maki and Kgatho, and many others like you might grow up and live peacefully and happily in a free country where all its people, black and white, would be bound together by a common loyalty to a new South Africa. I gave you a brief account of her family background and career and the many occasions in which she has been sent to jail. I ended the letter by giving you the assurance that one day Mummy and I would return and join you, perhaps at 8115 Orlando West or may be in some other 'home'. It may well be that she may come back with her poor health worse than it is at present and needing much nursing and care. It will then be your turn to look after her. Your love and affectionate devotion will serve to heal the deep and ugly wounds caused by many years of hardship and may prolong her life indefinitely.

The second letter contained the sad news of the death of Buti Thembi in a car accident near Cape Town and I gave you deepest sympathies on behalf of Mummy and me. I do hope that some good friend was able to tell you of this family tragedy soon after it had happened, and that you have already recovered from the shock.

Kgatho has not gone to the University of Fort Hare this year and does not even appear to be studying at present. In March I wrote and asked him to give me an explanation. I also wrote to Uncle Paul Mzaidume in April requesting him to arrange with Fort Hare for Kgatho to be admitted even though it was somewhat late. It is possible that my letter never reached them, just as you did not receive yours. Maki has passed the Junior Certificate and is now doing Matric. She plans to visit me sometime this month when the schools close. If she does come then I will be seeing her for the first time since 1962. I managed to see her and Kgatho for a few seconds through the gauze wire of a police van outside the entrance to Pretoria Jail during the Rivonia Trial in June 1964. I last saw our brave and beloved Mummy in December 1968. She was arrested on the 12th of May last year about two weeks before she was due to visit me. Her visits brought me joy and inspiration and I always looked forward to them. I must confess that I miss her very badly. I also miss you, darlings, and hope you will be able to write me long and nice letters in which you tell me everything about yourselves: your health condition, the classes in which you are this year, the position you held in your class in the last examination, the place where you spend your holidays.

I have in my cell the lovely photo that you took during the 1965 Christmas with the Orlando West High school in the background. I also have the family photo which Mummy sent in March 1968. They make it somewhat easy for me to endure the loneliness of a prison cell and provide me with something to cheer and inspire me every day. I long for your latest picture but I suppose that will not be possible for some time. Perhaps one day, many years from now, Mummy will return, and maybe it will then be possible for her to arrange for me to have the little things that are precious to my heart. That day will bring moments of joy and song for me, and for you Zindzi and Zeni, for Maki and Kgatho, and for our devoted relatives and faithful friends who will have looked after you for all the years when she was away.

The dream of every family is to live together happily in a quiet peaceful home where parents will have the opportunity of bringing up the children in the best possible way, of guiding and helping them in choosing careers and of giving them the love and care which will develop in them a feeling of serenity and self-confidence. Today our family has been scattered; Mummy and Daddy are in jail and you live like orphans. We should like you to know that these ups and downs have deepened our love for you. We are confident that one day our dreams will come true; we will be able to live together and enjoy all the sweet things that we are missing at present. Tons and tons of love, my darlings.

Daddy

LETTER FROM NELSON MANDELA
TO HIS SISTER LEABIE PILISO

1st June, 1970

My dear Nkosazana,

Your letter of March 9, 1969 duly reached me and I was pleased to hear of the role that Jonguhlanga continues to play in helping to solve the difficulties which my absence would have brought on you and the rest of the family.

I received the news of your marriage with mixed feelings. A happy marriage is the ambition of all human beings, and that you had found your life partner gave me real joy. As I have already expressed my feelings and views in another letter which contained my congratulations to you and Sibali,[184] I do not consider it necessary to add here anything on this aspect of the matter. It is sufficient to say that it is a source of real pride to me to have yet another brother-in-law. My only regret is that many years may pass before I see him. Although the news of your marriage pleased me very much, mine was pleasure mingled with worry and concern because I know well how uneasy a girl with national pride could be when the conclusion of the marriage was not accompanied by the usual traditional rites. Accordingly, it was a great relief for me when I heard that Jonguhlanga had bought you the required articles and that he had arranged for you to be formally escorted to your new kraal. Jonguhlanga has a large family and heavy responsibilities, and it is a measure of the deep love and devotion to us all that he was able, in spite of his numerous obligations, to give you the assistance you describe in your letter.

In October 1968 I sent a long letter thanking him for organising Ma's funeral and for the heavy expenses he personally incurred on that occasion. Nobandla wrote and gave me a lengthy report on the proceedings. About a week before I received Nobandla's letter Sibali Timothy Mbuzo[185] had visited me for the express purpose of giving me a first-hand account of the passing away and of the funeral of Ma. It afforded me much consolation to hear from him that large crowds had turned up to honour her at the graveside. I was particularly happy to be told that you were able to attend. Ma was very attached to you and her death must have been exceedingly painful for you. I hope that you have now completely recovered. Tellie came down last October and told me that

---

184. Name for brother/brother-in-law.
185. Nelson Mandela's cousin.

you and Baliwe[186] had managed to attend Thembi's funeral in Johannesburg, another family disaster which shook me violently. I should have liked to attend both ceremonies, but in my current circumstances it is not easy to carry out such wishes. Incidentally, in connection with Ma's funeral I also wrote to Daliwonga,[187] Nkosikazi NoEngland, Vulindlela, Wonga, Thembekile ka Tshunungwa and Guzana and thanked them for their own role.

I thought I would discuss the question of the child with Nobandla when she visited me in May last year. I fully grasped the importance of the whole question of removing her from Mount Frere and had hoped to arrange with Nobandla that she be sent to the same boarding school as Zeni and Zindzi. But as you are now aware she was arrested on May 12 almost a fortnight before she was due to visit me, and she is still in prison. Since her arrest I have experienced considerable difficulties in arranging our household affairs. Almost every one of the letters I write appears not to reach its destination. I have not been able to establish contact even with Zeni and Zindzi in spite of repeated efforts I am making and of several letters that I have written to them. I shall keep on trying to contact a friend who, in Nobandla's absence, will be the most suitable person to help straighten out our affairs, and shall keep the question uppermost in my mind. By the way, Zeni and Zindzi must feel at times very lonely and homesick, and I feel sure that a cheerful letter from you once or twice a year would keep them bright and hopeful. You could always write to them care of Mrs Iris Niki Xaba, PO Box 23, Jabavu, Johannesburg.

In March I wrote to Sibali, Mrs Timothy Mbuzo. Today I am sending a special letter to Mhlekazi Sidumo. He never replied to the one I sent him in May 1969. I suspect that his was one of the numerous letters from me that inevitably 'go astray,' especially since Nobandla's arrest. You may phone or write to Sisi Connie Njongwe, Station Road, Matatiele, and tell her that it was a real pleasure to receive her inspiring letter and to get news about the family. Let her know that in August last year I received a letter of condolence from Robbie and Zuki, and was disturbed to learn that Jimmy[188] had removed a disk and subsequently fractured a leg. Connie never even as much as hinted at this in her letter. Tell them that I know just how tough and courageous Jimmy is, and that I have not the slightest doubt but that he is still the same cheerful man who is always full of self-confidence and hope. I will be writing as soon as that can be arranged. Connie will inform Robbie that I was just about to reply to

---

186. Another of his three sisters.
187. His nephew Kaiser Matanzima.
188. Connie's husband.

their sweet and encouraging letter when weather conditions in their territory worsened. I shall drop them a line as soon as conditions improve.

Tons and tons of love.

Yours very affectionately,

Buti Nel

LETTER FROM NELSON MANDELA
TO THE COMMANDING OFFICER ROBBEN ISLAND

2nd June 1970

<u>Attention: Col. Van Aarde.</u>

I refer to the discussion I had with you on the 25th May 1970 and should be pleased if you would approve of the registration of the 2 letters attached hereto.[189]

The letter to Sidumo Mandela is the exact copy of the one I wrote and handed in for posting on the 4th May 1969, and which apparently never reached. It deals, among other things, with matters relating to the title deeds of our quit-rent lot as well as payment of tax. The second one is addressed to Mrs Xaba, my sister-in-law, and is meant for my daughters jointly, one of whom is 11 years and the other 10. Letters previously written to them did not reach. You are aware of the present circumstances relating to my wife and household affairs, and I consider it necessary to ensure the safe arrival of the letter through registration.

I hope you are giving attention to the question of the expected visit from my eldest daughter during the present month, and I apply formally for an hour's visit.[190]

[Signed] Nelson Mandela 466/64[191]

---

189. Note in another hand writes here: 'Approved 3.6.70'.
190. Note in another hand: 'Approved'.
191. Note in another hand in Afrikaans: 'Regard as special letter'.

LETTER FROM NELSON MANDELA
TO WINNIE MANDELA

20th June 1970

Dade Wethu,

Indeed, 'the chains of the body are often wings to the spirit.' It has been so long, and so it will always be. Shakespeare in *As You Like It* puts the same idea somewhat differently:

> 'Sweet are the uses of adversity,
> Which like a toad, ugly and venomous,
> Wears yet a precious jewel in the head.'

Still others have proclaimed that 'only great aims can arouse great energies.'

Yet my understanding of the real idea behind these simple words throughout the 26 years of my career of storms has been superficial, imperfect and perhaps a bit scholastic. There is a stage in the life of every social reformer when he will thunder on platforms primarily to relieve himself of the scraps of indigested information that has accumulated in his head; an attempt to impress the crowds rather than to start a calm and simple exposition of principles and ideas whose universal truth is made evident by personal experience and deep study. In this regard I am no exception and I have been victim of the weakness of my own generation not once but a hundred times. I must be frank and tell you that when I look back at some of my early writings and speeches I am appalled by their pedantry, artificiality and lack of originality. The urge to impress and advertise is clearly noticeable. What a striking contrast your letters make, Mhlope! I hesitate to heap praises on you but you will pardon my vanity and conceit, Ngutyana. To pay you a compliment may amount to self-praise on my part [as] you and I are one. Perhaps under the present conditions this type of vanity may serve as a powerful lever to our spirits.

During the 8 lonely years I have spent behind bars I sometimes wish we were born the same hour, grown up together and spent every minute of our lives in each other's company. I sincerely believe that had this been the case I would have been a wise man. Every one of your letters is a precious possession and often succeeds in arousing forces I never suspected to be concealed in my being. In your hands the pen is really mightier than a sabre. Words flow out freely and naturally and common expressions acquire a meaning that is at once challenging and stimulating.

The first paragraph of your moving note, and more especially the opening line, shook me violently. I literally felt every one of the millions of atoms that make up my body pulling forcefully in all directions. The beautiful sentiments you have repeatedly urged on me since my arrest and conviction, and particularly during the last 15 months, are clearly the result more of actual experience than of scholasticism. They come from a woman who has not seen her husband for almost 2 years, who has been excluded from her tender children for more than 12 months and who has been hard hit by loneliness, pining and illness under conditions least conducive for recovery, and who on top of all that must face the most strenuous test of her life.

I understand perfectly well, darling, when you say you miss me and that one of the few blows you found hard to take was not hearing from me. The feeling is mutual, but it is plain that you have gone through a far more ravaging experience than I have ever had. I tried hard and patiently to communicate with you. I sent you a long note on Nov. 16; thereafter a Xmas card; and again a letter on Jan. 1 – all were written at a time when you were an awaiting-trial prisoner. After Feb. 13 I was informed that I could not communicate with you and my earnest plea for a relaxation of this particular restriction was unsuccessful.

Your illness has been stubborn and persistent, and I would have expected to be given a proper medical report by the Prisons' Department to help ease my mind. Brig. Aucamp gave me a very generalised account which disturbed me intensely. I was shocked to learn that you had to be hospitalised and to actually see evidence of your present state of health in your sloppy handwriting. I believe you completely when you say that you have shrunk to Zeni's size. It was some sort of relief to hear that you have been seen by numerous specialists and that blood tests have been taken. But I know, Mntakwethu,[192] that every piece of your bone, ounce of flesh and drop of blood; your whole being is hewed in one piece out of granite, and that nothing whatsoever, including ailment, can blow out the fires that are burning in your heart. Up on your feet! Onward to duty! My love and devotion is your armour and the ideal of a free South Africa your banner.

A few days after your arrest in May last year I asked for a special letter to my attorney in connection with the following urgent matters:

1. The appointment of a caretaker for the house and for the payment of rent;

---

192. My love.

2. The appointment of a legal guardian for the children;
3. The making of arrangements for the maintenance, upbringing and education of the children;
4. The making of arrangements for the raising of funds for your education, toilet and other requirements in the event of your being found guilty and imprisoned;
5. The making of arrangements for the raising of funds for my own education, toilet and other requirements during your absence in jail.

Although I have made repeated representations on several occasions the application was not granted. I have, however, now instructed Mr Brown of the firm of Frank, Bernard and Joffe in Cape Town to give immediate attention to these matters. I agree with your suggestion that Father Leon Rakale and Uncle Mashumi[193] be appointed joint guardians of the children. I should like to add Uncle Marsh's name. I wrote him an urgent letter on February 3 in connection with the house. I doubt if he ever received it. He never responded. When Kgatho visited me on Jan. 31 he indicated that he and Tellie were in favour of Lulu (Mxolisi's sister) moving into the house. I informed Uncle Marsh of this fact and indicated that I would be happy if she did, provided you approved.

Mxolisi visited me last Saturday and says they have not heard from Marsh. Perhaps you would like to discuss the matter with him and Niki when they next pay you a visit. I doubt if Mashumi received my note written on Nov. 19 and rewritten on Apr. 4. I asked him to give me a report on Zeni and Zindzi and to help get Kgatho to varsity. I received no reply from Mashumi as well.

Kgatho is at home and I have no proper information as to why he failed to go to Fort Hare. I made the necessary arrangements for payment of fees and allowance and when he came down in Jan. he confirmed that everything had been fixed and that he would leave for varsity on Feb. 14. I believe he is not working. My letter to him on March 31st produced no response.

I have written 3 letters to Zeni and Zindzi. I now know that the first two never reached them. The 3rd one was written on June 1st. I have received no information whatsoever on them since your arrest save and except the reports you gave me. Of course Niki's letter of Sep. 9 informed me that they were well.

I, however, hope to straighten out the whole affair with Mr. Brown soon and will arrange for you to be regularly informed.

I have raised the question of my paying you a visit once more and I can tell you nothing at present apart from saying that Brig. Aucamp has promised

---

193. Mashumi Paul Mzaidume.

to discuss the matter with the Commissioner. Speaking frankly, I think the Commissioner has been unusually hard and has not shown the consideration and assistance that I normally expect from him in circumstances of this nature.

Dade Wethu, I wish I could have been in a position to tell you something that could gladden your heart and make you smile. But as I see it we may have to wait a long time for that bright and happy moment. In the meantime we must 'drink the cup of bitterness to the dregs.' Perhaps, no I am sure, the good old days will come when life will sweeten our tongues and nurse our wounds. Above all remember March 10.[194] That is the source of our strength. I never forget it.

Tons and tons of love, Mhlope, and a million kisses.

Devotedly

Dalibunga

---

194. 10 March 1957 is when Winnie Madikizela and Nelson Mandela went on their first date.

LETTER FROM NELSON MANDELA
TO ATTORNEY MR BROWN

23 June 1970

<u>Attention Mr Brown</u>

Dear Sirs,

I should like you to attend to the following urgent matters at your earliest possible convenience.

1. The appointment of a legal guardian for our minor children, Zenani and Zindziswa, aged 11 and 10 respectively;
2. The making of arrangements for the children's upbringing, maintenance and education;
3. The appointment of a caretaker for our house No 8115 Orlando West, Johannesburg;
4. The making of arrangements for the raising of funds for my education, toilet and other requirements.

I would appreciate an urgent interview with your Mr Brown to discuss the whole matter.

Kindly treat the matter as extremely urgent.

Yours faithfully

[Signed] Nelson Mandela

LETTER FROM NELSON MANDELA
TO HIS SISTER-IN-LAW JANE XABA

June 29, 1970

Our dear Ndyebo,

You were staff nurse when we parted and I believe you have since risen to become sister. You are doing well and I congratulate you with a warm heart. I would like to tell you that your progress is a source of real joy to us. I hope it will be possible to rejoice with you again some time in the near future when you will have become a fleshy matron – slow-moving and grave as befits one with the status of first lady in a hospital.

I was happy to see you on Oct. 12 '68 when you visited Mkhiwa.[195] We had last met the night in '61 when Zami ordered me to drive you from Bara to Mofolo. About 3 months before this you and I had spent a whole Sunday morning at Jabulani on the tracks of the gentleman you kindly recommended for the purpose of laying our floor tiles. Soon thereafter I went my way and later you flew to England for an advanced course. I welcomed the news of your departure as I felt sure that further training would enhance proficiency and ensure promotion to more responsible positions. I had hoped then that on your return I might have the privilege of listening to your impressions and experiences. But as we now know that was not to be for some time. Of course, one day I'll be back and although these impressions will have probably gone stale, it will be a great pleasure for me to be able to resume our usual chats. Until then!

I hardly hear anything about Dudu these days. You will recall that we fetched her from Granny in Alexandra for Zeni's birthday in Feb. '61. She was growing well and struck me as alert and good-mannered. I should naturally be glad to hear something on her progress. On June 13 I was fortunate enough to catch a glimpse of an old college mate, Monica, who came to see Mkhiwa. She was a contemporary of the late Phyllis Mzaiduma, Victoria Kabane, Edna Kgomo (now a Mrs Bam), Caroline Ramolohloane, Louisa Kumalo, Dineo Mofolo, Clarisa Mzoneli, Ulrica Dzwane, Musa Msomi, Nomoto Bikitsha and several other talented women who played an important role in college affairs those days, made great impact on us and who are distinguishing themselves in various fields. Monica was then studying science and still stands out in my

195. Jane Xaba's brother.

memory as a gifted and promising young maiden who could stand up at a moment's notice and deliver a first class speech. I was accordingly very sorry when I subsequently learnt that it had not been possible for her to complete the course. But she seems to have lost none of those virtues which endeared her to us 30 years ago. The consistency with which she has looked after Mkhiwa during the past 7 years shows the considerable depth of her feelings and portrays a good image of herself.

Perhaps one day in the course of the next 4 years I may have the luck of seeing Nkomo, Nomonde and Jerry, Thembsi and Mhlekazi Ncapayi, piccanin Jane and hubby, and Kwezi. From scraps of information gleaned from numerous conversations we have had with Mkhiwa, I have formed some mental picture of each one, and I do look forward to meeting them some day. I was never present to meet the omnipresent Hlope, but Mkhiwa has one of her latest photos. She looks serene as a seraphim, perfectly innocent and possesses great charm. I suspect this may be the source of her tremendous pull on others. Now and again I see in official publications available here pictures of our good friends of bygone days – Siko, the ever-smiling eleganté. On some occasions she appears wrapped in traditional costume, sucking away at a long pipe and haranguing poor nurses against the evil of superstition. Other times she is playing angel in Bochabela's Paradise Hall, or else is simply shown as ibhinqa elinesidanga esinomsila. I am glad to see her taking an active interest in some special questions and note her happy frame of mind. The other day I learnt that her Makwedinana was matriculating and wish him and sisters well. I believe Thanti is teaching somewhere in Lesotho. I am sure she is still as pleasant, warm and cheerful as we have always known her to be. Unfortunately, I never had the fortune of meeting all her children. But I know Lindelwa, the youngest (I am told she no longer is [the youngest]). Way back in the fifties Thanti holidayed in Johannesburg. Lindelwa and I became very friendly and we frequently drove around together. She must have blossomed into a full-size Amazon and I should love to see her again and to develop the friendship we started almost 15 years ago. George, formerly in charge of Tladi, is a person for whom I have great admiration and affection. She had done a lot for the family and we owe her a debt which will not easily be repaid. A few years back I heard that she had been offered a medical scholarship abroad and was surprised to note that she did not accept. She and my youngest sister, Leabie, had a raw experience in '64 and I should have liked to write to her directly. But in our present circumstances such gestures are not always possible or expedient. I like her to know that I highly value her friendship and that I always think of her. I am told that Millie now lives elsewhere. You had been together for so long that the house must look different in her absence. To all of them I send my fondest regards and sincerest good wishes.

To you I must confide that I miss the happiness I have found in sharing life with Zami. I have not seen her for 18 months and Zeni and Zindzi for 8 years. Kgatho visits me regularly and Maki writes often. But I have had nothing about Zeni and Zindzi since May last year. To come to grips with real life can be a terrifying experience. But the human body and the human soul has an infinite capacity for endurance and life goes on all the same. Zami has neither doubts nor hesitations and is full of hope and confidence. To both of us life has become the hope of the moment when we will return to strive as before for the realisation of our ideals and the fulfilment of our dreams. In the meantime, tons and tons of love.

Very sincerely,
Nel

LETTER FROM NELSON MANDELA
TO WINNIE MANDELA

July 1 1970

Dade Wethu,

Thoko saw me again last April. In Feb. she sent me R10 for 'pocket money' as she put it. The second visit was much easier than the first. Then she still bore signs of one whose energy had been drained by the shock of death and whose nerves have been wrecked by prolonged brooding over the ghastly experience that had befallen her so early in her married life. Although I was meeting her for the first time, it was easy to notice that I was seeing a shadow of her real self. The visit almost upset my own balance especially when she showed me Thembi's picture. The feeling of anguish and depression that had hit me so viciously when I received the horrible news of his death returned and began to gnaw away mercilessly at my insides. Once again I had come face to face with the ugly reality of life. Here was a green girl who had just turned 25 and who looked up to me to say something that could console her; something that might take away her mind from grief and give her some hope. This was one of those occasions which tend to emphasise just how little we know about real life and its problems in spite of all the literature that we read and the stories we listen to.

Things were altogether different in April. She looked grand and cheerful and could even use her injured arm. I thoroughly enjoyed the visit. When I think of the disasters that had invaded us over the past 21 months, I very often wonder what gives us the strength and courage to carry on. If calamities had the weight of physical objects we should long have been crushed down, or else, we should by now have been hunch-backed, unsteady on our feet, and with faces full of gloom and utter despair. Yet my entire body throbs with life and is full of expectations. Each day brings a fresh stock of experiences and new dreams. I am still able to walk perfectly straight and firmly. What is even more important to me is the knowledge that nothing can ever ruffle you and that your step remains as fleet and graceful as it has always been – a girl who can laugh heartily and infect others with her enthusiasm. Always remember that this is how I think of you.

I believe that you have been charged and that you will appear again on Aug. 3. On June 19 I met Brig. Aucamp and he gave me the assurance that I am free to discuss the case with you and to give you the necessary advice and encouragement. In the first charge I was a co-conspirator and a count referred to certain conversations which were to have taken place when you visited me. I am ready to testify on behalf of all of you whether or not I am still cited as a co-conspirator, as long as counsel deems my evidence relevant and necessary. It will be a real pleasure for me to be of some help to you and your fearless comrades in striking the blows you have waited so long to deliver and in turning the tables against those responsible for the multitude of wrongs that are being wantonly committed against you. The various pleas tendered during the last trial were quite appropriate and pleased me very much – my fist is clenched. They portrayed you as determined and conscious freedom fighters who are fully alive to their social responsibilities and who have no delusions whatsoever about the sort of justice dispensed by the country's courts nowadays, both inferior and superior. The first trial collapsed because you pulled no punches and asked no mercy. The onslaught against you this time may be more vicious and vindictive than the last trial, and calculated to smear rather than to establish guilt in the usual way.

You people have shown extraordinary alertness and amazing stamina during the last 13 months, and my remarks may be altogether redundant. But in these hectic days when the adversary is plotting cunningly and laying traps in all directions we are called upon to be extremely cautious and vigilant; and there is nothing wrong in drawing attention to the dangers that lie ahead, even though such dangers may be plain for all of us to see, we fight against one of the last strongholds of reaction on the African Continent. In cases of this kind our duty is a simple one – at the appropriate time to state clearly, firmly and accurately the aspirations that we cherish and the greater South Africa for which we fight. Our cause is just. It is a fight for human dignity and for an honourable life. Nothing should be done or said which may be construed directly or indirectly as compromising principle, not even the threat of a more serious charge and severe penalty. In dealing with people, be they friends or foe, you are always polite and pleasant. This is equally important in public debates. We can be frank and outspoken without being reckless or abusive, polite without cringing, we can attack racialism and its evils without ourselves fostering feelings of hostility between different racial groups.

These are matters we ought to discuss in absolute confidence and no third person ought ever to know about them. Any impression that I lecture or give pious advice will fill me with a sense of shame. You know, darling, that I never even attempted to do so before. That I have to run this risk today is a measure of the unusual times in which we live and the great issues that are at stake. It is men and women like yourselves, Mhlope, that are enriching our country's history and creating a heritage for which future generations will feel really proud. I know that, even though on the morning of Aug. 3 you may have shrunk to a size much smaller than that of Zeni, and even though life itself may be oozing out of you, you will try to muster just enough strength to be able to drag your thinning body to the courtroom to defend the ideals for which many of our patriots over the last 500 years have given their lives.

I have already written to Brown re the children and am expecting him soon. Is Nyanya in or out? Can she visit me? Tons and tons of love and a million kisses, darling.

Devotedly
Dalibunga

LETTER FROM WINNIE MANDELA
TO NELSON MANDELA

2/7/70

Mfowethu,[196]

I still cannot believe that at last I've heard from you darling. You will notice the very difference in the handwriting, the hypnotising effect your lovely letters have on my scarred soul. All it needed was its natural drug after all. Although my state of mind is not highly receptive at the moment I have tried as best I could to photostat your last letter in my mind, as you know I haven't the privilege of keeping your letters, I'm just given enough time to read them.

I take it you were told I was remanded in absentia on the 18th of June with 18 others on alleged charges under the Terrorism Act. I was so deeply hurt by not being fit to be with my colleagues. I have been seeing the defence team with them though but the indictment has not been served yet. Last Thursday I saw Niki and Uncle Marsh, I was thrilled darling, it was a lovely reunion disturbed as they were by my appearance. From now henceforth I should improve each day. I do not know yet whether the reports from the various specialists are available [but] I shall let you know as soon as I have been advised of same.

As you say, our goal is [a] free Africa my love I have never had any doubts about that. You flatter me so much when you referred to your 'self praise', vanity which I call my natural drug Hugo once said, 'No power on earth can prevent an idea whose time has come.' How right he was. During the gruelling experience of solitary confinement I have since discovered so many truths! I've had enough time to play back in my mind the tape recording of our strange life in this most historical period one has ever lived.

On our twelfth wedding anniversary[197] I lay on my back gasping for breath with a temperature of 103. I did not fail however to go through the ceremony twelve years ago when a trembling little girl of 23[198] stood next to you in a shabby little back veld church in Pondoland and said, 'I do'. I often wonder if your memory of me isn't that of that little girl. I recalled with all emotions and affection your reassuring and firm grip as you slipped the ring on my finger. It was not to you only that I said, 'I do'. I[t] was to you and all what you stand

---

196. Brother.
197. 14 June 1969.
198. Winnie Mandela's official date of birth is 26 September 1936 which would make her 21 at the time she was married, but it is a guestimate as she is not sure of her exact date of birth.

for. The one without the other would have been incomplete for me. The huge congregation sang an unusual hymn for a wedding. 'Lizalise idinga lakho … Zonk'itlanga zonkiziwe, Ma zizuze usindiso … Ngeziphithi-phithi zethu, yonakhele imihlaba.'[199]

The hymn was composed and sung by Rev Tiyo Soga the day he landed where you are in Cape Town on his return upon the failure of their mission abroad in the delegation that went to make representations for a better deal for the African in the Union Constitution of 1910 to the head office of the colonial settler government. Until then he had not realised how beautiful his country was and he sang praises on the spot. After the wedding, the wedding guests were rounded up and questioned. In the words of my late grandfather, 'Has the time come when the white man must determine who our children should marry and where?' The events looked unimportant, yet whether we are allowed to speak the truth or not, one single spark will always start a prairie fire. It was not long before my place of birth was on fire! It is still under Proclamation 400 to this day.[200]

We were hardly a year together when history deprived me of you. I was forced to mature on my own. Your formidable shadow which eclipsed me left me naked and exposed to the bitter world of a young 'political widow'. I knew this was a crown of thorns for me but I also knew I said, 'I Do' for better or worse. In marrying you I was marrying the struggle of my people. Yes, the thorns sometimes pricked so hard that the blood from the wounds covered up my eyes and the excrutiating pains blinded me for a while. Although I staggered across the path of freedom with pain, I staggered forward and never doubted my goal even when the crown was nailed by my people at times, this was only history. I would not have been worthy of their great love without such. When the tortuous minutes, hours, months dragged by gnawing at the inner cores of my soul I remembered that 'an army of principles will penetrate where an army of soldiers will not'. I also realised that honour and conviction are more binding than any oath. I also learnt that 'Even gold pass[ed] through the assayer's fire, and more precious than perishable gold is faith that has stood the test'. So much for that strange life of ours my love!

Uncle Marsh has been battling to see you since my detention. Unfortunately his applications do not receive the first consideration. There are urgent family matters which he has to discuss with you. It seems we need your co-operation now. Would you kindly advise whoever is concerned that you request Uncle

---

199. Fulfil your promise ... Let all the nations of the world, Receive salvation ... Behold our nation, And forgive its misdeeds.
200. Similar to the Terrorism Act, Proclamation 400 was used to proclaim emergency regulations and detain people without trial. It was introduced in 1960 and used by the Matanzima regime in Transkei.

Marsh to be the next to see you. I understand there is quite a long queue at the moment. The girls did not come home even during these last holidays but they are fortunately on his passport now and he is visiting them next weekend. I must say I am terribly disturbed by this, they are too young to be torn away from the security of a family. It was enough of a hardship to bring them up without you. Everytime I imagine how they must be feeling without both of us I get a relapse. One of those blows I referred to in my last letter.

All the Waterford documents are with Mr Carlson whom you also know has been battling to see you. I understand [he] and you had a lengthy discussion with Brig Aucamp on this matter. I have every confidence in Mr Brown whom I met during the case I had in 1967. It seems to me there will be quite a few problems we have at home. All the people he has to deal with are in Johannesburg. I quite agree with you that we should include Uncle Marsh amongst the guardians for the children and of course they will all act jointly with Uncle Allan Nxumalo who has been absolutely wonderful to them. They spent their last holidays with him again, he fetched them from the school once more. By the way he is still Minister of Health. Won't you ask for a special permission to write and thank him? One feels so small when so much is done without a word from the parents.

I was shocked to learn Kgatho has not gone to Fort Hare nor is he working. It also seems the family problems that have since arisen have no immediate solution. I find this subject disturbing and have suggested that it be left to you and Marsh to discuss urgently. The situation is getting out of control when one needs the clarity of mind to concentrate on the case. You know how much is involved in preparing for a mass trial and the amount of responsibility on my shoulders at the moment. There are certain feelings during such times which perhaps only you and I know but cannot put in words, suffice to say one cannot help but simply express them as the bitter sweetness of unjust suffering.

That reminds me once more of your remark upon 'the flow of the pen' and the 10th of March. But what you said about the wish that we were born the same hour! It's the other way around my love otherwise there wouldn't have been such a bitter struggle for filling up the gap. I am aware that my own infinitesimal contribution to the cause of my people will perhaps be worth one incomplete sentence in the books of the history of our country but even that is enough for me so long as it shall not be washed down the gutter of time. I know that when I get what I am fighting for I will get it forever and those who cling desperately to it swimming against the tide, fear losing it forever. I am lucky for I have seen the dawn of the day Rev T Soga serenaded. No amount of brutality meted out to me and my people will change the course of history.

There were times when I missed you so much during the presentation of our case last time. I remembered when you once roared at me 'Zami you are undisciplined'. Someone in the defence team used the same words when we were arguing over a certain point ... The same person said when I submitted my notes the following day over the same argument, 'you have definitely take a wrong profession, the pen is your profession even if I don't agree with you.' I laughed when Mr Bizos shook his head saying, 'She is an amazing character'.

When you get the childrens' school reports please study them with a view to asssisting them with the choice of their subjects. Kgatho and Maki struggled so much because we did not do so on time. Zeni wants to be [a] doctor and Zindzi wants to be a teacher. Zeni is quiet, spotlessly clean, stands for hours in front of the mirror to make sure she is well-dressed, fond of cooking, sewing and very choosy about friends. She has stuck to Nombeko whom she befriended during their babyhood. Zindzi will have not less than twenty friends in our small yard, she conducts a holiday school, pugnacious, an embarrasing extrovert with ready-made views at the age of nine. 'Mummy do you know children have brains too? When I say I do not want a thing, I do not want it, stop putting cabbage in my food.'

On the night of 11th May 1969 when we were eating supper five days after their return from school she burst out at table, 'I want my Daddy' and she cried herself to sleep, little knowing that was my goodbye to them, that the outburst was an omen in fact. It was a well chosen period to break down a mother of young children!

(I think you should study their reports and Waterford prospectus jointly to assist in the choice of subjects.)

I was so happy to learn you have renewed your application to see me. I really cannot understand why there is so much harshness. I do agree that the Commissioner has honestly been rather hard on us. I have not seen you since the 21st of December 1968, what more would one want from us when we are now both prisoners?

There is complete chaos over our home at the moment, only Kgatho and Nomfundo are there, a very unsatisfying arrangement. As long ago as November last year a couple was put on the permit by Niki with the assistance of the Ngakane's[201] who are related to it. I approached one of the couple, I know them very well too. I did so to enable Kgatho to proceed to university without any difficulty. On several occasions when the couple tried to move in there were difficulties deliberately created. I am surprised that Kgatho raised

---

201. Neighbours.

the problem with you early this year, he is aware of all the details. However we have decided that the matter must have full understanding on all parties concerned, this must be discussed urgently by you and Marsh before you even instruct on this. I am very grateful to Nkosazana Telia who has also tried her best to settle this.

Yes my love at the moment there is nothing we can do but swallow the cup of bitterness but one day we shall swallow it no more and that is the day whose dawn I have seen. One day we shall have a normal family unit too for no man with any manhood in himself can lead a normal life in an abnormal society. In the words of the late Luther King 'it is no better to be maladjusted in a mal-adjusted society'. He goes on to say 'the American negro is tired of being told to keep cool for he knows you can keep so cool in the long run you end up in the deep freeze'.

Darling, lots of love and a million kisses with sixteen million salutes to you.

Forever yours,
Nobandla

LETTER FROM NELSON MANDELA
TO FRIEND AND FORMER COLLEAGUE DOUGLAS LUKHELE

August 1, 1970

My dear Duggie,

Our children, Zeni and Zindzi, aged 11 and 10 respectively, are at 'Our Lady of Sorrows,' a Roman Catholic boarding school at Hluti. We are extremely disturbed because, since Zami's detention in May last year, we have heard nothing about them. Information reached me that they spend their holidays with Allan. I should have liked to write directly to him and [his] wife, to thank them for the hospitality, but I am not sure whether having regard to his present position, I am free to do so. I [would] like them to know that Zami and I are sincerely grateful. I believe Mrs Birley,[202] now lecturing in a British university, had arranged scholarships for the children at Waterford for next year. I have written them 3 letters and sent a birthday card, but none seems to have reached. Please investigate and give me a detailed report, preferably by registered letter, at your earliest possible convenience.

Letters from me hardly ever reach destination and those addressed to me fare no better. I am hoping that the remorseless fates, that consistently interfered with my correspondence and that have cut me off from my family at such a critical moment, will be induced by consideration of honour and honesty to allow this one through. I know that once it reaches your hands my troubles will be virtually over.

You know that I am essentially a rustic like many of my contemporaries, born and brought up in a country village with its open space, lovely scenery and plenty of fresh air. Although prior to my arrest and conviction 8 years ago I lived for two decades as a townsman, I never succeeded in shaking off my peasant background, and now and again I spent a few weeks in my home district as a means of recalling the happy moments of my childhood. Throughout my imprisonment my heart and soul have always been somewhere far beyond this place, in the veld and the bushes. I live across these waves with all the memories and experiences I have accumulated over the last half century – memories of the grounds in which I tended stock, hunted, played, and where I had the privilege of attending the traditional initiation school. I see myself moving into the Reef in the early forties, to be caught up in the ferment of

---

202. Lady Birley, wife of Sir Robert Birley, the former head of Eton.

the radical ideas that were stirring the more conscious of the African youth. (Incidentally it was at this stage that I first met Allan, then a clerk at Union College.) I remember the days when I served articles, licking stamps, daily running all sorts of errands, including buying hair shampoo and other cosmetics for white ladies. Chancellor House! It was there that OR[203] and I became even more intimate than we were as college mates and as [Youth] Leaguers. Around us there developed new and fruitful friendships – Maindy, Zubeida Patel and Winnie Mandleni, our first typists; the late Mary Anne, whose sudden and untimely death greatly distressed us; Ruth, Mavis, Godfrey; boxing Freddy and Charlie the upright and popular caretaker and cleaner who never missed a day at Mai-Mai.[204] For some time you battled almost alone and against formidable difficulties to keep the firm afloat when OR and I were immobilised by the Treason Trial. I even recall the strange incident that occurred when you visited Zami and I at our home in Orlando West in Dec. '60. As you approached the gate a bolt of lightning split out with such tremendous force that Zeni, then only 10 months [old], was flung to the ground where she remained motionless for some seconds. What a relief it was when she came round and started yelling; it was a close shave. Your presence at the DOCC[205] on that occasion put a new and deeper meaning to your magnificent stand at Winburg and added more weight and lustre to the eulogies that have since been heaped on you in memory of your outstanding service to the womenfolk.

Lenvick! There you established yourself with Manci as articled clerk and [were] ably assisted by the smooth and energetic Joe Magame. I have not forgotten the good things you did for me personally those days. I was still involved in the T.T.[206] and during adjournments you kept me busy by giving me work, and it thus became possible for me to assist Zami in some way to keep the home fires burning. I hope one day I shall be able to reciprocate. Anyway I was very happy when I was informed that your fatherland, the beautiful country which is full of so much promise and potential, could now avail itself of your talents to the fullest extent. I was even more pleased to be told that you were now [a] member of your country's Senate. But I knew at the same time that it must have been a grievous blow for you to sever connections with a country you had chosen to be your permanent home and to be cut off from a community you had served so faithfully and courageously. These and other reminiscences, occupy the long and difficult moments of my present life.

203. Oliver Tambo.
204. Market in Johannesburg.
205. Donaldson Orlando Community Centre in Soweto.
206. Treason Trial, 1956–61.

Spiritual weapons can be dynamic and often have an impact difficult to appreciate except in the light of actual experience in given situations.

In a way they make prisoners free men, turn commoners into monarchs, and dirt into pure gold.

To put it quite bluntly, Duggie, it is only my flesh and bones that are shut up behind these tight walls.

Otherwise I remain cosmopolitan in my outlook, in my thoughts I am as free as a falcon.

The anchor of all my dreams is the collective wisdom of mankind as a whole. I am influenced more than ever before by the conviction that social equality is the only basis of human happiness. We and the children of Mswati and Mbandzeni are linked by a million threads. We have a common history and common aspirations. What is precious to you touches our own hearts. It is in this light that we think of Sept. 6 – an historic event that marks the close of an epoch and the rise of a people whose national pride and consciousness helped them to survive the changes of fortune brought by the imperialist era to our Continent.

It is around these issues that my thoughts revolve. They are centred on humans, the ideas for which they strive; on the new world that is emerging, the new generation that declares total war against all forms of cruelty, against any social order that upholds economic privilege for a minority and that condemns us, the mass of the population, to poverty and disease, illiteracy and the host of evils that accompany a stratified society.

Remember me to Ntlabati, Leslie's wife, Andrew and wife, Stanley Lollan, Maggie Chuene, Regina Twala, Wilson and Gladys if they are still around. I am particularly grateful to Wilson for looking after my son, Kgatho, after he had been expelled from school for organising a strike, and for all the help he and Gladys gave him.

Let everyone keep well and be of good cheer; my fist is firm!

Yours sincerely
Nel

LETTER FROM NELSON MANDELA
TO WINNIE MANDELA

August 1, 1970

Dade Wethu,

Can it be that you did not receive my letter of July 1? How can I explain your strange silence at a time when contact between us has become so vital?

In June I learnt for the first time that you had been confined to bed for 2 months and that your condition was so bad that you did not appear with your friends when the case came up for formal remand. Is your silence due to a worsening of your health or did the July letter suffer the fate of the 39 monthly letters, letters in lieu of visits and specials that I have written since your arrest on May 12 '69, all of which, save 2, seemed not to have reached their destination? Not even Kgatho, Maki, Zeni, Zindzi, Tellie, Ma of Bizana, Marsh and Mashumi responded. I am becoming increasingly uneasy every day. I know you would respond quickly if you heard from me and I fear that you have not done so because you either did not receive the letter or you are not fit to write.

The crop of miseries we have harvested from the heartbreaking frustrations of the last 15 months are not likely to fade away easily from the mind. I feel as if I have been soaked in gall, every part of me, my flesh, bloodstream, bone and soul, so bitter am I to be completely powerless to help you in the rough and fierce ordeals you are going through. What a world of difference to your failing health and to your spirit, darling, to my own anxiety and the strain that I cannot shake off, if only we could meet; if I could be on your side and squeeze you, or if I could but catch a glimpse of your outline through the thick wire netting that would inevitably separate us. Physical suffering is nothing compared to the trampling down of those tender bonds that form the basis of the institution of marriage and the family that unite man and wife. This is a frightful moment in our life. It is a moment of challenge to cherished beliefs, putting resolutions to a severe test.

But as long as I still enjoy the privilege of communicating with you, even though it may only exist in form for me, and until it is expressly taken away, the records will bear witness to the fact that I tried hard and earnestly to reach you by writing every month. I owe you this duty and nothing will distract me from it. Maybe this line will one day pay handsome dividends. There will always be good men on earth, in all countries, and even here at home. One day we may have on our side the genuine and firm support of an upright and straightforward man, holding high office, who will consider it improper to shirk his duty of protecting the rights and privileges of even his bitter opponents in the battle of ideas that is being fought in our country today; an official who will have a sufficient sense of justice and fairness to make available to us not only the rights and privileges that the law allows us today, but who will also compensate us for those that were surreptitiously taken away. In spite of all that has happened I have, throughout the ebb and flow of the tides of fortune in the last 15 months, lived in hope and expectation. Sometimes I even have the belief that this feeling is part and parcel of my self. It seems to be woven into my being. I feel my heart pumping hope steadily to every part of my body, warming my blood and pepping up my spirits. I am convinced that floods of personal disaster can never drown a determined revolutionary nor can the cumulus of misery that accompanies tragedy suffocate him. To a freedom fighter hope is what a life-belt is to a swimmer – guarantee that one will keep afloat and free from danger. I know darling that if riches were to be counted in terms of the tons of hope and sheer courage that nestle in your breast (this idea I got from you) you would certainly be a millionaire. Remember this always.

By the way, the other day I dreamt of you convulsing your entire body with a graceful Hawaiian dance at the BMSC.[207] I stood at one end of the famous hall with arms outstretched ready to embrace you as you whirled towards me with the enchanting smile that I miss so desperately. I cannot explain why the scene should have been located at the BMSC. To my recollection we have been there for a dance only once – on the night of Lindi's wedding reception. The other occasion was the concert we organised in 1957 when I was courting you, or you me. I am never certain whether I am free to remind you that you took the initiative in this regard. Anyway the dream was for me a glorious moment. If I must dream in my sleep, please Hawaii for me. I like to see you merry and full of life.

I enjoyed Fatima's[208] 'Portrait of Indian S. Africans' – a vivid description of Indian life written in a beautiful and simple style. With characteristic modesty she describes the title in the preface as still pretentious for a book that only skims the surface. But the aspects that form its theme are skilfully probed. She raises an issue of wider interest when she points out that 'differences that divide are not differences of custom, of rituals and tradition, but differences of status, of standard of living, of access to power and power-gaining techniques.

---

207. Bantu Men's Social Centre in Johannesburg.
208. Fatima Meer.

These are the differences that have at all known times determined the destinies of persons and people, and the same people and the same cultures have at one point enjoyed high privilege and at another none.' The book contains chapters which touch on other fundamental matters and I fear that some of her observations on current public questions may spark off animated debates. I welcome the brutal frankness of her pen, but it may be that once she elects to raise such matters her duty is not only to comment but to inspire, to leave her fellow countrymen with hope and something to live for. I hope you will be able to read the book before the case ends. It is a brilliant work written by a brilliant scholar. I thoroughly enjoyed it.

Mr Brown, our Cape Town attorney, should have been here on July 29 in connection with the question of guardianship of the children. The sea was very rough and this may probably be the reason for his failure to turn up. I am hoping that he will come soon. In the meantime I am writing to our friend, Duggie Lukhele, requesting him to check on them and to give us a detailed report. I shall certainly keep you informed of developments. Do not allow yourself to be agitated by the chaos in our household affairs and by the difficulties we are having in communicating officially and openly with each other. This is a phase in our life that will pass and leave us still there, and perhaps even growing stronger. I almost forgot to tell you that my second application to see you was summarily rejected, notwithstanding the fact that I had cited your present illness as one reason for renewing the application. The Commissioner did not even consider it his duty to allay my fears by giving me a report on your condition. There was a time when such experiences would make me wild; now I can take them calmly. I have become used to them.

Keep well, my darling; do not allow yourself to be run down by illness or longing for the children. Fight with all your strength. My fist is firm. Tons and tons of love and a million kisses.

Devotedly,
Dalibunga

LETTER FROM NELSON MANDELA
TO NOFUMAHADI ZUKISWA MATJI

August 1, 1970

Our dear Zuki,

The death of Thembi was a bitter blow to me for he was an intimate friend. The relationship of father and son was but the foundation stone upon which we were building more intimate connections and it really hurt me to know that I would never see him again.

There was a time during the last 8 years when nothing could ever ruffle me and when I felt secure and in perfect control of myself. Thembi was gradually taking over the family responsibilities and was helpful in many ways. He had become very attached to Zami and to Kgatho and sisters he had become an idol. Then came '68 and '69 when the skies suddenly fell upon me. I lost both him and Ma and I must confess that the order that had reigned in my soul almost vanished. Exactly 2 months before Thembi's death my Zami was put under lock and key where she still is, and our household affairs plunged into unbelievable chaos. Up to the present moment I do not know where Zeni and Zindzi (aged 11 and 10 respectively) are and who maintains them. Every one of the letters I have written them in the last 15 months has not reached. Probably the car and furniture have been repossessed and the telephone disconnected.

My funds have been completely drained and I have had to give up a couple of necessaries which make life here comparatively easy. I cannot even manage an eye-test for reading glasses. At times I am tempted to feel that this is too heavy a cross to bear and it is against this background that I regard Robbie's[209] cheerful letter. Its warmth and simplicity touched my heart and raised my spirits.

Robbie refers to Thembi and Kgatho's visit when you were at Sekake's. What a strange coincidence. The letter arrived while I was reading about old times in Lesotho, Matatiele, Cedarville and Kokstad; about Sekake, his father Sekwati and Lehana, ou Letsie, Lerothodi and Masupha, Mhlonto and Mditshwa, Makawula, JoJo and Mqikela. In the past 8 years I have read more on S.A. history and geography than I ever did in my whole life, and this has made me curious and anxious to tour the country and to visit all the places which have

---

209. Robert Resha.

aroused my interest. I do not know how I will ever raise the funds for that purpose. I have always been more needy than the proverbial church mouse, and the position will certainly be much worse on my return. However, remote problems can have no bearing on my present hobby of castle building. But this strange coincidence Zuki! Sekake and Sekake's. Is it possible that research, experiment and observation may establish telepathy as an empirical study?

The death of Masango and Maroyi was a terrible tragedy which intensely affected us. Robbie must have found it extremely painful not to be able to pay his last respects to such dedicated fighters. Jimmy and Connie are wonderful people for who I have the highest regard. Some of the most pleasant moments in my life were spent in their company. In the early fifties Jimmy was hot and sharp and attracted great interest. Later on he seemed to cool off and the knife-edge sharpness that once characterised him was blunted; but he has never faded from those of us who worked closely with him. Connie is a lady in the full sense of that term; always gentle and courteous, kind and decent in every way. They are always in my thoughts and I was very sorry to hear that he had a disk removed in addition to a fractured leg. I was pleased to note that the beautiful friendship that kept your respective families close to each other is still growing strong and deep. I shall write to them soon. Meanwhile give them my love.

I was delighted to hear something about Khalaki, Kumani and Liz. Khalaki attracted me the first day I met him. He struck me as a modest and cautious lad of great promise. In the numerous discussions I have had with him on a variety of questions I was impressed by his ability to grasp at once the crucial aspects of a problem. He must have ripened a lot the 24 months he spent away from Bata and kids. With such a gifted girl on his side, he is well equipped to fulfil our wildest expectations. I should have long written to them if I knew their address. In Dec '68 I sent them a Xmas card care of Moses Tlebere, PO Box 190, Maseru. I should love to hear from them about the kids. I am confident that if they had been around this part of the world they would have visited us already. Khumani also made a great impression on me on the one occasion on which I met him. His calmness and steadiness reflected a measure of depth which appealed to me very much. During my travel in the Pafmecsa area early in '62, I was pleased to note that he was attracting interest even beyond our borders. Is he now married?

The name 'Elizabeth' has featured prominently in history. The house of the Spanish, Phillip II and his 'Invincible' Armada probably would still rattle in their grave when reminded of the year 1588. There is a lot of exciting history around our own Liz and her labours have not been in vain. Perhaps there are on God's earth other Phillip II's who are seized by nightmares when they think of her. Remember Paarl is only 40 miles away from us where she is regarded with the utmost respect and affection. To all of them I send my warmest love. I was sorry to hear that our erstwhile mutual friend is a mole that burrows no more. What a pity that such a shrewd and able man should now suffocate in his own timidity! Do you hear anything about Jack?

Robbie was very unkind to me. He never said a thing about the children. What is the purpose of a first letter from so close a friend which omits these matters? I have not had the privilege of meeting you and look forward to seeing you one day. At Healdtown[210] I was with Bangani, Ncoma and Botha – all Manyanis. Your relatives? Anyway, you must be a great girl to have extracted a promise from Robbie and what is even more important, in getting him to honour it. He has always been a connoisseur – only a woman who is a living symbol of those virtues that make a perfect spouse could have tamed him. His reputation as ravenous reader, clear thinker, orator, efficient administrator and man of action is well-known. Though cut off from friends and relatives he never ceased burrowing all the time. We will never forget him for he is a real grand guy. Treat him well, motlose ka mafura.[211] Let him feed on mofutswela,[212] lesheleshele[213] and motoho[214] – the dishes that have kept our people alive, vigorous and happy; that have produced king makers and martyrs. Zami joins me in sending you our love. My fist is firm.

Yours very sincerely,
Nel

---

210. High school.
211. Butter him up – porridge with butter.
212. Stiff porridge with milk.
213. Salt-free soft porridge.
214. Soft porridge.

LETTER FROM WINNIE MANDELA
TO NELSON MANDELA

3-8-70

Mfowethu,

On Friday the 31st I received your letter of 1 July. I hope you have received mine of the 2nd July. I find the telepathy between us quite fantastic. I seem to have been replying to all you said in yours in advance. I hope you also received your birthday telegrams darling. The invisible hand which has been directing our lives has made your birthday have tragic memories for it was the same date I got the painful news of our son whilst you got the news re mama's death on my birthday. Looking back, this strange pattern has been at work for years. In the first treason trial you were Acc No 23, in my humble 1958 trial I was accused No 23 and I was 23 years when we got married, etc. etc.

I was thrilled to learn Thoko has been to see you and is looking much better. I will be writing to her soon, I did not have the courage to do so all along. I could feel from your letter how shaken you must have been after seeing her, this is why I was afraid to even mention her in my letters for I know how it is to be gnawed by painful memories behind bars, yet one of the greatest ingredients of courage is hope, hope that after all these hard knocks of life one day we shall try to make Thoko forget her misery for there is nothing you could do for her from where you are. My soul will only be at peace when I have seen her although Kgatho has been keeping me informed on her up to date. I am so glad to learn she has recovered. I do know that after seeing you she must have felt the way I felt all through the years after seeing you. She must have also rediscovered the power of her soul, a renovation of one's spirit without which we cannot go on in life.

Today my love was one of my greatest days. What could be greater than the arrival of that moment 'to strike the blows we have waited so long to deliver and in turning the tables against those responsible for the multitude of wrongs that are being wantonly committed against us'. Life is burdened with a species of man that does not learn either from history or from his own experience. I was so tortured when all my family turned up in court today, all in traditional dress. Daddy sent mama and our sister-in-law MaNgutyana to represent him. They looked magnificent in our attire. I was allowed to see Kgatho only though. I will write to you when I have seen mama. I learn they are trying to make arrangements to visit the girls and you. Nyanya was released in December, she was also present. I spoke to Brig Aucamp today about your wish to see her. She will apply immediately. They have all been battling to do so since my detention but I now learn their applications are unknown.

Today was like the 10th of March.[215] If I were to write my biography I would say my life began on the 10th of March. Not until you have discovered what is worth dying for is life really worth living. I was discharged from hospital on the 27th of last month. My flesh is nothing more than sea shells washed up to the coast by heavy waves of stormy political seas, my soul like the sea will always be there. I would have been filled with shame if I was unable to get up and defend those ideals [that] my heroes and our patriots have sacrificed their lives for. I often thought I would never have forgiven myself if something had happened before this opportunity for I certainly did not deserve so honourable a departure. I am too small, the ideal is too great.

I now know the gravity of the last sentence in your last address. I had known its weight all along but it took me some time to discover the fact that there are only two worlds for us; in the one world life is priceless, in the other freedom is priceless and it can never be the other way round as far as I'm concerned. One of my interrogators said, 'Is any cause sacrosanct, least of all a thankless one like this', the same day the same lips said, 'The Afrikaners will fight to the last drop of blood to defend the Free State'. Our just cause is a difficult one. There are the absurd pathetic contradictions one has to put up with. It makes me think of a dying horse I once watched as a child, as it dies it kicks and these kicks are more violent as life departs from the body. Yet if my honour is at stake I will stop at nothing in challenging those last kicks.

Your remarks about the last trial and the present one are quite appropriate and highly appreciated. During the last trial I watched with horror man committing political suicide with a double edged sword sharpened on his side, cutting the one who attempted to deliver the blows more than it cut me. I watched men in billowing academic gowns, an achievement I would have given my life for, stooping so low in court that I thought he needs a ladder to look at the back of a worm, so narrow minded that if he fell on a pin with his face on it the pin would pierce both eyes. There was no difference in the trial of Socrates in 7BC and this one in the 20th century. I wondered if such a man ever worries about his epitaph, priding himself as he does over his grandfather's epitaph. I remembered not with pathos rather than bitterness that this is the absurd mind which argues that separate development is the Magna Carta of the African

---

215. The 10th of March 1957 was the day they had their first date.

people but what on earth does he achieve by lying to himself? If anything it makes my task so much easier.

I was reminded of a peasant's speech I once read, an old man who had never seen the door of a classroom. Referring to the SA situation he said something like this, 'my lord hears I shot an aeroplane with an arrow, he laughs, I laugh too, he thinks it's funny as so do I – when a man tells me he is stronger than the whole world I laugh. I think it's too funny.' He was facing the same charges I now face for having said to a state witness whilst driving past the Orlando Stadium looking at a football crowd – that they would be better off soldiers instead of playing football – perhaps the most terroristic of all my so-called activities is saying to the same poor soul – 'that I would fight in the front-line when the revolution started' this recurs in the present indictment.

Uncle Marsh who is still awaiting a permit to visit went to see the children two weeks ago. He visited me last week, he states that they are a little more cheerful now especially Zindzi who was overheard by the principal saying to Zeni, 'Mummy and Daddy are in prison they are not dead – we shall get them back one day – so what – stop crying Zeni'. Such is her spirit, Uncle will try to bring them back for the holidays to make them try and pick up weight. They are both run down physically. I wonder if you have now seen Mr Brown. I noticed your letter of June reached him on the 23rd of last month.

The great girls I am with who are a tremendous source of inspiration to me with all their clenched fists salute you and send their fondest regards, this goes for all my colleagues in fact. Thoko from Alexandra wishes to be remembered by you and Xhamela. I intimated to the defence what you said about being prepared to asssist us. Since the indictment now dates back to 1962 with Ramotse as accused, I imagine there will be all the relevance now, even more than the previous indictment.

Dad did get the bottle store, it's now run by Thanduxolo.[216] On the 1st of August his syndicate took over the Bizana Hotel, the only one, thereby depriving the white community of their only quenching place. With all the business networks he has it was quite a sacrifice on his part to send Ma and Sisi for the trial as they run the different shops.

At the moment darling all I can tell you is that I am being educated so much. No school would have taught me what we are going through. The experience is invaluable. I was moved almost to tears when the emaciated and sickly Shanti[217] refused to testify against me. Only a person who has gone through

---

216. Winnie Mandela's brother.
217. Shanti Naidoo.

solitary confinement would know the amount of sacrifice that lies behind that single decision, a real daughter of Africa.

Tons of love my darling and a million kisses

Forever yours
Nobandla

LETTER FROM WINNIE MANDELA
TO HER FATHER COLUMBUS MADIKIZELA

9.8.70

My Dear Daddy,

I hope you are as well as I have seen you in my dreams. Sometime in March I dreamt you were seriously ill, I was so upset that I tried to get permission to write to you, this was refused then. I was very happy to learn much later in June that you were a picture of health.

A million thanks for sending Ma and the family to attend my trial. I was overwhelmed with excitement when I saw her enter the Supreme Court on the 3rd. I could see however, that she was terribly shaken, this was made worse by the fact that she was refused permission to see me. On the 5th she visited me in prison and she broke down completely when I appeared. I must confess I was myself badly shaken especially when I noticed how strained she was. Her eyes were badly swollen, obviously she had been crying from Monday. I tried as much as I could to console her but I fear I was not very successful. It was one of those situations where words become too shabby to express one's feelings, especially when one is in the process of crossing one's Sahara of his or her life.

She wanted details of my health which I did not give her because of the state in which she was. I told her I would write and give her a brief account. I have a heart condition which I am told by the specialists is Sinus Tachycardia (nerve heart in literal terms). I was told it is due to acute mental strain and stress as a result of the hard knocks of life, the lean years and the bitter struggle of the past few years with [minor] children who were hounded in primary schools by the security branch, children whose mother was unemployed, abandoned and therefore could not exercise the parental duties.

I am told this condition is now chronic or permanent. I was admitted to the prison hospital on the 6th of May and was discharged on the 27th of July. This time I was told by the specialist that I had hyper-ventilation – a further complication (lack of carbon dioxide). As a result of this I lost a large amount of weight. I think this is what worried Ma a lot as she remarked repeatedly about this. I however feel much better with the present wieght she should not worry, I'll be alright. I am receiving good medical care now. Besides medicines the doctor prescribed a pint of milk and bread which I get daily. In the past few months I was terribly anaemic, I have now improved considerably.

I was happy to learn from Ma that the businesses are all doing very well. In a letter you wrote to me in 1956 you told me to make haste slowly. I hope this was a theory you found practicable in your wealth of life's experiences and that you are not straining yourself as you did in the past five years. Who are the other members of your syndicate which has taken over the Bizana Hotel? Since whites cannot buy liquor from Africans what's going to happen to their thirst? Are they to travel; to Port Edward or Kokstad for a bottle of beer? I hope this will not encourage illicit liquor trading which is bound to have [un]palatable consequences. Let us hope the standard of the village itself will not be lowered with Africanisation. It was coming up so well when I last saw it in 1962.

Ma tells me my kid sister is doing Std 4 and that she is giving her classmates the same trouble I used to give mine. Please tell her how proud I am of her. It is so consoling to me to know she will do all I would not do academically. I hope you are guiding her subjects to enable her to do medicine or law. Mummy should not forget to put [her] in her passport together with Zeni and Zindzi so that when they come down to spend the Xmas holiday mummy should take them straight back to school accompanied by Zukiswa. Besides, Ma should visit the school the children will be attending next year. They were awarded a bursary by Sir Robert Birley, the London educationist who is presently visiting the country. I am sure you must have read about him in the past two weeks. I was very friendly with his wife when they were attached to the Witwatersrand University. He will be visiting the children and will also make final arrangements for their admission to Waterford.

How is my eldest brother's stomach trouble? Has he been finally diagnosed? I hope he is looking after himself. Ma told me about Msuthu's tremendous progress. It was exciting to see Lungile looking so well for a change although I learn he is very lazy. I think you should be a little more firm with him to help him adjust himself to daily life. Please do not allow him to roam from business to business, he must have a firm position.

I have asked Ma to take care of my in-laws' children whom I am guardian of since my late mother-in-law's death. Because of lack of supervision and proper discipline in my absence the eldest is already in trouble. Ma must have told you of the complete choas in my domestic affairs to which I have no immediate solution being where I am with the possibility of being away for [a] number of years to come.

I hope you will not let Mxolisi's parents force him to do articles with just matric. He should do a degree first surely, he is very young and keen. How is Bandlakazi's progress and Pumla? Who is the principle of the local secondary school?

Ma should bring oranges if there are still some in the garden. She should also bring a whole bag of madumbe, I so enjoyed the ones she brought me with the chicken and cakes. I felt I was right back at home.

How is granny at Ludeke and Aunt Nomadabi and Uncle Mewana? Please give them all my love. Where is Nomawonga and Thandeka? Did Batshaka ever pay back her tuition fees? How are all my uncles? I've always had secret childhood admiration for Uncle Laneginya's carefree type of life and complete independence. I hope he is not anywhere near any of the bottle stores. I can well imagine him unable to serve customers because he would attend to himself first thing in the morning, then he becomes unbearably arrogant in that state. How is Uncle Peter's hypertension?

Sometime back Nelson wrote to say he had written to you, Ma and my eldest brother but that he had no reply. Did you all receive the said letters? I hope even though you might have received them late you did reply. You must have heard about the death of my eldest stepson a year ago. This news upset him a great deal especially so soon after mother's death. In a recent letter he recalled this incident in very sad terms, I realised that he is not over it although he takes all these things like a man. I will be glad when Ma visits him as she intends to. My own applications to see him have been unsuccessful so far. No responsible member of the family has seen him since these tragedies climaxed by my detention.

I look forward to seeing Ma once more on the 24th. She looked so lovely in traditional dress and I prefer her in it. I would have loved to have a picture of her in it. She should bring me Zuki's picture and my brother's kids pictures, especially the lot I'd not know. If she can manage I would like one of the bottle store as well, I know the other business.

Lots of love to all the members of the family,

Your loving daughter
Zanyiwe

LETTER FROM NELSON MANDELA
TO WINNIE MANDELA

August 31, 1970

Censor asked me to shorten the letter on the ground that it exceeded 500 words.

Dade Wethu,

Your note of July 2 was shown to me on Aug. 14 – 1 month and 12 days after you wrote it. It was the sweetest of all your letters, surpassing even the very first one of Dec. 20, '62. If there was ever a letter which I desperately wished to keep, read quietly over and over again in the privacy of my cell, it was that one. It was compensation for the precious things your arrest deprived me of – the Xmas, wedding anniversary and birthday cards – the little things about which you never fail to think. But I was told to read it on the spot and [it] was grabbed away as soon as I had reached the last line.

Brig. Aucamp attempted to justify this arbitrary procedure with the flimsy excuse that in the letter you gave his name for your address instead of your prison. He went on to explain that my letters to you were handled in exactly the same way, and that you were not allowed to keep them. When I pressed him for an explanation he was evasive. I realised there were important issues at stake which necessitate to the making of serious inroads on your right as an awaiting-trial prisoner to write and receive letters and a curtailment of my corresponding privilege. Our letters are subject to special censorship. The real truth is that the authorities do not want you to share the contents of the letters I write you with your colleagues there, and vice versa. To prevent this they resort to all means, fair or foul. It is possible that communications between us may be whittled down still further, at least for the duration of the trial. As you know, the privilege as far as my normal monthly letters to and from friends and relations practically disappeared with your arrest. I have been try-ing to communicate with Matlala since January last and with Nolusapho since November. On June 19 Brig. Aucamp explained that another department had instructed him not to forward these letters, adding at the same time that he was not in a position to give me reasons for these instructions, but that such instructions were not influenced by the content of the letters. This revelation solved the riddle of the disappearance of most of the letters I wrote over the past 15 months. The matter entails even more serious implications. I should like to be in the position where I can always rely on what officials tell me, but I'm finding it increasingly difficult to square up wishes with experience. Twice during July and early this month, I was informed that your letter had not arrived. I have now established that the letter was actually here when I was being given assurances to the contrary. I was also disgusted to hear from you that Marsh had been applying for a permit to see me and that he had been informed by the prisons department that there were long queues of visitors for me. Nothing could be further from the truth. I had only three visits during the past 8 months – in January, April and June. It is easy to understand why they are reluctant to allow Marsh to come down. He is in touch with you and a visit from him would not suit Liebenberg and the S.B.[218] who wish to cut me off from you. I have had numerous experiences of this nature and each one leaves me sad and disappointed.

Incidentally, I was told that you and your colleagues now enjoy better privileges. I asked for more details and was shocked to learn that even after you had been formally charged you were not allowed a change of clothing and food from outside. How can any honest and intelligent person justify this barbarism? To the best of my knowledge and belief, as an awaiting-trial prisoner you are entitled to clean garments and to food from relations and friends. These are not privileges but legal rights. The tragedy of the whole situation is the blissful ignorance on the part of the officials concerned of the implications of the offensive utterances they often make. I deeply resent to be told of so-called concessions which are invariably made so late in the day and which are so trivial as to cause more harm and bitterness than gratitude and appreciation.

But your marvellous letter! There are moments in the life of every couple that are not easily forgotten and the occasions you describe so feelingly, I recall with equal affection and I always think of them. The information on Zeni and Zindzi's manners and tastes interested me much. I should like to know more about them, and it will be a real joy for me when I break through and succeed in establishing contact with them. By the way, the other day I was reading the terrific telegram you sent 2 years ago on the occasion of my 50th birthday. It dawned on me that it will not be long before I become elder, the highest title which even ordinary men acquire by virtue of advanced age. Then it will be quite appropriate for me to purchase some measure of corpulence to bloat my dignity and give due weight to what I say. If obesity were my dream, I would have all the means of fulfilment at my disposal. To be able to swing my own pot belly all I need to do is take things easy and pack my wretched stomach

218. Security Branch of the South African Police.

with carbohydrates – mealie-pap at sunrise, mealies for lunch and mealie-pap at supper. But the trouble is your letters. They form a solid wall between me and senility. After reading one of them the natural processes seem reversed, and I am never certain whether I'm ageing or rejuvenating. The latter feeling appears dominant.

How I long for Amasi,[219] thick and sour! You know, darling, there is one respect in which I dwarf all my contemporaries or at least about which I can confidently claim to be second to none – a healthy appetite. There was a time when I could polish off enormous quantities of food in any order. I could start with pudding backwards and feel just as happy and contented at the end of it all. I well remember the painful remarks of a housewife who was also medical student at the time. She and hubby had invited me for dinner one day. I had built quite some formidable reputation as a meat eater. After watching my performance for some time as the heavily laden dishes on the table rapidly vanished one after the other, and I concentrating more especially on the meat, she decided to share with me the benefit of her immense learning. Bluntly she told me I would die of coronary thrombosis probably in my early forties. I was foolish enough to challenge her statement, and tried to support my argument with the sweeping declaration that thrombosis was unknown amongst our forefathers in spite of the fact that they were great meat-eaters; whereupon she promptly produced a huge textbook out of which she read out emphatically and deliberately the relevant passage. It was a galling experience. I almost immediately felt a million pains in the region of my heart. That tip, raw and tactless as I was, made me cautious, and although I still relished meat I reduced its consumption. But my appetite was still as sharp as ever and I did not lose my colours as hero in this field. I long for the wonderful meals you could prepare so carefully at home, putting your whole heart into it – fresh homemade bread, macaroni with mince meat, egg and cheese, ox tongue and tail; chops; liver and steak, porridge and honey with the high flavour that was always mixed with your dishes. Above all I long for Amasi – the food for which I loved to sharpen my teeth and to stretch out my tummy, the act that I really enjoyed, that went straight into my blood and into my heart and that produced perfect contentment. A human being, whatever his colour may be, whether he lives under a regime of Christians, Pharisees, hypocrites, heathens, or those who chose to flirt openly with the devil, ought never to be compelled toward the taking of meals as a duty. This is likely to be the case if the product is poor, monotonous, badly prepared and tasteless. If I can only have Amasi. You remember how we

---

219. Traditional drink of sour milk.

carried a calabash [on our] way back from Mbongweni. What a lovely trip, Mhlope! I'm sure we will do it again.

In the meantime I know that your courage will rise with danger and that you'll fight with all your might. Fight, as your gallant forefathers did from the Zuurveld to Ngwavuma, from Nxuba Ntaba Busuku, the Lulu to the land of Nyabela. Fight as worthy heirs of Mafukuzela, Seme, Makgatho, Rubusana and the constellation of heroes that have defended the birthright of our people. This Sept. 26 will be your second birthday in jail. May the next one find you free and happy. My warmest congrats! I think of you always, Ngutyana. I will join battle and do my best when counsel calls.

A million kisses and tons and tons of love to you.

Devotedly
Dalibunga

LETTER FROM NELSON MANDELA
TO HIS SON MAKGATHO MANDELA

August 31, 1970

Heit my Bla,

I don't know whether I should address you as son, mninawa or, as we would say in the lingo, my (pronounced meyi) sweet brigade. The bond of parent and child that has kept us together for 2 decades gradually weakens as you grow full size, whilst that of friendship becomes stronger and deeper. I'm beginning to see in you an intimate colleague with whom I can discuss hopes and despairs, setbacks and achievements, one with whom I can chat as an equal; to whom I can open my heart. It is to such a friend that I now write; to you Lewanika, my bla, as the guys up on the Rand would put it. To you I can write freely and forget about formal or elevated language.

You must be frightfully busy; I have not heard from you these past 7 months. I know you'll write as soon as you can. I should have liked to leave you alone, but I long for you and am anxious to hear how you are getting on. What is even more important is that this September 8th you will turn 20 and that alone is sufficient excuse for me to intrude. Naturally, it will not be possible for me or Mummy to be at home to organise a birthday party, give you our warmest love and special wishes, to sit round the family table and feast, sing merrily, tell stories and rejoice with you with a full heart. But we will be thinking of you. The family is very proud of you and watches your progress with real interest. May good things come to you, fortune and the best of health and achievement. I hope you now received the card that contains our greetings and good wishes.

I have been reminiscing a great deal these days and events from the past in which you prominently featured come to mind – active moments in the gymnasium with Jerry Moloi, Simon Tshabalala (He was brutally tortured by the Security Police in 1964 resulting in the breaking down of his health.), Joe Motsepe, Joe Mokotedi, Eric Ntsele, Freddie Ngidi, Selby Msimang and other wonderful boys; the pennies we spent to provide you with the pleasure of swimming at the Huddlestone Pool, accompanying Nyanya to see the presentation of King Kong at Milner Park, the amount of fish you consumed as we travelled together from Qamata to Johannesburg and legions of other episodes. I remember all these as if they occurred only the other day. Those were the days when you lived a happy life free of problems and fenced from all hardships and insecurity by parental love. You did not work, grub was galore, clothing was plentiful and you slept good. But some of your playmates those days roamed around completely naked and dirty because their parents were too poor to dress them and to keep them clean. Often you brought them home and gave them food. Sometimes you went away with double the amount of swimming fees to help a needy friend. Perhaps then you acted purely out of a child's affection for a friend, and not because you had become consciously aware of the extremes of wealth and poverty that characterised our social life. I hope you're still as keen today to help those who are hard-hit by want as you were then. It's a good thing to help a friend whenever you can; but individual acts of hospitality are not the answer. Those who want to wipe out poverty from the face of the earth must use other weapons, weapons other than kindness. There are millions of poverty-stricken and illiterate people, masses of unemployed people, men and women who are grossly underpaid, who live in dirty and overcrowded dwellings, who feed mainly on dikgobe, papa, mngusho, motoho and marhewu, whose children never drink milk and who are exposed to all sorts of disease.

This is not a problem that can be handled by individual acts of hospitality. The man who attempted to use his own possessions to help all the needy would be permanently ruined and in due course himself live on alms. Experience shows that this problem can be effectively tackled only by a disciplined body of persons, who are inspired by the same ideas and united in a common cause. Most of us never had the opportunities which are enjoyed by the present youth – a wide variety of progressive literature dealing with man's struggle to master nature's physical resources; the immortal classics that stress, on the one hand, the dependence of human beings upon one another, and on the other hand, the social conflicts that flow from distinctive interests, that split society into various strata. I was almost 35 when I began reading works of this nature systematically, and what a difference it brought to my own outlook! You appear more militant and a better democrat than I was at your age and hope you'll be selective in your readings. We shall discuss the letter more fully on your next visit. In the meantime, I hope you'll enjoy 'And Quiet Flows the Don' by Sholokhov. Did Tellie get her letter of March 6, 1970? I also wrote [to] you [on] 31.3.70 and to Maki on 1.5.70. Once again, hearty congrats on your 20th birthday. Keep den 8115 safe and clean.

Affectionately,
Tata

LETTER FROM NELSON MANDELA
TO THE MINISTER OF JUSTICE

14th September 1970

My wife was detained on May 12, 1969 and has been in custody ever since.

I last saw her in December 1968. Twice after her arrest, I asked the Commissioner of Prisons to make arrangements for me to meet her. The second application was made after I had received information that she had been hospitalised as a result of deteriorating health. Both applications were refused. I now make a special appeal to you to approve the request.

There are important and urgent domestic problems which we cannot properly solve without coming together. In examining the matter you will bear in mind that there is nothing in the law or administration of justice to preclude me as husband from having consultations with her while she is facing trial, political or otherwise. On the contrary, it is my duty to give her all the help that she requires. The fact that I am a prisoner ought not of itself to deprive me of the opportunity of honouring the obligations that I owe her. You will also bear in mind that she has been in custody for more than 15 months, 10 of which were spent in solitary confinement – a frightful experience which must have been primarily responsible for the worsening of her condition. I sincerely believe that the pleasure she would derive from a meeting between us would induce a speedy and complete recovery, and put her in a better position to stand trial.

In considering both applications, General Steyn failed to show that high sense of values and human feeling that I have come to associate with him as an individual during the last 8 years. I am willing to hope that you, as the executive head of the Department of Justice, are well instructed in the principle of rightness and equity and not to turn a deaf ear to this appeal, and that the whole bent of your mind will be used to uphold those virtues that your office symbolises.

(Signed) NRD Mandela
Nelson Mandela: 466/64

LETTER FROM NELSON MANDELA
TO WINNIE MANDELA

October 1, 1970

My Darling,

A respite at last! I received your unexpected telegram in which you informed me of your release. I am sure you were as surprised to be acquitted as I was when I received the wonderful news. I should have liked to reply also by telegram immediately upon receiving yours, but these conveniences are not available for me even on so important occasion as an acquittal on a capital charge. I had to wait for 2 weeks before I could send you my warmest congratulations for serving 491, and still emerge the lively girl you are, and in high spirits.

To you and your determined friends I say welcome back! Were I at home when you returned I should have stolen a white goat from a rich man, slaughtered it and given you *ivanya ne ntloya* to down it. Only in this way can a beggar like myself fete and honour his heroes.

You are back and in accordance with my promise I bid good-bye to 'dadewethu' and return to 'My darling', to you dear Mhlope. This is the salutation I have used since Aug. '62, and I regretted it much when I had to abandon it.

Now that you are back I long for you even much more than I did when you were in. I fought hard to see you in the knowledge that such a meeting would do you a lot of good. But I did so also to save myself from catastrophe. There were times when I felt and responded like one in whom something had suddenly snapped. I could hardly concentrate and the picture of you rotting away in some dingy and isolated apartment with nothing to read and nobody to whom you might talk was unbearable. Your release relieved me, but it worsened my pining. I can no longer wait. I want to see you badly; it is now my turn to shrink to a size less than that of Zeni. When will you come? How I wish I could have a contact visit, where I could hug you, feel the warmth of your blood, smile straight into your eyes, chat to you normally without having to shout before I could be heard, as happens at present.

I long to see you in a peaceful and decent atmosphere, as a man and wife should when discussing tender domestic affairs after a separation of almost 2 years. But those who bear the cross ought never to squeal if the going is uphill, and I shan't. How is your health? Have you seen Zeni and Zindzi? What news will you bring me?

Incidentally, several hours before I received your exciting message I had handed in a letter addressed to the Minister of Justice asking him to allow us to meet. I imagine me still fighting long after the battle had been won. If your plea had been dismissed by the court and my application to the Minister refused, I would probably have appealed to a bone-thrower, or beseeched the Divinitus or turned to Marx. Luckily I did not have to choose between these alternatives.

I was sorry to learn that Ramotse remained behind. May he also have luck when the case goes to trial.

You have heard by now that our friend Mr Denis Healey, accompanied by the British ambassador, saw me on Sept. 19. I was pleased to see him again. He told me that you had paid a visit to Helen[220] and Shanti.[221] He also told me that that evening you would attend a ball given in his honour. I was very happy to hear this because after the ugly experience you had recently, you need relaxation and a lot of fun. Do enjoy yourself but beware of sprees if you can. It is a strange coincidence that you should have chosen to visit the Josephs and the Naidoos at the moment when they were very much in my thoughts.

I wish you had met Shanti's father, Naran, a courageous person who was widely known for his dedication and simplicity. We were arrested together in June 1950 and detained for some hours before we were released. When we reached their Doornfontein residence we were hungry and tired. Amma, wearing that free and easy smile of hers, presented us with a meal of crab and rice. It was my first time to see these creatures cooked, and the mere sight of them made me sick and everything inside me – my gizzard included – began protesting violently. You know, darling, that I never give up easily on such matters. I tried to be as graceful as was possible in the circumstances and even dared to chew 1 leg or 2. It was a delicate adventure. Thereafter I became much attached to the Naidoos and enjoyed crabs very much.

Shanti was then a mere nipper. I was to see her grow into a fearless girl who followed closely on the father's footsteps. But I never suspected that she had such strength of character, pluck and endurance.

As for our friend, Helen, I believe she is one woman who would continue to swing the sword even beyond the grave; that is if death allows her victims freedom to engage in these posthumous activities. With her background, qualifications, social status and opportunities she hardly had any reason to ruin her brilliant career by following the course she chose. She had the franchise,

---

220. Helen Joseph.
221. Shanti Naidoo was detained for six months and forced to stand for five days and nights but had refused to testify against Winnie Mandela. She was sentenced to two months.

could belong to any respectable party and express herself freely on any public questions. Only a highly principled person, completely dedicated to the ideals of freedom would make this fatal decision. I have the highest regard for her. She certainly will be one of the very first persons I shall visit when I return, just as you and Nomvula did the day after your release. She can dish out and take punches, and I'm sure she will still be slogging it out when the people of S.A of all races lay her remains to eternal rest. Give her, Amma and Shanti my warmest love ...

Darling, your friends have impressed me tremendously. I was not the least surprised by David, Elliot, Mqwati, Rita, Douglas, Thoko, Martha, and Livingstone. One day I shall have the opportunity of hearing something on Samson, Jackson, Nomvula, Paulos, Joseph, David Dalton, Victor, George, Joseph Chamberlain, Simon, Owen and Samuel and Peter. Fondest regards to them all. I'm proud of you darling and you are more to me than all the world. I expect wonderful stories from you when I return home. One day we will pack up. Then we will be free from the troubles of this world.

A million kisses and tons and tons of love.

Devotedly,
Dalibunga

LETTER FROM WINNIE MANDELA
TO NELSON MANDELA

26.10.70

Mfo Wethu,[222]

Although I still have had no reply to all my letters dating from the 2nd July, 3 August etc. I am writing once more. I was assured by Brig Aucamp that he had personally given you the letters but that to his knowledge there were no replies, that was just before our release.

Today I arrived at my shack at 12 noon to find the house locked. I was from my doctor for my daily treatment, then I decided to go and report as usual only to find Nyami in custody, arrested for staying with me allegedly without a permit. There was a slip as well at home for a letter from you which must have arrived after her arrest. The case will be on the 27th and mine on the 29th for an alleged violation of the order besides the appeal on the 2nd of November. My sisters and their husbands have been called for questioning and to make statements I understand for having visited me.

After bailing Nyami we went to fetch your letter. What a lovely surprise! Although parts of the contents were a strange anti-climax. It's amazing how this pattern of gross harassment peculiarly coincides with so many other forces. I keep repeating that the infinitesimal experience of the brutal two years has made me completely immune to misguided calculations due to lack of touch with reality and present situation often due to the refusal sometimes quite unconsciously on the part of the old established order to accept the fact that 'the old order changeth yielding place to the new'. Resistance to the position of rubber stamps is sometimes misconstrued and costly. I am quite aware that my original tactics have not always impressed the old order. They are no imitation of someone else's. I believe with our unique problems in our country only history will prove those who are right, right and those who are wrong, wrong. Different situations have always needed different tactics. In an amused manner I am reminded of the Greek philosopher Socrates who once lit a candle in broad daylight and went from house to house. The Greek population was amazed and they asked if the great man was mad. When asked what he was doing he replied, 'I am looking for an honest man!'

My views when I underwent that minor brutal test of the durability of my

---

222. An isiXhosa word meaning brother.

ideals and my experiences with the outside world now that I am temporarily out are such that I need not comment on the criticisms in Nyami's letter. Time and history attends to such things. My only concern at the moment is that you should join us soon and you will be in a better position to diagnose thalido-mide babies with modern stethoscopes and modern medical facilities. Any specialist who diagnoses a patient purely on the prescription and history of a medical practitioner or his own examination of ten years ago is tantamount to committing murder. I am not aware of the patronage of the mere handful, I only heard such remarks at Compol building under interrogation. What we know is the patronage of the black brotherhood of man, locally and interna-tionally. It is the first time I learn of the inability to hold friends. Almost half the people mentioned in Nyami's letter have security branch records which compelled them to withdraw if they wished to work and maintain their fami-lies or avoid leading the kind of life I lead in and out of court yearly. Bangilizwe and Vulindlela were interrogated, Nombulelo was detained, Leabie was de-tained, Tellie interrogated up to date, Ralangobuso was interrogated, Niki is daily threatened with loss of her job if she keeps visiting me, Marsh has already lost one very good job, Nali and Sef[223] fled and their persecution started when they lived with me, Gabula fled after his detention because he lived with me, George was detained because of me, if Sally wanted to keep her shops the sensible thing was to keep away, Mohla and Ishy were banned and they left.

Whilst inside I received numerous messages of apology from your Ndlangisa and have had thousands such from such circles – in fact not apologies but more of confessions now that we are out and pleadings for forgiveness. There comes a time in life when history completely kills personal life. When one talks of pursuit of pleasure at times like this it simply reminds me of my six days and nights of interrogation and the fantastic photostat record I have in my mind of that experience. In one of your letters I said any man who leads a normal life in an abnormal society is himself abnormal. If it was a few years back I might have been surprised at these remarks, I'm no longer surprised by anything for I know I chose the life of insults, hardships, and tears which have long dried up – myself with the full knowledge that it was for the better or for the worst for my people.

It is quite illogical to anticipate a return of the 1961 atmosphere where my own sister, my own brothers have to appear in a court of so-called law charged with staying with me without permits! I was in fact not surprised that Nyami was picked up this morning after reading the letter. I need no chances from

---

223. Winnie Mandela's sister and her husband Sefton Vutela.

members of my family for the returns of such an atmosphere, I need to be left alone by those who are responsible for wanting to see both of us behind us – it is then that one could nurse such dreams. One paragraph of the letter is censored – what a pity.

I have not received any of the letters darling. My last letter from you was in June 1970 although I kept writing. I hope you received the R100 I sent you. Am so sorry my love I could not do this when I was incommunicado. Dad is seriously ill at King Edward Hosp. I dashed down to see him before my house arrest. He looked terrible and has upset me terribly. I also visited grandpa and grandma's graves and mama's at Bizana. Mpumelelo killed an ox. The whole Mapgutyana's are praying for your return and predict that it will be soon. I visited Fatima[224] we had a royal time. She gave me lovely books. She sends her fondest regards. She was refused permission to see you when she was already in Cape Town. Her eldest daughter is now doing architecture at Natal University. I spent some time on dad's side although I had intended visiting many friends.

Our shack looks like it was hit by a tornado just within two years of my absence. We have to start from scratch fixing up everything if and when I get a job. At the moment there are no prospects at all. David A[225] had written to find out if you have any requirements or whether you need financial aid. Before I was banned Adie and Paul[226] phoned on behalf of everyone wishing us luck in the appeal and they sent their fondest regards. Mary[227] sent a lovely telegram.

In a way during the past two years I felt so close to you. It was the first time we were together in similar surroundings for that length of time. Eating what you were eating and sleeping on what you sleep on gave me that psychological satisfaction of being with you. It does not matter if there is such meanness that you can hardly be given cards and telegrams, as you once said in one of your letters which I do not have – perhaps I'll give you something better one day. A friend brought the girls for two days last week, they look terrible but will recover soon if we win the appeal. Zeni took things very badly and they were terribly affected by not returning home since my detention.

Zindzi is now a pianist so you'll sing together my love! I expect to see you as cheerful as ever my love! Am still battling to see you once more darling and how I look forward to it. I have beaten you to it, I have more white hair than you now. The first day I saw a mirror in prison I did not know the woman I was

224. Fatima Meer.
225. David Astor, the editor of the *Observer* in London.
226. Adelaide and Paul Joseph, activists in exile in England.
227. Mary Benson, activist in exile in London.

looking at! With white hair at 36? The blue bags beneath the eyes are slowly disappearing.

Do you remember what you said at the Fort when I visited you for the first time after your arrest? You thundered at me, 'This is not the woman I married, you have become so ugly' and then you sent me a magazine on the 'Reigning Beauties of the World – the Women and the Power behind politically successful men.' Most of them were wives of the independent heads of Black States. I was furious – I had taken such a lot of trouble to look nice that day!

How I miss you Mntakwethu. Love from all of us my darling.

Forever yours,
Nobandla

LETTER FROM NELSON MANDELA
TO THE COMMANDING OFFICER OF ROBBEN ISLAND

1 November 1970

Attention: Major Huiseman

Some of the matters I discussed with Major Huiseman on the 25th October have been given attention, for which I am grateful. I now refer you to those which were either not dealt with at all, or which were insufficiently considered.

1. No information has been given to me as to whether or not a letter was received from my wife. I cannot believe that she has not written to me since her release on September 15, and I should be pleased if you would give the matter your personal attention.

2. (i) A letter from my brother-in law, Marshall Xaba, dated 24th August 1970 indicates that my children's photographs and school reports had been posted to me sometime before the letter was written. Although it is now more than two months ago that the material was sent, it has not been given to me.

    (ii) I ask you to reopen the question of the letter of 22nd April from Kenneth Stofile, whose arrival here was not only confirmed by two experienced officials of the Censors' Office, but also by the writer thereof in a second letter written on 12th May, and which was delivered to me last June. It is unsatisfactory to attempt to dispose of the matter by merely telling me that there is no record of the letter. The circumstances are such that its fate should be known to the Censors. Please consider the whole matter against the background that there have been several other incoming letters which I never received, particulars of which I have given you on more than one occasion.

3. On 29th June 1970 I wrote to Jane Xaba. She is the same person who wrote to me in October last year, and whose letter I also never received. For an unknown reason the letter of 29 June was referred to Pretoria. Towards the end of July I showed a copy thereof to an official from the Censors' Office who expressed surprise that the letter was sent to Headquarters since its contents dealt exclusively with family matters. On August 19 Brigadier Aucamp assured me that his office had posted it straight to the addressee. October 10, Mrs Xaba visited her brother, Fikile Bam, and informed him that she never received my letter. You will see from its contents that the matter was

handled unfairly from the beginning, and I should be glad if you would allow me to send her a copy.

Would you be kind enough to give me a record of all incoming letters addressed to me that were referred to the Head Office during 1969 and 1970.

4.   In the letter referred to in paragraph 2 (i) above, my brother-in-law informed me that he had renewed his application for a visiting permit. Has he been granted a permit and, if so, for what date? I am also informed that my mother-in-law, Helen Madikizela from Bizana in the Transkei, made several applications for a permit, but that she received no acknowledgement. In this connection I should be please if you would give me full details of all applications made to visit me since May 12, 1969, and which were not approved, and the reasons, if any, for your refusal.

<u>Has a fresh application for a visiting permit been made by my wife?</u>

5.   On October 23 Lt. Nel informed me that no material had been received from Mr Denis Healey. On the 19th September the British Ambassador promised to send me the material, and General Nel had indicated that he would have no objection in me receiving it. In view of the undue delay. I should be pleased if you would kindly allow me to send a registered letter to the Ambassador reminding him of his promise.

6.   The letter that I wrote to my wife on October 1 went astray before it had been posted. On the 27th October I handed in a copy with a request that it be sent by registered post. Please arrange for me to be given the registration slip as well as those for the following letters.
(i) To Makgatho Mandela dated 31 August 1970
(ii) Mrs ZK Matthews dated 1 October 1970
(iii) Miss Nonyaniso Madikizela dated 1 November 1970

You are fully aware of the circumstances of my family, with particular reference to the formidable difficulties we are experiencing in communicating with one another. I ask you to investigate the matter seriously and objectively, and to arrange for me to be given reasonable and respectable explanations.

I deeply appreciate the help you have already given me and regret that I have to add to your heaving pressure of duties.

[Signed] NR Mandela
Nelson Mandela 466/64

LETTER FROM NELSON MANDELA
TO THE HEAD WARDER OF ROBBEN ISLAND

24 Desember 1970

Hoofbewaarder Van der Berg
Hospitaal,
Robben-Eiland

Ek sal dit hoog op prys stel as u die twee aangehegte briewe aan die aandag van die geneesheer sal bring.

Ek het alreeds die aangeleentheid van my aansoek vir heuning met u bespreek.

[Signed NR Mandela]
Nelson Mandela: 466/64

[Chief Warder Van der Berg
Hospital
Robben Island

I would appreciate it if you could bring to the attention of the doctor the two enclosed letters.

I have already spoken to you about my request for honey.]

[Note from official in Afrikaans]

Ek is nie familie van die Donder nie. Ek het al herhaalde kere vir hom gese hy mag nie 'n brief aan my addreseer ie ek is ook nie die B/O nie.

[I am not family of this scoundrel. I have told him repeatedly that he can't address letters to me. I am not the C/O (Commanding Officer).]

[another note from official]
B/O Sien D/G se nota op aansoek. Vir u goedkeuring asseblief.

[C/O See D/Gs note on the request. For your approval please.]

LETTER FROM NELSON MANDELA
TO THE MEDICAL OFFICER OF ROBBEN ISLAND CARE OF THE
COMMANDING OFFICER

24th December 1970

<u>Attention Medical Officer</u>

My medical report will show that my blood-pressure has for several months remained dangerously high, and I frequently complained of headaches and dizziness.

I have been put on a daily treatment of 6 improved Rantrax (50) and 6 Aldimets, the effect of which is to make me tired and sleepy during working hours. On several occasions when I go out with the span, I have to ask the warder-in-charge, much against my will, to allow me to lie down both in the fore- and afternoon. To the best of my knowledge and belief, the pressure has not risen beyond the level it reached on 14 September 1970. On the contrary, there has been a slight improvement and even the headaches are abating.

I contribute the improvement to the treatment and the complete rest that I am having. I have explained my position fully and frankly to the Medical Officer, Chief Warder Fourie and the warder-in-charge of the section. Some time back I was ordered to remain inside for a specific period, and when that period lapsed, I returned to work, but fared no better. The headaches and dizziness reappeared as well as the feelings of fatigue and drowsiness. I stayed inside and immediately reported to Dr Going who promised to go into the matter.

I am restating the position because I consider it proper that you should be fully aware of my health condition, and I trust that in examining the position you will be influenced solely by health and humanitarian considerations.

[Signed] NR Mandela
Nelson Mandela 466/64

LETTER FROM NELSON MANDELA
TO THE MEDICAL OFFICER OF ROBBEN ISLAND CARE OF THE
COMMANDING OFFICER

24 December 1970

Attention: Medical Officer

I should be pleased if you would kindly reconsider your decision rejecting my application for leave to order 4 lbs of honey per month on health grounds.

I have been shown your comment on my previous application in which you stated that I did not need the honey requested. You will recall that I had earlier shown you a pamphlet of the SABC which contained an address by Dr McGill. I drew your attention to some paragraph but missed the crucial statement contained in page 5 thereof which I am anxious that you should now read.

A perusal of my medical report will reveal that although I have been put on treatment with a higher potency, and although the rising of the pressure has been halted, it is far from being normalised. In re-examining the whole question, I ask you to bear in mind that applications of this nature raise not only medical issues, but also those of psychology, etc. I trust that you will give me an opportunity to discuss the matter with you again if you consider this second application inadequate for the purpose of inducing you to reconsider your decision.

[Signed] NR Mandela
Nelson Mandela

OC[228]
The treatment he is on is the best that modern medicine can provide. Honey is not a therapeutic substance for hypertension. I therefore refer you to my previous comment on this matter. I am prepared to see Mandela at any time to recheck his blood pressure.

---

228. Note from prison official.

LETTER FROM NELSON MANDELA
TO THE MINISTER OF JUSTICE

13 May 1974

Dear Sir,

I should be pleased if you would treat this matter as one of the utmost urgency. I should have liked to have made these representations more than two months ago, but due to my current circumstances and the measured pace at which government departments are accustomed to move, it has not been possible for me to write earlier than today.

1

In this connection, I should be grateful if you would

(a) Grant my wife, Mrs Winnie Mandela, House no. 8115 Orlando West, Johannesburg, a permit to acquire a firearm for the purposes of self-defence.

(b) Request the Minister of Police to order members of the South African Police in dealing with my wife to confine themselves strictly to the execution of their duties according to law.

(c) Use your influence with the City Council of Johannesburg to relax their influx control regulations and to allow my brother-in-law, Mr Msuthu Thanduxolo Madikizela, and his wife to live permanently with my wife at 8115 Orlando West, Johannesburg.

(d) Arrange with the Minister of Police for members of the South African Police to guard the house daily from 7pm to 6am until my brother-in-law and his family join my wife.

(e) To request the Minister of Interior to furnish my wife with a passport to enable her to holiday abroad.

(f) Grant my wife and me a two hour contact visit for the purpose of discussing the special problems outlined here.

2

My wife is a person upon whom notice has been served under the provisions of the Suppression of Communism Act, 44 of 1950. I have not had the opportunity of seeing the actual text of the abovementioned notice, but to the best of my knowledge and belief, she is prohibited from attending gatherings, entering a factory, an educational centre or similar places. Though she is free to take up employment within the urban area of Johannesburg, she is otherwise confined to Orlando Township and is not permitted to enter the rest of the area in Johannesburg known as Soweto.

3

In terms of the abovementioned notice, and with the exception of our two daughters now aged 15 and 13 respectively, no person is allowed to visit the house during certain specified hours. As the children were then and still are, away at a boarding school for the greater part of the year, this meant that she had to live all alone in the house.

4

Towards the end of 1970 and again on 27 May 1971 I wrote to your predecessor, Mr PC Pelser, requesting him to grant me an interview to enable me to discuss with him my wife's house arrest and its implications. In this connection I wish to refer you to the following passage in my letter of 27 May 1971:

> 'I consider it dangerous for a woman and detrimental to her health to live alone in a rough city like Johannesburg. She suffers from an illness which is caused by worry and tension and which has on occasions rendered her unconscious. Believe me when I say that I have since September last year lived in a real nightmare. She has visited me thrice since her release from prison, and the harmful effects of many nights of loneliness, fear and anxiety are written across her face. She looks pale and spent. I am further told that her hardships have been carefully and fully explained to you, without success, by herself as well as her legal representative. I cannot get myself to accept that you could remain indifferent where the very life of another human being is actually involved, and I ask you to relax the notice to enable her to live with friends and relatives.'

In addition, I raised other family problems which I considered serious and repeated the request for the interview.

5

I was informed by the Commanding Officer at the time and by Brigadier Aucamp, that both letters had been forwarded to your predecessor. I regret to advise you, however, that Mr Pelser did not even favour me with the courtesy of an acknowledgement to say nothing of a reasoned reply.

However, sometime after the May 1971 letter had been forwarded my wife informed me that the notice had been relaxed and that she could now live with such relatives or friends as were qualified to remain within the urban area of Johannesburg in terms of its influx control regulations. She further informed me that although the terms of the notice were still restrictive, some of the problems about which I had complained in my second letter had somewhat eased.

6

In pursuance of the aforementioned relaxation our friends, Mr and Mrs Madhlala, came to live with my wife. To the best of my knowledge and belief, [the] Madhlalas were not associated with any of the political organisations that fight against racial oppression generally and the policy of Separate Development in particular. In spite of this, the Security Police repeatedly dragged them to their headquarters and subjected them to gruelling interrogation. As a result of this harassment they were reluctantly compelled to leave our place. The news of the experience of the Madhlalas at our house spread far and wide and people, including close friends who would readily agree to reside with my wife, took fright and are now unwilling to do anything that may attract the attention of the Security Police so much so that today there is hardly any person who is willing to share the type of life my wife is forced to lead.

7

The one and only person who is still prepared to live with my wife is Mr Madikizela, and I must request you to use your influence with the City Council of Johannesburg to give him permission to live at 8115 Orlando West. I must add that prior to his endorsement out of the urban area of Johannesburg, Mr Madikizela, stayed with my wife.

8

The fears I express in my letters to your predecessors were not unfounded. On several occasions my wife has been the subject of brutal night attacks from criminals whose identity is unknown to us. In this connection I wish to quote from a letter she wrote to me on 6 December 1972.

'You must have perhaps heard from our mutual informer of the serious events which have left me quite shaken. Briefly, the house was broken into whilst I went home with the children to see my sick father. All our little valuable possessions were taken, the strange thief did extensive damage to the house, smashed to pieces what he could not take, tore down paintings from the walls, broke our glass partition, smashed the glass doors, removed books and personal documents …

Then at 3.30 am Sunday morning two weeks ago, three black men gained entry into the house through the same window which I had not fixed because the police had not taken the statement of the burglary. They tried to strangle me with a cloth. Had he not taken a deep breath as he bent over my neck to tie the cloth I would not have heard anything. I did not know I could scream so much, they switched off the light and fighting them off in the dark saved me. I sustained slight injuries. I was given police protection for a few days whilst an urgent application was made for some-one to stay with me. My attorneys applied for Msuthu and Nonyaniso temporarily whilst the Minister is deciding on Msuthu. However, I was subsequently granted permission for a Mr & Mrs Ntsokontsoko whom I met at work, they have been given 7 days at a time and their permit is expiring tomorrow. Our problem is that no one is prepared to share my kind of life, the situation is far worse now.'

I also quote from her letter of 20 March 1974:

'The last attempt on my life on the 9th (i.e. 9 February) has left me quite speechless … The damage to the house was quite extensive. I have been battling to repair what can be repaired, the garage doors need complete replacement. The hatred with which iron doors were torn apart like pieces of wood is indescribable. It is a mystery to me how the house doors took so long to give in with such a heavy impact on them.'

These events show that the effect of the restrictions placed upon my wife and the persistent refusal of the Johannesburg City Council to allow Mr Madikizela to stay with her, have made her an easy target to a mysterious type of thug. An Alsatian dog, which she acquired at the end of 1970, was poisoned and killed quite obviously by a person who has considerable experience in dealing with dogs that are trained to do police duties and to accept food from one person only.

All the fears I expressed to your predecessor have been confirmed and today my wife lives in perpetual danger and acute anxiety. I am reluctantly compelled to request you to give her a permit to acquire a firearm for purposes of self-defence, a request which I hope you will consider fair and reasonable, having regard to all the circumstances. I might add that last year a man attempted to stab her in the streets of Johannesburg in broad daylight and she was saved only by the intervention of friends. The man was subsequently arrested, but I have been told that the charge was later withdrawn.

9

In the light of my wife's experiences I must ask you to arrange for the house to be guarded by members of the South African Police daily from 7 pm to 6 am until Mr Madikizela moves in.

I must point out that from all the reports I have received the Security Police have acted towards my wife in a manner which I cannot accept as a proper execution of their duties. She is shadowed wherever she goes, taxi-men whom she hires to convey her to and from work are frequently interrogated and those who come to stay with her persistently harassed. Generally their attitude is hostile and on occasions positively provocative. Your intervention could give her some respite and ease the strain.

10

In spite of all her bitter experiences my wife has no intention whatsoever of leaving the house. But I think it advisable for her to be furnished with a passport to enable her to travel abroad on holiday. Getting away from Orlando for a month or two might ease the strain and benefit her health immensely.

11

I must add that although I have now completed eleven years of my sentence, and although I have reached 'A' Group, the highest classification a prisoner may attain, I have never been given the privilege of a contact visit with my wife. I have been forced to discuss serious domestic problems across a glass partition, and under difficult conditions where I have to shout to be heard even in regard to highly confidential matters. Moreover, the one hour allocated for the visit is too short a period, if account is taken of our special problems. I must accordingly ask you to allow me a two-hour contact visit, with all the normal liberties and courtesies associated with such visits, for the purpose of discussing these special problems.

12

I am quite certain that if you think that my representations are reasonable and substantial, and you consider it your duty to help, all red-tape will be brushed aside and our problems could be solved with a stroke of the pen.

13

It would be quite easy for you to reject each and every one of the requests I have made. You could, for example, point out that the question of the relaxation of influx control regulations is a matter outside your competence and within the jurisdiction of the Johannesburg City Council. You could adopt the same attitude towards my request in regard to the South African Police and passports, and tell me that my wife and I should apply directly to the appropriate authorities. You could even go further to rub it in by adding that my wife, in fighting racial oppression, has deliberately invited all the troubles she is now experiencing, and that the Security Police, in giving more than ordinary attention to her movements and activities, are carrying out their normal duties under the law.

14

I am well aware that, in view of all the circumstances, my representations will have to be approached cautiously and carefully, and that a decision either way will carry a heavy responsibility. Your official capacity may demand that you should pay attention to policy and security considerations which will result in grave injustice to specific individuals. I am also aware that the decisions you arrive at in your Ministerial capacity may frequently clash with your own personal feelings in matters of this nature.

15

The representations contained in this letter are made in the knowledge and certainty that they can be approved in such matter and under such conditions as will not endanger the security of the State or the public interest.

Above all, is the fact that the central issue in this matter is that the life of another human being, of a citizen, is at stake. I feel confident that in examining my requests you will allow humanitarian considerations to override all others, and do everything in your power to enable my wife to lead at least a normal and happy life.

Yours faithfully.
Nelson Mandela 466/64

LETTER FROM NELSON MANDELA
TO THE MINISTER OF JUSTICE

25 May 1974

Dear Sir,

Further to my letter of 13 February 1974 in connection with the attempts made on my wife's life, I have to advise that on 22 May 1974 I received the following disturbing telegram from her:

> 'Another vicious attack 12 am today police investigation no arrest one face assailant seen house helper nearly died we are all right children returning to school 26/5 cheer up you are our force of strength all our love'

In my letter of 13 February I should have added the following passage from my wife's letter of 29 April 1974:

> 'I hope you have taken some steps towards the question of my younger brother Msutu. The state of anxiety in which I always am when the children are around is unbearable. Although I have learnt to expect anything to happen to me, I cannot bear the thought of the dangers my children are exposed to. My would-be killers struck four days after the children left for school last time. As a result they did not settle down at all this term, especially Zindzi who seems more scared than Zeni.'

You will readily appreciate when I say that I am very concerned about the whole matter and should be pleased if you would treat it as one of the utmost urgency.

Yours faithfully,
Nelson Mandela 466/64
CONFIDENTIAL

LETTER TO 'SECURITY'
FROM THE COMMANDING OFFICER OF ROBBEN ISLAND[229]

PETITION TO THE MINISTER OF JUSTICE: NR. 913 NELSON
MANDELA

1.   The abovementioned prisoner had an interview with His Honourable
     The Minister of Justice on the 27th December 1974 during the
     course of which he discussed his requests in his previous petition
     in more detail. He was informed about the outcome of his petition
     but is apparently not satisfied and submit[ted] another request to the
     Honourable Minister – a copy of which is attached hereto.

2.   His petition does not include any new information or evidence and
     it seems he wants to argue about the merits of his application and
     under these circumstances it is recommended that his request to pe-
     tition The Honourable Minister not be approved.

OFFICER COMMANDING
[hand-written note]
S. O. (Security)

1.   We must submit a submission to the Commissioner stating that
     background of his previous requests and results.

2.   Recommend that it would be waste of the Minister's time to send
     the attached letter any further and that the prisoner be informed ac-
     cordingly.

[signed and dated 24.2.75]

---

229. The letter has a stamp on it dated 24 February 1975.

LETTER FROM NELSON MANDELA
TO THE MINISTER OF JUSTICE

12 February 1975

Dear Sir,

Extracts from your letter of 13 January 1975 addressed to the Commanding Officer were read out to me.

I note (a) that my request for my wife to be granted a firearm licence was carefully considered but that you were unable to approve it; (b) that no complaint against any member of the South African Police (the Security Branch included) had been made by my wife and that no member of the South African Police (the Security Branch included) was specifically employed to watch her activities; (c) that due to shortage of manpower, the request that you arrange for members of the SAP to guard her house daily could not be acceded to, and if protection was really deemed necessary by my wife, she could be advised to approach one of the numerous private organisations which undertake services of this kind; (d) that the request that my brother-in-law be permitted to live with her was still under consideration.

In this connection I should be pleased if you would be good enough to reconsider your decision on the question of the firearm licence. It should be a matter of real concern to the police authorities that, despite persistent attacks on the house and family, the SAP with all their training, skill and experience, and with all the vast resources and modern facilities at their disposal for tracking down criminals, the culprits involved in this particular case should still be at large. I have no clear information to indicate who is really responsible for persecuting my family. When I discussed the matter with you on 27 December 1974 you repudiated any suggestion that the SAP might in any way be involved and, in the absence of concrete evidence one way or the other, I could not take the matter any further. I must also accept your statement that, owing to shortage of manpower, the SAP cannot guard the house as requested. But I cannot appreciate why you should be reluctant to assist my wife in acquiring a firearm when the police have been totally unable to give her protection in the face of a serious threat to her life.

There are literally thousands of South African women, including blacks, who have lawful access to firearms in spite of the fact that they lead normal family lives, enjoying the protection of able-bodied men whose residential areas are, comparatively speaking, well-patrolled by members of the SAP and who are not exposed to any kind of danger whatsoever. You even seem to doubt whether protection is really deemed necessary by my wife notwithstanding the detailed particulars on the matter already furnished.

Bearing in mind the viciousness of the last two attacks in particular, growing concern on my part for the safety of the family is, to say the least, not unreasonable. Her health has already broken down and there are disturbing reports that the children are finding the strain difficult to bear. It seems to me that the only solution in these circumstances is to grant her a permit to acquire a firearm. I should add that even if you should be good enough for my brother-in-law to join her, which I trust you will do at your earliest possible convenience, she will still require possession of the weapon. He cannot be expected to defend the family against armed thugs with bare hands. I believe my wife would be willing to submit any reasonable conditions subject to which you might grant the permit. The firearm could for instance, be inspected at the house by the SAP at their convenience. Alternatively, she would probably be prepared to hand it to the SAP at 7am and collect it at 5pm daily. The second alternative would be quite onerous and would also deprive her of protection during daytime, and I hope you will not impose it. But it may be that she would be prepared to accept even such a stringent condition if she would thereby be able to defend herself at night. These conditions should meet any security problems the SAP might have in this regard. I might also add that I am unable to advise her to approach any of the private organisations which undertake services of this kind, solely because she cannot afford the fees charged by such organisations. She is due to be released from prison on April 13 and I must tell you that I am deeply troubled by the fact that she may have to go back to the house to face all over again the ordeals she has experienced in the past before anything is done to ensure her safety.

I was sorry to learn that you were unable to grant me permission to write to Mr Bram Fischer[230] concerning his illness. I must remind you once more that he is a friend of long standing and has been good to me and family in numerous ways. I am told that his illness is a serious one and fear that I may never see him again. Writing to him now may be the only chance I have to tell him just how much his friendship has meant to me, and to let him know that at this critical time in his life my sympathy and thoughts are with him. Few things would be sweeter in his adversity than little words of comforts and encouragement from a well-wisher. Such sentiments may give him the courage

---

230. Advocate Bram Fischer who defended Nelson Mandela and his colleagues in the Rivonia Trial was himself sentenced to life imprisonment in 1966. He contracted cancer in April 1975 and was sent from prison and placed under house arrest in his brother's house in Bloemfontein. He died on 8 May 1975.

and strength to fight back, and perhaps even help to save him altogether. The fact that my letter would be subjected to a double censorship should allay the anxiety that anything objectionable on security grounds may pass between us. I leave the matter entirely in your good hands again.

It was indeed very kind of you to allow me to acquire Piet Meiring's 'Ons Eerste Ses Premiers'. I am really eager to go through it. The only difficult[y] I might experience in this regard is that reading such material often tends to whet one's appetite. Perhaps one day I may be able to thank you personally for the gesture.

Finally, I should like you to know that it was a pleasure for me to be able to exchange views with you on matters of mutual concern. Your statement that the problems of our country will be solved by blacks and whites together coincides with my own views. Carried to its logical conclusion, and objectively applied, such an approach could provide a solid basis for harmonising the common efforts of all South Africans in working out lasting solutions. I sincerely hope your efforts in this regard may bring rich rewards. Mag dit goed gaan![231]

Yours sincerely,
Nelson Mandela 466/64

It has been [a] valuable experience for me to watch powerful organisations and highly-placed individuals clubbing together for the specific purpose of destroying a virtually widowed woman; how all these can stoop so low as to bring to my notice all sorts of details calculated to dim the clear image I have about the most wonderful friend I have in life completely baffles me. My consolation has always been that you've kept your head, held the family tight together and made us as happy and optimistic as circumstances would allow a girl who's live[d] under heavy and sustained pressure from all directions. Of course, dear Mum, we're but human Zeni, Zindzi and I and we'd like you to be highly praised by all and all the time just like the lady who rose from the valley of the Caledon in the 1820s. But the more you're slandered, the more attached to you do I become. These are not the things we should even mention in our correspondence to each other. But we live 1 000 miles apart, see each other rarely and for short periods and with all the jazz around your ears you may even wonder what Madiba thinks. Only because of this do I think I should, nonetheless, say to you that I LOVE YOU ALWAYS.
— NELSON MANDELA IN A LETTER TO WINNIE MANDELA, 19 AUGUST 1976

---

231. Go well.

Winnie Madikizela-Mandela

When the pages that make up this journal were returned to me after so many years I did not want to read them. I was afraid. There are memories you keep in a part of your brain; it is part of those things that hurt so much you do not want to remember. Getting it back after more than 40 years probed that particular part of the brain that had stored it.

I never thought I wanted to revisit those times. But at the same time I was glad that one could have a glimpse, a little peek through that window of darkness and relive those times for the sake of posterity, to be able to tell our children and grand-children what we went through.

I was fearful to go through that again, afraid of hurting myself and hurting my children because in hindsight you cannot help but think, 'What did I do to my children?'

That is the truth; that was the physical experience. That was why I was so scared to revisit that period because seeing those pages of handwritten notes and diaries brought back that fateful day. My children, Zindzi and Zeni, were clinging to my skirt crying, 'Mummy, Mummy don't go.' It was about 2.30 or 3am and they were used to these knocks. The authorities would knock at the door, knock at the windows, kick the doors in and break the windows. But that day I knew I was going for a long period of time. So I went into prison against that background and I did not know whether the children would survive. I did not know where they were going to take them to because the police who arrested me never even asked me where they should take them. It was God's luck that at that age they remembered my elder sister's name. Zeni was ten years old and Zindzi was eight. I learnt after a month that they were actually with my elder sister.

I already had a bag. I always had this bag packed because the children were too young to bring me clothes in prison and I had been arrested so often. I was not permitted to have an adult at home because I was under house arrest and speaking to me was tantamount to having leprosy – you were infecting yourself because you were bound to be arrested. So I ended up not communicating with people, trying to protect them. This even applied to my own family. I could not even take the children to my sister.

I did not know what my fate would be because we were part of an experiment – the first ever to be detained under Section 6 of the then Terrorism Act. They were using me as a barometer, a political barometer. If they could arrest this number one terrorist and number one terrorist's wife then they could measure the political heat in the country and how the country was going to react. After Madiba's arrest, he was in prison for life and I was this 'communist' who was continuing where others had left off. So arresting me was the highest point in their lives – they knew they had completely thwarted opposition to their nationalist government policies. I was aware that I was being used as a barometer to test the reaction of the country. If they could take his wife, when there was so much noise when he was arrested and jailed for life, what did the nationalists have to worry about thereafter? They were going to just sit back and rest and rule forever.

So I was arrested in that atmosphere and I knew my fate was in those people's hands and I knew no one would have the courage to open their mouth because apartheid meant murder in those days. If you dared oppose the nationalists, you were dead. Once this lawyer came to me at midnight to find out how I could help him leave the country. I was doing a lot of that in those days. The Security Branch happened to get this information and they detained him in John Vorster Square. The following day he was dead. That is how vicious apartheid was then – our lives were nothing.

When we arrived at Pretoria Central Prison, we were all held in a certain section of the prison. Then I was removed and placed on death row, in that cell with three doors – the grille door, then the actual prison door and then another grille door. The sound of that key when they opened the first door, the first grille door, was done in such a way that your heart missed a beat and it was such a shock. You had been all by yourself with dead silence for hours and hours and hours and suddenly there would be this K-AT-LA, K-A-T-L-A. That alone drove you beserk; that alone was meant to emphasise the fact that 'we are in control, not only of your being, but your soul as well and we can destroy it'. Solitary confinement is worse than hard labour. When you do hard labour you are with other prisoners, you can tolerate it because you all dig together, you communicate and you are alive. Solitary confinement is meant to kill you alive. It is the most vicious punishment that you could wish on your worst enemy.

You are imprisoned in this little cell. When you stretch your hands you touch the walls. You are reduced to a nobody, a non-value. It is like killing you alive. You are alive because you breathe. You are deprived of everything – your dignity, your everything.

We were held incommunicado. We were not allowed to even see a lawyer. In those days we were completely at their mercy. Some families never knew that their loved ones died after they were detained. We were lucky to be alive and it was purely because of my name that I survived because the easiest thing for them at the time would have been to kill me, which they threatened every day. 'Oh you're still alive?' They would come in every day and say, 'You're still alive? We don't know if you will be alive tomorrow.'

They honestly believed that it was impossible for a black woman to have this kind of stamina, to be this stubborn. Because they were meant to break us and they could not believe that anyone would resist them like that?

When we were released the first time I had red lips from pellagra and my skin was peeling because even when you tried to eat you brought up because you were very, very hungry. We were supposed to be awaiting-trial prisoners but they did not treat us as such. Our lawyers had to make an application to the Supreme Court for us to be brought food and then when they brought this food if it was bread they would break the bread. They were searching to see if there was anything hidden in it. They would break the fruit open so you got your food in pieces – just to humiliate you and to show that you are a nobody. They reduced you to such levels.

They still searched you in your cell despite the fact that you had nothing other than the clothes you were wearing, two blankets and a mat. We had a plastic bottle with two-and-a-half litres of water for the whole day. That was your ration for the day and you drank from the bottle – there was no glass, you drank from that. Then you wiped your face with that and you just wiped your armpits and yourself. One of our lawyers, George Bizos, had to apply for us to wash. An application had to be brought before the Supreme Court for months to allow us to wash properly.

Solitary confinement was designed to kill you so slowly that you were long dead before you died. By the time you died, you were nobody. You had no soul anymore and a body without a soul is a corpse anyway. It is unbelievable that you survived all that. When I was told that most of my torturers were dead, I was so heartbroken. I wanted them to see the dawn of freedom. I wanted them to see how they lost their battle with all that they did to us, that we survived. We are the survivors who made this history.

When I was in detention for all those months, my two children nearly died. When I came out they were so lean; they had had such a hard time. They were covered in sores, malnutrition sores. And they wonder why I am like I am. And they have a nerve to say, 'Oh Madiba is such a peaceful person, you know. We wonder how he had such a wife who is so violent?' The leadership on Robben Island was never touched; the leadership on Robben Island had no idea what it was like to engage the enemy physically. The leadership was removed and cushioned behind prison walls; they had their three meals a day. In fact, ironically, we must thank the authorities for keeping our leadership alive; they were not tortured. They did not know what we were talking about and when we were reported to be so violent, engaged in the physical struggle, fighting the Boers underground, they did not understand because none of them had ever been subjected to that, not even Madiba himself – they never touched him, they would not have dared.

We were the foot soldiers. We were their cannon fodder and it was us who were used as their political barometer each time they wanted to find out how the country was going to react. They tortured us knowing that it was going to leak to the country and they wanted to test the reaction. Tata could not comprehend how I had become so violent in the eyes of the police. They knew that I was involved with the military wing of the ANC and they knew I was a leader of the struggle underground. They knew I saved soldiers who infiltrated into the country.

But we learnt all kinds of tricks to protect ourselves against them. I learnt then that 'the nearer the danger, the safer the place', which is the first thing they are taught in the military. It was him, Tata, who always repeated that 'the nearer the danger, the safer the place', so I hid the cadres next to the police stations. Not one of those cadres was arrested, and they were right under their noses. If I had a very dangerous unit, which was in the high command and involved in special operations, I hid them around the police station. And they could not catch me because I discovered that the only way to survive those days was to operate alone. There was always a danger of getting someone killed by merely associating with them. That is why I never knew their real names. I never knew the names of the units that infiltrated the country. When they came into the country I gave them my own combat names so that they did not coincide with the names they used in the camps and they would not know who was who. These are people who are generals in the South African army today who hold the highest offices in government but they must tell that story themselves.

We and the enemy hunted each other at sunset – our daybreak was 6pm. We operated right through the night; it did not matter where I was. Daybreak was nightfall. We reversed the hours in the same way we had to reverse the values of society.

Zindzi and Zeni would ask questions, especially Zindzi. She was a very troublesome child; she had a very enquiring mind. Her sister did it in a more sombre and dignified way. Zeni was always the princess. She was born like that. When her father used to play with her as a baby, he addressed her as 'Princess'. That is how she became 'HRH' and she is still HRH today. That is how we addressed her. Zindzi was a tomboy and she was always asking, 'Ma, you know? You know you are a liar.'

'Why darling?'

I always give the example of Tat'uSibeko, my next-door neighbour, a Zulu from Zululand and one of those real traditional types. And so Zindzi came in, she was about five or six, and she said, 'Mummy you said all the daddies are in jail. Why are the daddies in jail?'

I said, 'Because they are fighting for us to also be able to live in town.' You could not use the word 'free' because the children did not understand. 'They want us to have nice houses and also live next to the shops in town.'

And then she said, 'But then why is Tat'uSibeko next door at home? Why hasn't he gone to fight for that?' And then she went on to say, 'But Mummy, the other children say people who are in prison are bad people.'

What do you say? This is a five-, six-year-old with an enquiring mind. Both of them would confront me with these questions so the values of society were reversed to the extent that as they grew older the fathers who were not in jail were 'collaborators' – it was 'wrong' not to be in jail, you were a 'collaborator'. It was right to be in prison; it was not that if you steal you would be arrested and you would go to jail. You could not use that example so we had to use religious examples and say, 'You know if you do wrong things your angel is watching. You know God does not want you to do bad things, that's why we have to pray, that's why we have the Lord's Prayer. You mustn't do bad things.' We could not use imprisonment for right and wrong because then they would have regarded their father as a criminal and how would you get that out of a child's mind? No matter how she gets educated later on in life, what you teach the child as a mother in the formative years is what sticks. There was propaganda from the nationalists that their father was terrorist – he was a killer.

And how do you change those values later on in life? People do not realise how tough it was to bring up children in those years. They have led conflicted lives and they have turned out to be who they are. You do not know how many times parents like us fell on our knees and thanked God that they turned out to be who they are. It was touch and go – the child could have turned out to be a criminal. In fact, the child could have grown up to blame you. When they discovered the truth, they could have told us, 'How dare you?' So, 'Mummy and Daddy gave us up and chose the world and chose the country, chose to fight for the people? These people?' Can you imagine what that would have meant to our families if they had turned out to have such questioning minds? At what point do you, as a parent, decide that you would fight for a cause that is thankless sometimes, but you know you are fighting for human dignity?

When Tata was arrested in 1962 and I got my first banning order, it had no name – 'Mandela's wife' was banned and confined and the rest of the world did not know who I was. I could never say anything that was from myself, my own mind. It was possible they did that deliberately, but my reaction was that if you have arrested the man you must destroy what he left behind. I took that as a direct attack on women and that we were useless – our husbands were our voices and in their absence the struggle would end. To the prisoners, if they did not have the support of their families that would have been their end. I realised how important the support of family is when you are in prison.

When Tata was arrested on 5 August 1962, I decided, 'I will fight them to the last drop of my blood. I am going to fight them and I am not going to let them break me. I will never let them break me.' I was aware of the fact that suddenly I discovered, 'Oh, I have no name now' – everything I did as 'Mandela's wife'. I lost my individuality: 'Mandela's wife said this', 'Mandela's wife was arrested'. It did not matter who the hell I was; it did not matter that I was a Madikizela; it did not matter that I was a human being. And it was understandable to the oppressor that whatever they did to Mandela's wife, she deserved it. So I thought, 'My goodness I've grown up a princess in my own home; I come from the Royal House of Pondoland; and suddenly I've lost my identity because of this struggle. I am going to fix them. I will fight them and I will establish my own identity.' I deliberately did that. I said I was not going to bask in his shadow and be known as 'Mandela's wife'; they were going to know me as Zanyiwe Madikizela. I fought for that. I said, 'I will not even bask in his politics. I am going to form my own identity because I never did bask in his ideas.' I had my own mind.

I realised that, my goodness, if you are married you lose your identity completely. I became a nobody and I had grown up walking tall in my home. I had been taught by my mother and my father that I must walk tall. I am me; I am black; I must be proud of my blackness. My father taught me the history of our country; he taught me about the nine Xhosa wars; he taught me the role the Pondos played in the liberation struggle; he taught me what happened when the 1820 Settlers came into the country and how Van Riebeeck landed in the Cape in 1652. I heard all this history from my father and then I came here; I am a nobody. Not on your life. No, I am going to be who my father taught me to be. I am going to walk tall. My grandmother, my father's mother, was one of the 29 wives of my great-grandfather, who was a chief. My grandmother was the first woman to wear shoes in Pondoland in those days and when she bragged about these shoes it turned out that they were sneakers. But she was the first of the chief's wives to wear shoes and she hated the people who came with silky hair, blue eyes and with those light skins. She hated them because she had been a shopkeeper. She was the first of the chief's wives to have one of those stalls in the rural areas – I do not remember now what they used to be called. But she was the first to own a shop and when these people came, she lost that shop, she lost that land. She hated them. My mother was light skinned, very light skinned, and as a result we were not our grandmother's favourites because most of my sisters had the same skin as my mother. My grandmother was very, very anti-white. So you can imagine me having this grandmother, with my father teaching me this history and I grew up learning that we must walk tall, that in fact Africa is ours, and Africa was stolen from us by these people who came and took our grandfather's land.

There were these two backgrounds and then I come to Johannesburg. I was a young social worker. I got married to this man and here I was taken back again to my grandmother's days when she taught me to walk tall. So when the authorities banished me to Brandfort as far as they were concerned that was just the last act to bury me forever, but I was never as active as I was in Brandfort. I presented a public picture that I was in banishment and the international community was singing our name all over the world. I recruited from the Free State like you have never known. The apartheid system formed the homelands and each homeland had its own pseudo passport called *incwadama yoku ndwendwela* (small book of visiting). These travel documents were not recognised by any other country in the world, not even by the protectorate sister states. So the people would travel to these bordering countries and leave this so-called travel document at the border and they had an arrangement with the homeland governments that the people would be allowed to go to those countries and when they returned to South Africa then they would pick these documents up. Every week I had soccer teams from Brandfort going to play in Botswana and Lesotho. Brandfort was close to both Lesotho and Botswana. They left those travel documents at the borders and they never came back. The authorities were so stupid not to realise that they were not coming back into the country. They were so keen to have these pseudo travelling documents recognised that it never occurred to them that there must have been bags full of these travel documents at the borders. I recruited more people from Brandfort than I had ever done in Soweto.

Because I was under house arrest in Brandfort, I had to sign in at 6pm every day. Especially over weekends, I would sign in at 6pm and then get back to the house, change, dress like an auntie who was selling apples and get into the car, a different car. I sometimes went to Soweto. I recruited right through the night in Soweto from Brandfort. At about 5am I was back on my bed, sleeping, and they always came to check at around 5.30am. By 6am they are in front of the house to see if I was going to get up and I would go out – the toilets were outside – and yawn and stretch myself. I would act as if I had been sleeping – meanwhile I had been in Soweto the whole night. They taught us to do things like that. We really became criminals.

It was a thankless job; you were not fighting to gain anything personally – at least those of us who were not aspiring to positions in government and to enrich ourselves. Those of us who were so young in the struggle were hooked. It was like opium. Fighting for freedom in the ANC was the greatest thing in your life. You knew there could not have been any greater reward than the freedom of your people. We did not know it was a thankless job and people were fighting to be presidents.

I would do it all over again. I realised that that is what a liberation movement is all about actually. That is why it is called a 'struggle'. Those who were fighting for their own positions and things were really fighting differently from us. You accept the fact that there will always be the Oliver Tambos, the Chris Hanis, the Nelson Mandelas and the Sisulus of the day. My personal mentor was always Tat'uWalter Sisulu whom I grew up worshipping as a young bride because he was like a father to Tata and Tata revered him. When I was newly married, Tat'uSisulu sold watches and jewellery. He was so humble. We would go and pick him up every day. He lived in an ordinary house in the township and we hardly realised what would ultimately happen to those people. We never had dreams of them being in government and being presidents and that is why up to his dying day Tat'uSisulu never wanted any position in government. He refused and even turned down positions within the ANC. He was that type of person: unassuming, fighting for the liberation of his country. The liberation of your fellow man was the greatest reward and that is how Tat'uWalter used to talk and that is how Chief Albert Luthuli was and I was so blessed to know all of them.

I used to cook for them, these big men. I only realised their stature long thereafter. I just worshipped them as my leaders. I used to cook for J.B. Marks and Moses Kotane in that little house in Orlando. I even used to cook for Gatsha Buthelezi when he would come with the king of the Zulus and they would have dialogues with Tata through the night. At that time they were starting to form Inkatha, which was originally a structure that was meant to be used in the light of the Youth League. Buthelezi was going to use Inkatha to fight apartheid from within. That is why originally the colours of Inkatha were the colours of the ANC. He was one of the greatest fighters in his day and he was entrusted, with Matanzima, with fighting the system from within. And that is what people do not know.

Looking back as a parent, you feel you do not deserve this forgiveness because you cannot explain yourself to the children and you fear that they would never understand. You are lucky that they understand so much anyway; that they do not begrudge you. And what makes things difficult, of course, is when they see that what is happening today to other people is all about enrichment and it was never about self-sacrifice. They cannot even understand why I live in Soweto, really. They do not understand that it was a statement on my part. I made a conscious decision that I was going to live in Soweto instead of moving to the suburbs. I fought for my children to lead the kind of normal life they could live anywhere, but I will die in Soweto. The only time I am in the suburbs is when I am in hospital.

I felt strongly that this journal and these letters needed to be published in this way, exactly as they were written at the time, so that my children and my grandchildren and whoever else reads them should please see to it that the country never ever degenerates to levels such as those. It is for their future. Right now, people like myself who come from that era become petrified when we see us sliding and becoming more and more like our oppressive masters. To me, that is exactly what is happening and that is what scares me.

Throughout the years of oppression, I think my feelings got blunted because you were so tortured that the pain reached a threshold where you could not feel pain anymore. If you keep pounding and pounding on the same spot the feeling dies, the nerves die. I can feel us sliding back to that right now.

Johannesburg
November 2012

Twenty Years in the Life of Winnie Mandela

1957

Winnie Mandela, a twenty-year-old social worker from Bizana in the Transkei, meets Nelson Mandela, a young lawyer who is banned and on trial for high treason.

1958

Marries him when he is given four days off his banning order and restriction to Johannesburg to return with her to her family home in Bizana for the ceremony. She participates, while five months' pregnant, in an anti-pass protest and is arrested and detained for two weeks.

1959

Gives birth to her first daughter Zenani.

1960

Gives birth to her second daughter Zindziswa.

1960

The ANC is banned, making it illegal to promote its aims.

1961

Her husband is acquitted of treason and goes underground.

1962

Is banned and restricted to Johannesburg for two years. Her husband is arrested and sentenced to five years in prison.

1963

Is arrested for breaking her ban by attending a gathering. She is acquitted. Her husband is put on trial for sabotage.

1964

Her husband is sentenced to life imprisonment with Walter Sisulu, Ahmed Kathrada, Govan Mbeki, Raymond Mhlaba, Denis Goldberg, Elias Motsoaledi and Andrew Mlangeni.

1965

Is banned for five years and restricted to Orlando township. She is forbidden from preparing any document and requires special permission to visit her husband.

1966

New restrictions forbid her from participating in the preparation of printed material.

1967

Is acquitted on a charge of resisting arrest.

1967

Is sentenced to twelve months in prison for failing to give her name and address to the security police. The sentence was suspended for three years but she had already spent four days in prison.

1968

Her mother-in-law dies and she attends the funeral. Nelson Mandela is visited on Robben Island by his wife for the last time before her arrest.

1969

At 2am on 12 May, she is detained by police under the Terrorism Act. In July, while in prison, she receives news that her stepson was killed in a car accident. She is charged for promoting the aims of the ANC.

1970

On 16 February charges are withdrawn, but she is immediately re-detained and charged. On 15 September she is acquitted and released. She applies for a permit to visit Nelson Mandela on Robben Island and is given 3 October 1970 as the date. On 30 September her banning order is renewed for five years. She is also placed under house arrest. She has to be at home from 6pm to 6am on week days and between

2pm and 6am on weekends and public holidays. She is forbidden from receiving visitors other than her children. The local magistrate refuses to allow her permission to leave Johannesburg to visit her husband. In October the police raid her home and find Peter Magubane, a banned person, her sister, Nonyaniso, and her brother-in-law. She is charged for breaking her banning order. Nonyaniso is arrested for being in Johannesburg 'illegally' and her brother-in-law is charged for not having a pass. She successfully applies to visit her husband. They have only 30 minutes together.

1971

Is sentenced to twelve months in prison suspended for three years for communicating with a banned person in her house. The conviction and sentenced are set aside on appeal.

1972

On 25 April she wins her appeal against her sentences for receiving visitors to her house in October 1970. One of the visitors was her brother-in-law, Marshall Xaba, who called at the house to collect a grocery list. Another was her sister, Nobantu Niki, and the third was another banned person, Peter Magubane. Her conviction and sentences of six months and twelve months are set aside on appeal.

1973

Is sentenced to twelve months suspended for three years for having lunch with her children in a vehicle in the presence of a banned person.

1974

Her sentence is reduced on appeal to six months, time that she serves in Kroonstad Prison.

1975

Her third banning order expires. In April 1975 she is released from Kroonstad Prison.

1976

Is detained without trial for four months after the Soweto uprising.

1977

Her banning order is renewed for five years. She only has ten months 'freedom' from banning in thirteen years. She is banished to Brandfort, a rural backwater in the Orange Free State province, where she knows no one and does not speak the local language. (In 1985 she defies the banning order and returns to Soweto.)

Sixteen Months in the Life of Winnie Mandela

12 MAY 1969 TO 14 SEPTEMBER 1970

12 May 1969

Is detained under the Terrorism Act of 1967, which allowed for indefinite detention as well as indefinite interrogation. Caleb Mayekiso, one of the detainees, dies in detention on 1 June 1969.[232]

26 May – 30 May 1969

Is interrogated continuously.

18 July 1969 (Her husband's 51st birthday)

Police ask her, 'Who is Thembi Mandela?' When she answers that he is her stepson, they say, 'He's dead.'[233]

28 October 1969

Appears for the first time in court with 21 others. Their attorney Joel Carlson says, 'When I first saw them they had not been able to have a bath or a shower for nearly two hundred days.'[234] Maud Katzenellenbogen, who had befriended her after her hus-

---

232. Caleb Mayekiso, who had been an accused in the 1956 Treason Trial, was detained on 13 May 1969 and died eighteen days later.
233. She clearly did not receive the letter from her husband telling her about his death.
234. Carlson, *No Neutral Ground*.

band Moosa Dinath met Nelson Mandela in prison, tries to arrange an attorney, Mendel Levin, to defend her. It transpires that he was a supporter of the ruling National Party. From prison, Nelson Mandela urges her to have Joel Carlson defend her.

1 December 1969 – the trial starts at the Old Synagogue, Pretoria

List of accused:

1. Sampson Ratshivande Ndou
2. David Motau
3. Nomzamo Winnie Mandela
4. Hlengani Jackson Mahlaule
5. Elliot Goldberg Shabangu
6. Joyce Nomala Sikakane
7. Manke Paulus Matshaba
8. Lawrence Ndzanga
9. Rita Anita Ndzanga
10. Joseph Zikalala
11. David Dalton Tsotetsi
12. Victor Emmanuel Mazitulela
13. George Mokwebo
14. Joseph Chamberlain Nobandla
15. Samuel Solomon Pholotho
16. Simon Mosikare
17. Douglas Ntshatshe Mvembe[235]
18. Venus Thokozile Mngoma
19. Martha Dlamini
20. Owen Msimelelo Vanqa
21. Livingstone Mancoko
22. Sexford Peter Magubane

Defence: Adv. David Soggot and Adv. George Bizos. Instructed by Joel Carlson
Prosecution: J.H. Liebenberg and D.W. Rothwell
Judge Bekker

They are charged under the Suppression of Communism Act and the Unlawful Organisations Act, including furthering the aims of the ANC and conspiring to commit sabotage. No acts of violence are alleged. All the accused plead not guilty and as this transcript from the court record shows:

---

235. Douglas Mvembe, 73, was tortured for three days. He was hanged by handcuffs and rope to a window grating.

Accused No. 3 wishes to address the court.

ACCUSED NO. 3: With due respect to you, My Lord, I would like to draw your attention to the fact that I have been under detention in the past six months in terms of Section 6(1) of the Terrorism Act, an Act which I regard as unjust, immoral, soul-corrosive and physically destructive. Twenty-four days after my detention I lost a colleague of mine who could not go through the trial we have already gone through behind bars and that was Caleb Mayekiso, a colleague of mine. My Lord, I find it difficult to enter any plea.

BY THE COURT: Well, then for the purpose of record I will enter a plea of not guilty. Is there anything else you wish to say?

ACCUSED NO. 3: I would just like to say, My Lord, I find it very difficult to enter a plea because I regard myself as already being found guilty.

BY THE COURT: I think you are wrong in that assumption. I will enter a plea of not guilty.

Accused No. 6 also indicates that she wishes to address the court in English.

ACCUSED NO. 6: My Lord, I feel the same as Accused No. 3.

BY THE COURT: Just tell me your name, please.

ACCUSED NO. 6: It is Joyce Nomafa Sikakane.

BY THE COURT: I forgot to ask No. 3 her name. What is your name?

ACCUSED NO. 3: Winnie Mandela.

ACCUSED NO. 6: My Lord, I feel the same as Accused No. 3, Winnie Mandela, but I am going to enter a plea of not guilty.

BY THE COURT: In your case, too, I will enter a plea of not guilty.

*   *   *

The 22 are also accused of arranging the funerals of two anti-apartheid activists and the illegal display of ANC flags.

Judge Simon Bekker, whom Nelson Mandela had encountered during the 1956 Treason Trial, presides. The prosecutor, J.H. Liebenberg, tries to prove that the ANC was an integral part of the Communist Party and that Mrs Mandela was in touch with the ANC in London.

The court hears twenty witnesses for the prosecution including Briton Phillip Golding who admits to having been tortured. Nonyaniso Madikizela, Winnie Mandela's 18-year-old sister who had been threatened with long imprisonment if she did not testify, tells the court she had been tortured. Mohale Mahanyele, the assistant librarian at the United States Information Service in Johannesburg, testifies against the accused.

Detained activists Shanti Naidoo and Nondwe Mankhala refuse to testify and are sentenced to two months in prison. As Nelson Mandela is named as a co-conspirator, attorney Joel Joffe applies to see him on Robben Island. His application is refused so he applies to have him subpoenaed. The case is remanded until Monday, 16 February 1970.

16 February 1970

Attorney General Kenneth Donald McIntyre Moodie comes to court and announces he is withdrawing the charges.[236] Judge Bekker tells the accused they have been acquitted and are free to go. Before they can leave, the police re-detain them. Advocates George Bizos and David Soggot fail in their attempt to prevent the security police from confiscating the group's written statements. Attorney Joel Joffe unsuccessfully applies for a court injunction against torture.

12 May 1970

The Black Sash and university students protest to mark a year since the accused were detained. About 1 200 people march through the streets of Johannesburg and 354 are arrested.

18 June 1970

Winnie Mandela and three others do not appear in court. She is in hospital. Manke Paulus Matshaba has suffered a mental breakdown and Victor Emmanuel Mazitulela and Livingstone Mancoko are released and then disappear. They are joined by Benjamin Ramotse.[237]

3 August 1970

The twenty accused are charged with 540 offences, which are almost identical to the 528 on the previous charge sheet. Nelson Mandela's name no longer appears as a co-conspirator.

A new list of the accused:
1. Benjamin Sello Ramotse
2. Sampson Ratshivande Ndou
3. David Motau
4. Winnie Mandela

---

236. Relatives and friends immediately applied for an interdict against further assaults but it was not granted.
237. Benjamin Ramotse was injured in the 16 December 1961 explosion at the launch of MK, which killed fellow operative, Petrus Molefi. Ramotse was detained and charged with sabotage. He estreated his bail and left the country for military training.

5. Jackson Mahlaule
6. Elliot Shabangu
7. Joyce Sikakane
8. Lawrence Ndzanga
9. Rita Ndzanga
10. Joseph Zikalala
11. David Dalton Tsotetsi
12. George Mokwebo
13. Joseph Chamberlain Nobandla
14. Samuel Solomon Pholotho
15. Simon Mosikare
16. Douglas Ntshatshe Mvembe
17. Venus Thokozile Mngoma
18. Martha Dlamini
19. Owen Vanqa
20. Sexford Peter Magubane

Defence: Adv. Sydney Kentridge, Adv. George Bizos, Adv. David Soggot and Adv. M. Kuper
Prosecution: J.H. Liebenberg and D.W. Rothwell
Judge Viljoen

24 August 1970

The defence enters a special plea that the court has no jurisdiction to try Ramotse because he had been kidnapped by the then Rhodesia Police and was handed over to the South African Police. In addition, the defence pleads against the duplication of charges for which the accused had already been acquitted.

14 September 1970

Viljoen decides the case against Ramotse should proceed but that the remaining nineteen are free to go. Police threaten to arrest the jubilant group so they go to Joel Carlson's house to celebrate.

30 September 1970

Mrs Mandela's banning order is renewed for five years and she is placed under house arrest. She is forbidden from leaving her house from 6pm and 6am during the week and from 6pm to 2pm on weekends and public holidays and cannot receive visitors or engage in political activity.

7 November 1970

She is allowed to visit her husband on Robben Island. They have only 30 minutes to discuss all the events and issues of the last 23 months since they had last seen each other.

Acknowledgements

Without Advocate David Soggot's encouragement I would not have written this journal in prison, and without the efforts of his widow Greta Soggot to return it to me, this book would not have been published. I thank them both.

I am grateful to Ahmed Kathrada for writing the Foreword.

My granddaughter Swati Dlamini and Sahm Venter, of the Nelson Mandela Centre of Memory, helped me to go through the journey of bringing to the fore this deeply buried part of my history.

I also thank the Nelson Mandela Centre of Memory for safeguarding my journal and for providing letters from its archive for this book.

My thanks go to my publishers Terry Morris and Andrea Nattrass and their team at Pan Macmillan.

For their constant love and support I thank my children, grandchildren and great-grandchildren.